HEIRESSES

THE LIVES OF THE
MILLION DOLLAR BABIES

HEIRESSES

LAURA THOMPSON

ST. MARTIN'S PRESS
NEW YORK

First published in the United States by St. Martin's Press, an imprint of St. Martin's Publishing Group

HEIRESSES. Copyright © 2021 by Laura Thompson. All rights reserved. Printed in the United States of America. For information, address St. Martin's Publishing Group, 120 Broadway, New York, NY 10271.

www.stmartins.com

The Library of Congress Cataloging-in-Publication Data is available upon request.

ISBN 978-1-250-20273-4 (hardcover)
ISBN 978-1-250-20274-1 (ebook)

Our books may be purchased in bulk for promotional, educational, or business use. Please contact your local bookseller or the Macmillan Corporate and Premium Sales Department at 1-800-221-7945, extension 5442, or by email at MacmillanSpecialMarkets@macmillan.com.

Originally published in the United Kingdom by Head of Zeus Ltd, an Apollo Book

First U.S. Edition: 2022

10 9 8 7 6 5 4 3 2 1

CONTENTS

INTRODUCTION

"The rich are different from you and me."

"Yes, they have more money."

Apocryphal conversation between F. Scott
Fitzgerald and Ernest Hemingway

IN FICTION, IN general, the heiress does not have a very good time of it.

Take, for instance, the pallid little figure of Anne de Bourgh in Jane Austen's 1813 novel, *Pride and Prejudice.* Anne is the only child of the widowed Lady Catherine de Bourgh, and as such will inherit the superb estate of Rosings Park. Meanwhile the Bennet girls at the center of the novel—Jane, Elizabeth, Kitty, Mary, and Lydia—are hamstrung by genteel poverty because their family estate, worth £2,000 a year, can only be passed on to a male heir. Lady Catherine states that she can see "no occasion for entailing estates away from the female line"; which might be seen as admirable proto-feminism, were it not for the arrogance of the speaker. From her, it sounds like mere self-validation and—strikingly—like a put-down of the novel's heroine, Elizabeth Bennet.

For Lady Catherine is threatened by Elizabeth. Why should she be? Anne is an heiress: supremely marriageable, in an age when marriage was seen as a woman's natural destiny. By rights she is the greatest prize among the group of young women—the

Bennet girls, Caroline Bingley, Charlotte Lucas—who fight to succeed in this polite and unyielding arena.

Yet Anne is the most insignificant of them all. Described as "pale and sickly," she sits near-silent at the Rosings dinner table and is glimpsed like a ghost inside her carriage. There is no sense that her fortune makes her happy or blessed; in fact there is scarcely any sense of her at all.

By contrast, Elizabeth blooms. Her personality is the life force of the novel. She is physically at ease with herself, and her sense of humor—"I dearly love a laugh"—is delicately anarchic. Most importantly, she has a sense of self-worth that no insult or reversal can touch. This worries Lady Catherine, for it suggests that her own scale of values is not the only one in town. Here is a girl without fortune, an anti-heiress as one might say, who simply refuses to countenance the idea that she should feel inferior on that account. Instead, and without in the least meaning to do so, Elizabeth suggests through her artless confidence that Anne de Bourgh is *her* inferior.

And indeed, when it comes to marriage—the means by which a young woman proved her worth—Elizabeth does triumph; thereby more than justifying Lady Catherine's unease. The intention had been that Anne de Bourgh should marry her cousin, Darcy, whose Pemberley home is on the splendor level of Rosings. A union of two estates, therefore, rather than two individuals; wealth calling to wealth, as was perfectly normal practice. Elizabeth, however, is the rogue factor. Like Lady Catherine, Darcy feels threatened by her (who *is* this girl?) but he is also beguiled. His aunt, meanwhile, has forgotten that a man as rich as Darcy can marry whomsoever he chooses, and has absolutely no need of an heiress as terminally insipid as Anne.

For all its reputation as a love story, *Pride and Prejudice* is really a novel about money. Those who have it—Anne, Darcy, his sister Georgiana, his friend Bingley—are set against those who do not; the haves represent a winning post that the have-nots seek to reach. For example Darcy's friend Colonel Fitzwilliam, well born but without fortune, is attracted to Elizabeth but says to her: "Younger sons cannot marry where they like," to which she blithely replies: "Unless where they like women of fortune, which I think they very often do." That is a tease, but it is also the truth: Fitzwilliam is on the hunt, and his quarry cannot be Elizabeth.

As a man of honor he will not behave like the amoral Mr. Wickham, who attempts a shortcut—one extremely familiar in Austen's time—by plotting to elope with Georgiana Darcy. Meanwhile, Charlotte Lucas shackles herself to the barely tolerable Mr. Collins, which to her friend Elizabeth is scarcely less shocking. But Charlotte accepts that marriage is a "preservative from want," and in doing so shows better sense than Elizabeth, who turns Mr. Collins down; a dangerous thing for a poor girl to do. Collins makes a very fair point when he says: "Your portion is unhappily so small that it will in all likelihood undo the effects of your loveliness and amiable qualifications."

What stops his words from coming true is the fairy tale element of *Pride and Prejudice*; the fact that, in the end, romance conquers the finance-based narrative, Darcy decides that it is the poor girl or nobody, and Cinderella goes to a lifetime of Pemberley balls. Anne de Bourgh—briefly presented as Darcy's natural mate—disappears almost completely from the reader's consciousness to be remembered, just, as an etiolated presence trapped in a drawing room dominated by her appalling mother.

Her fate beyond the book is hard to imagine. Health permitting, she would probably have been married off, to a husband of whom her mother approved; as an heiress, she would not have lacked suitors. Yet precisely because she is an heiress—pure and simple—it is impossible to think that she would have been wanted for any other reason. Poor, pale, undersized Anne de Bourgh: she seems weighed down by her inheritance, well-nigh obliterated by it. No clearer contrast is possible with Elizabeth Bennet, who represents freedom in a way that is somehow connected to her lack of money.

Elizabeth is loved not for what she has, but for what she is; she is loved, as the phrase has it, *for herself*. No wonder *Pride and Prejudice* has become so popular among the "you're worth it" generation. Indeed the lengths to which the wildly eligible Darcy goes to win Elizabeth—paying off and putting up with her embarrassing relations, proposing for a second time despite a rejection that he can scarcely credit—have an outlandishness worthy of Richard Curtis. Austen's great literary gift solidifies the happy ever after, makes clear that it is also the culmination of a series of moral choices. Nevertheless I never read the book without thinking: my God, Elizabeth, would you have gotten this lucky in real life?

* * *

In fiction, however, the penniless heroine—which means all of Jane Austen's protagonists except Emma Wodehouse, who has £30,000—is allowed to be in a fair fight with the heiress, her implicit enemy. She is given qualities that the heiress lacks because, in fiction, fortune alone cannot be allowed to carry the day. If it does, as when Marianne Dashwood loses her beloved Willoughby to a rich girl in *Sense and Sensibility*, this proves to be a blessing in disguise: Willoughby was not worth having.

Furthermore, as Austen makes clear, had Willoughby not been financially "all to pieces" he would have chosen Marianne every time. The woman whom he does marry—Sophia Grey, possessor of the enormous sum of £50,000—is again a cipher, but a still more unappealing one than Anne de Bourgh. The reader is told that she is "not handsome," that she is "jealous as the devil." Unlike lovely passionate Marianne, she has nothing to offer beyond the fact that she is an heiress; therefore, any victory that she scores is a hollow one.

But let us turn the tale around, and imagine—say—a novel entitled *Sophia, or Avarice and Advantage*, in which events are seen through the eyes of Miss Grey. Would her jealousy not seem reasonable, pitiable even, given that she knows all too well that it is only her money that keeps Willoughby by her side? And would she not, like the impoverished heroine, become a sympathetic figure? She would, of course. Such is the nature of narratives.

And yet, even when the story is told from the heiress's point of view, still it seems to be weighted against her. Her inheritance is her fate and, as in the old Muslim proverb, she wears it around her neck like a collar and chain (albeit one deliciously bejeweled). She suffers, and she suffers, and then she suffers some more. Unlike the bright-spirited poor girl, she is permitted no true transformative freedom, nor indeed much happiness.

Take Catherine Sloper, for instance, in Henry James's 1880 novella *Washington Square* (or, as it was bluntly titled on stage and screen, *The Heiress*). Catherine has $10,000 a year, and the promise of $20,000 a year more when her father dies. Wonderful! She is pursued by a young man named Morris Townsend, whose attentions dazzle her; Morris is glamorous, Catherine mild and homely. Still better! Lots of money and a desirable husband: only the rarest of women would have asked for more. This, then, could have been Catherine's happy-heiress ending; were it not for the fact that her father—the ice-cold spanner in the works—perceives her suitor to be a gold-digger, and threatens to withdraw her inheritance should she marry. The threat is designed to find Morris out. For why should he want Catherine, except for her money?

And therein lies the existential question at the heart of this piercing little fable, which itself contains the essence of the heiress's dilemma. How is she to know her own intrinsic worth, when everybody around her is so distracted by externals? How—especially in matters of love—can she ever be sure that she is wanted *for herself*?

As a woman of the nineteenth century, deprived of the right to pursue her own destiny (much more on this later), Catherine Sloper must accept that others will decide that question for her. Later fictional heiresses were at least allowed to do so for themselves; as for instance in Agatha Christie's 1967 novel *Endless Night*, which contains a superbly convincing sketch of a "poor little rich girl"—murder victim Ellie Goodman—who longs for a freedom beyond luxury hotel suites and Krug on tap in VIP lounges, and marries a sexy penniless young man rather than a family-approved blue blood. Ellie chooses to believe that her husband truly loves her, which he certainly seems to do. At the same time it is somehow clear that she knows he might not. She accepts this uncertainty as her heiress's burden, which is inescapable, however free she becomes. As with Linnet Doyle, the heiress victim in *Death on the Nile* (1937), her "self" is inseparable from her money, and indeed both women are murdered because of it. For why else would an heiress be killed?

Again, their lives are at the mercy of their inheritance—although they are at least in charge of it. Ellie causes ructions with her marriage to a Carnaby Street Morris Townsend, but she goes ahead anyway: an eighteenth-century-style elopement directed by the bride. Linnet has a sound business head, but she too chooses to bestow herself upon a good-looking pauper whom she hardly knows. These are twentieth-century women, and they have agency. The irony is that this very independence may lead them straight to the kind of men who plagued their heiress forebears.

As, for instance, in Jean Rhys's *Wide Sargasso Sea*, set in Jamaica in the 1830s: the story of the first Mrs. Rochester, the "mad woman in the attic" in *Jane Eyre*. When seen from her own point of view, rather than that of Charlotte Brontë's novel, this woman—Antoinette, a Creole girl whom Rochester married for her dowry—is beautiful, lovable, and deeply vulnerable. Not, as with Rhys's other female protagonists, because she has no money; but because she has it.

The marriage to Rochester quickly goes wrong. Antoinette's old nurse, Christophine—the voice of sanity, and of a woman who has to work for everything that she has—says to her: "I keep my money. I don't give it to no worthless man . . . But look me trouble, a rich white girl like you and more foolish than the rest. A man don't treat you good, pick up your skirt and walk out."

To which Antoinette replies: "I am not rich now, I have no money of my own at all, everything I had belongs to him . . . That is English law."

It was, too. "It's shameful," says her aunt, of a system that gives a woman no legal protection. The only protection is that of a husband; to whom all power has been given, in the form of money. Christophine asks Rochester to return half of Antoinette's dowry and leave her in peace: "You think you fool me? You want her money but you don't want her. It is in your mind to pretend she is mad."

Pretending that the heiress is mad . . . This trope, this terrifying ploy, also sits at the heart of Wilkie Collins's 1859 novel *The Woman in White*. Laura Fairlie, a young woman with £20,000, marries a heavily indebted baronet named Sir Percival Glyde (doing so in accordance with her "father's wishes": another trope, as for instance with Shakespeare's heiress Portia and those wretched caskets). Through a campaign of intimidation Sir Percival tries to make Laura sign the money away. Eventually she is carted off to an asylum. She is peculiarly helpless and voiceless, as insubstantial as the "woman in white" doppelgänger who haunts the narrative. Once more, the money that should be her strength has rendered her vulnerable.

What makes *The Woman in White* so interesting—especially to the modern reader—is that her loyal protector is a woman: her half-sister Marian Halcombe, as glorious in her good sense as Christophine, as staunch as Laura's little dog, who snaps his suspicion whenever Sir Percival comes near. Marian is described as "ugly," by which the reader understands that she does not conform to nineteenth-century ideals of femininity. She views Sir Percival with a ferocious terror: "Men! They are the enemies of our innocence and our peace—they drag us away from our parents' love and our sisters' friendship—they take us body and soul to themselves, and fasten our helpless lives to theirs as they chain up a dog to his kennel."

Marian's words are for Laura, whose outrageous suffering she feels as if it were her own. She herself, with no husband and without means, is free from such torments. Marian can deal with any man; Laura, perforce, must let men deal with her. There is an ambivalent comment upon this—upon the fact that women who marry potentially lose everything by doing so, and receive who knows what in return—at the end of *Washington Square*, when Morris and Catherine meet again, years after her father pushed him to desert her:

Morris stood stroking his beard, with a clouded eye. "Why have you never married?" he asked abruptly. "You have had opportunities."

"I didn't wish to marry."

"Yes, you are rich, you are free; you had nothing to gain."

"I had nothing to gain," said Catherine.

Any more suffering heiresses? Oh, most certainly. There is Milly Theale in Henry James's *The Wings of a Dove*, evaporating in the heavy Venetian air, with a fortune that cannot save her from death, indeed almost seems to be dragging her toward it... There is Maud Ruthyn in Sheridan Le Fanu's *Uncle Silas*, condemned by another of these perverse fathers to spend a purgatorial period in a Gothic mansion, peopled by grotesques who crave her inheritance... There is Lady Glencora in Anthony Trollope's *Can You Forgive Her?*, madly in love with the handsome gambler Burgo Fitzgerald, obliged instead to bestow her fortune upon the ducal heir Plantagenet Palliser, a man as austere as his name... There is Ernestina Freeman in John Fowles's *The French Lieutenant's Woman*, trapped by advantage in a vapidity that she herself recognizes, and no match in attraction for the soulful, dispossessed Sarah Woodruff... There is Polly Hampton in Nancy Mitford's *Love in a Cold Climate*, beautiful as the day and eating her heart out over her mother's lover, on whose pointless account she is disinherited...

One could go on, and on. One could also pick out random heiresses in the later medium of cinema, and discern the same lurking themes: Katharine Hepburn in *The Philadelphia Story* (1940), a patrician Newport goddess who must get raging drunk, lose her dignity, and admit to being "an unholy mess of a girl" before she can achieve redemption; Barbara Stanwyck in *Polly Fulton* (1948), whose husband despises her as a symbol of tainted capitalism; Joanne Woodward in *A Kiss Before Dying* (1956), pursued for her fortune and murdered when she falls pregnant, which will cause her to be disinherited; Miriam Hopkins in *The*

Richest Girl in the World (1934), who pretends to be her own secretary in order to find out if Joel McCrea loves her *for herself* . . .

And one could ask: where is the heiress whose inheritance brings her straightforward pleasure? Why is she so much more of a victim than the poor girl?

Because, goes the logic, it is only fair that the heiress should be unfairly treated. If she were to get the happy ending—if wealth were shown to triumph—then it would seem an affront against principle, against the Sermon on the Mount and against all those millions of readers who want to believe that the tortoise will overtake the hare. And because—is this a surprise?—it is *based upon fact*. The marriage of Elizabeth Bennet to Fitzwilliam Darcy may be a poor girl's fantasy, made convincing by literary genius. But the lives of Sophia Grey and Catherine Sloper, of Antoinette Cosway and Laura Fairlie . . . touches of melodrama notwithstanding, they are rendered with brutal realism; and yes, such a phrase can be applied to the rich. These fictional heiresses are not written merely to gratify the reader. They are recognizable figures, and they had real-life counterparts. The quietly mythic character of Catherine Sloper—for instance—grew from a story confided to Henry James by his friend, the actress Fanny Kemble, about a naive girl who had become engaged to Kemble's glamorous brother, and whose father was threatening to remove her inheritance on this account. The plot of *The Woman in White* was inspired in part by the case of Louisa Nottidge, who was placed in an asylum by family members seeking to control her money. *Endless Night* was not based upon any murder in particular, but one would almost be spoiled for choice when it comes to examples of rich women preyed upon—sometimes murdered— for their wealth.

This book will tell the stories of such heiresses; whose suffering did not stop when they acquired the right to control what they owned. To say that money does not bring happiness may be a consolation deployed liberally by storytellers. It may also be a truism. Quite often, however, it is the simple truth; one in which the heiresses themselves all too frequently believed, and which thereby became a self-fulfilling prophecy.

* * *

Why heiresses, incidentally, rather than heirs?

Because, in this regard, it really is different for girls.

The word may come across as retrograde, like poetess, but then so too is the concept. It derives from a time when money plus femaleness equaled something noteworthy, even contradictory. In the days before women acquired an identity in law—notably through the Married Women's Property Acts, passed in the United Kingdom in 1870 and 1882—wealth was in conflict with their gender. Money meant power, but femaleness meant its absence. An heiress was only created in the first place when there was no man to inherit.

Indeed from the moment a woman accepted a proposal from a man, they became one person: him. A wife's identity was legally subsumed into that of her husband. He had almost complete control over her body, and their children were his to command. He was entitled to all her property (unless a marriage settlement said otherwise, although even those were not inviolate) and could claim any of her earnings and rental income. The argument ran thus: "were she remitted to give away, or otherwise settle her property, he might be disappointed of the wealth he looked to in making the offer."[1] In other words, if a man were good enough to marry you, it was really better not to upset him.

The flip side of this was that if a woman committed a crime— short of murder or treason—in her husband's presence, the legal presumption was that she was innocent because he had coerced her to do it (this belief lingered into the twentieth century*). A husband was also responsible for his wife's debts. So there were benefits to being completely infantilized, if one could stand it. A counterview comes from the Beadle in *Oliver Twist*, who—when reminded that "the law supposes that your wife acts under your direction"—replies: "If that's the eye of the law, the law is a bachelor"; a majestic riposte, except that the Beadle's wife did not belong to the class of woman oddly flattered by privilege.

Later came the women whose wealth was their own, legally and incontestably, but who—not always, but often enough—allowed it to ruin their lives anyway. They were not prey in the real, dangerous way of those earlier heiresses. Yet their vulnerability was intense. It came from the people who surrounded them, who just as before had an eye to their money (laws change, people do not), but more than that it came from within: as if, as per the Aristotelian theory, an inheritance were an example of the flaw that leads to tragedy.

There are—needless to say—plenty of men whose lives have descended, post-inheriting, into a series of calamitous tableaux straight from Hogarth: the gaming tables, the divorce court, the heroin needle. But this book is about the particular relationship between women and their money. Some were able to make use of it. Others were not. As the world changed, and they acquired hitherto unimaginable rights, so the nature of

---

* In 1922, for instance, a woman named Elsie Yeldham lured a man to a remote forest with the promise of sex, where her boyfriend killed and robbed him. He was hanged but her death sentence was commuted; despite her active role in the crime, the judge deemed that she had acted under the male influence.

their vulnerabilities shifted. This is true for women as a whole, but with heiresses the truth is writ large; not least because they should have the means to avoid it.

To take two of the most famous twentieth-century examples: why did Christina Onassis (shipping heiress) and Barbara Hutton (Woolworth heiress) have such godawful lives? Why the terrible choices in men? Why the fundamental lack of confidence? External circumstances afflicted them both—desperate bereavements, hellhounds on their trail—yet the damage was also, indubitably, within. Christina thought of herself as physically undesirable, but a woman with $500 million can surely find a better solution than vats of Diet Coke and four dodgy husbands. Barbara had been made to feel unattractive by her first husband—Alexis Mdivani, a professional seducer thrust upon her by his scheming sister; *Les Liaisons Dangereuses* transported to 1930s Biarritz—and from that point onward seems to have been trapped in tendencies both anorexic and dependent. But why marry him in the first place?

These women were not stupid. Christina played a large part in running the Onassis shipping empire. Barbara, a woman of exquisite taste, wrote poems. One night at the Paris Ritz in 1957 she sat in her suite—a birdlike figure, somewhat drunk, surrounded as ever by opulence, luxury, surfeit, superfluity—as her friend Noël Coward read her words aloud to her: "Actually some of them are simple and moving," he wrote in his diary. The entry was suffused with slightly exasperated pity: "her money," it concluded, "is always between her and happiness."

Yet it shouldn't have been. Should it? Why *should* money bring unhappiness, when it facilitates what most of us crave: a life that can be one's own plaything? Exasperation is indeed the order of the day, reading about Barbara's infernal jewel-drenched misery while braced for the arrival of one's latest electricity bill.

No doubt workers at Woolworth felt a still stronger emotion when, in 1938, they went on strike for a weekly wage of $20 as the papers filled with pictures of Barbara, holidaying in Cairo with her second disastrous husband, the Danish count Kurt Haugwitz-Reventlow. In a clever PR move, the strike committee sent a telegram to Egypt—"WOOLWORTH STRIKERS IN NEW YORK ASK YOUR INTERVENTION"—which naturally went unacknowledged.

Barbara returned to her new home in England, Winfield House in Regent's Park (now the US ambassador's residence in London), on which she had spent almost $7 million, rebuilding and adding improvements, including two ten-car garages, a six-room nursery suite for her baby son, and a statue of herself in the "Tudor garden." *Life* magazine ran a photograph of this statue, alongside an article that advised its subject to "forget the counts who spend her money and remember the Woolworth counter girls who earn it." An easy shot, of course. Quite likely Barbara never even saw that telegram.* As the granddaughter of the man who created Woolworth, it may have seemed that she could do something about the pay of its employees, and perhaps some people would have tried; nevertheless, she held no position from which to dictate company policy. It was not actually her fault that she was rich, the "Million Dollar Baby from the Five and Ten Cent Store," as the 1930s popular song had it. But the unhappiness that her heiress status brought her, which does indeed inspire pity as well as irritation: where did that come from?

* * *

---

* According to C. David Heymann's *Poor Little Rich Girl* (Hutchinson, 1985), Count Reventlow pocketed the telegram and "conveniently forgot to give it to her"; unproven, but not unbelievable.

In Dorothy Parker's 1941 short story "The Standard of Living," two young stenographers play a game about what they would do if they were to inherit a fortune; the punch line is that their original fantasy figure of $1 million has to be raised to $10 million, when they learn the real cost of the kind of jewelry worn by heiresses. Who, aside from the *richissime*, has not done something along these lines? Who has not imagined how they would spend ten million or, these days (so liberal with their zeros), one hundred million? I have certainly done it. I have itemized the house on Cheyne Walk, the apartment on the Upper East Side, the cryogenic chamber, the Stubbs, the fittings at Givenchy, the animal sanctuary.

Would all that make me happy? Well: to be honest I think it might.

The Hutton-type heiress, however, is not made happy by these things, because for her they exist without context. They are cut off from the effort that earned them, the desire that yearned for them, the fear that they would never be attained, and the terror that they might be lost. They are simply there. The heiress has never had to *imagine* what it would be like to be rich, and she cannot know the value of what she has never been without. "There is no moment when you say 'I'm afraid I can't afford that one,'" as the poor-boy narrator puts it in *Endless Night*, trying to understand his wife's near-infinite wealth, the incomprehensibility of the fact that money, in itself, does not make her happy.

Similarly, the heiress has never experienced longing or need, so she cannot appreciate the absolute joy that comes with assuaging those feelings. The payment that soaks up outstanding bills, the windfall that buys a piece of designer clothing: those miraculous changes in circumstance, like sunbursts upon a gray sky, mean nothing to an heiress. Her life is without shade, therefore it is without the blessed relief from shade. It is a procession of sumptuous similarity. "Oh God, not another fucking beautiful day," as the American Alice de Janzé famously greeted the sight of a sunlit morning at her house in Kenya: the heiress's authentic cry of despair about her own state of accidie.

For most of us, much of our lives are spent in earning money, thinking about money, worrying about money, dreaming of money. It really does take up an awful lot of time. What to do, therefore, when that imperative is removed? The day still has to be filled, but the kind of pleasures that mean such a lot to the working person—a long weekend in Venice, say—have somewhat less resonance to somebody who can travel to a suite at the Cipriani on a last-minute whim and very possibly owns a couple of Canalettos. There is no anticipation, no aftermath, because every day is spent, metaphorically, in a suite at the Cipriani.

The removal of need should make life much more interesting, given that one has all the time in the world to study the piano, read the complete works of Shakespeare, save the world . . . And some heiresses have, indeed, been compelled to fill that time. Others, not so much. It is as though the smooth lack of context, imparted by inherited wealth, renders meaningful things oddly meaningless. The simplest way to fill a day is, therefore, with money. Hours can pass in a flash when there is no restriction on spending. What one actually *does* isn't the point. Drugs, of course, take up quite a lot of time, and don't mar one's silhouette in the Chanel. They also help with the unvarying blankness through which the heiress travels every day, as through vast beautiful rooms that have been furnished by somebody else.

As for the effect of this absence of longing: it is surely an unnatural human condition, not to feel need, because the heiress seems to be on an existential quest for that very sensation. It is as if she is hungry for hunger. And, having no material needs, she has an immense amount of time and energy to invest in the need for emotional fulfillment. For love.

Everybody hopes for it, of course. Everybody wants to meet somebody who will love them *for themselves*. But for the heiress—who has time on her hands and mistrust in her heart—finding that person can have an added layer of significance. Always there is the question, the one posed in Henry James's *Washington Square*, and still more relevant in an age of alarmingly free choice: where, within the chateaux and the couture, lies my intrinsic worth? In restless search of an answer to this conundrum, Barbara Hutton married seven times, although by the end this had surely become a mere reflex. Could anybody have married playboy-gigolo Porfirio Rubirosa—previously husband to another heiress, Doris Duke, from whom he received $25,000 a year in alimony—in a serious frame of mind?

The only one of the seven who treated Barbara properly—as if she were a person, separate from her heiress status—was the film star Cary Grant, whom she married in 1942. Clearly he did not need her money. He married her for something closer to the "real" reasons that she wanted—although fulfillment is not so easily accepted, even when it is there for the having—and he took nothing after they divorced three years later. Generally, however, living in the heiress's orbit is not good for the moral character. In fact it is quite astonishing what the prospect of a slice of an inheritance will do to people, who become suddenly ignited with a hot flame of cupidity, and behave in ways that they would never have done had the dollar signs not started flashing in their eyes.

There is a further, still weightier moral issue: should an heiress even exist in the first place? Or should inheritance tax—which has been around in the UK since 1796—level the playing field, taking the unearned penthouse from a single individual in order that thousands of others might benefit? It is a profoundly serious question; although it is not the concern of this book. What does arise, however, is whether the heiress *herself* thinks that she ought to exist.

When the heiress was only poorly protected, misery was—in the main—inflicted upon her, but later she became adept at inflicting it upon herself. So was this another expression of the rebalancing principle found in fiction? In other words: did all that masochistic behavior derive, at heart, from a subterranean guilt about being an heiress in the first place?

Unearned wealth has by definition been earned by somebody else. Some of the earlier heiresses had wealth that derived from plantation ownership; a specific immorality that was not specifically examined, any more than was the equality principle in general. Some of these women displayed altruism, a philanthropic instinct. Nevertheless injustice, which they themselves so often experienced, was only gradually perceived to be something systemic. Only as the nineteenth century came to an end, bringing with it those great legislative shifts toward rights for women, did the bigger picture start to emerge; and its significance permeated even the gated community of the megarich.

Somebody—a lot of people—had worked to produce their wealth. At some point in the past there had been an intrepid and industrious ancestor, such as Frank Winfield Woolworth with his five-and-ten-cent stores, and now there were a vast number of employees, working all hours for an annual wage that might just buy one's Ascot hat. Unless completely without sensitivity— which was certainly not the case with a woman like Barbara Hutton—the heiress would have felt some guilt about this.

Guilt could be channeled, of course, and money redistributed. There are heiresses who have chosen charity and patronage:

richesse oblige. A smaller number have chosen dissent and rebellion: a forceful denial of the system that bred their inheritance. Barbara took neither of these paths—she was too defined by her millions to do so—yet the level of her spending does imply a semiconscious desire to be rid of it all. To become as one with the Woolworth counter girl, in fact, whom a few years earlier she herself might have been. "I'm only one generation removed from the women of my family who washed their own dishes and made their own clothes," as she put it in 1938.[2] At the same time, it has to be said that she *liked* spending, and had a fine aesthetic taste in clothes, jewels, houses, interior design, and art. Much of what she bought was beautiful as well as valuable: Ching dynasty porcelain, *famille rose*, sculpted Arabian horse heads set in gold and decorated with precious stones, haute couture, a string of black pearls originally owned by the mother of Louis XIV. She was also extraordinarily generous; although that too has the air of a desire to offload—if a passing acquaintance admired a ring she would almost force it upon them, which is redistribution of a kind. The real point, however, is that none of what she owned seems to have brought much happiness. And heiresses surely know that they are the lucky ones, and therefore *ought* to be happy; a knowledge that can only bring still more guilt?

* * *

Great wealth has a mythic quality. It is the modern equivalent of rank in Shakespearean tragedy. And this confers a theatricality, a *scale*, upon the lives of these women, who were able to traverse the world with such ease, who had space—mansions, triplexes, cars the size of studio flats—and who had choice, a near infinity of it. They could buy history, as with Barbara's black pearls, or as when—in 1908—the American heiress Evalyn Walsh McLean acquired the Hope Diamond, first owned by Louis XIV. This gray-blue stone was said to carry a curse; which sounds like something out of Rider Haggard, although the Hope Diamond certainly brought ill luck to most of its owners. Evalyn's son was killed in a car crash, her daughter committed suicide, and her publisher husband went into a mental institution. Of course the curse had nothing to do with any of this. Nevertheless, the diamond was a symbol—of a spending urge that contributed, in part, to Evalyn's griefs, and of an inheritance that controlled her life while appearing to liberate it.

The scale of the heiress's life is part of what makes it so mesmerizing to behold. It is like watching a giant melodrama, one that arouses feelings of amazement, envy, bafflement, frustration, and—above all—Schadenfreude. Almost always the trajectory of the story is downward, but then it starts from such a high point. An heiress! The very word sounds light, golden, aeolian. It conjures a slender creature sheltered within vast estates, delicate feet on Aubusson carpets, horses and servants both equally devoted. A fairy tale, in fact, but one that all too often ends badly.

When the heiress makes her appearance in fiction, she creates expectations: of jeopardy, of comeuppance, of a righting of injustices, of a figure who will be disliked or pitied. Similarly when she features in the media, with the magical word liberally deployed in headlines: Heiress Marries, Heiress Elopes, Heiress Dies. An inheritance of a few thousands will license the use of the term. Lesley Whittle, for instance, the teenager who in 1975 fell victim to a vicious killer known as the "Black Panther," was routinely described as an heiress. Heiress Kidnapped. Heiress Found Dead. Her family was extremely well-to-do, to be sure, with a large detached house in the Midlands, and she was seized for a ransom of £50,000. Her late father had given her some £80,000; technically, therefore, she was an heiress. There is no fixed amount of money at which the term becomes applicable. Nevertheless it carries a Rockefeller sheen, and it was used in reports of the case as a signifier—a means to emphasize, as if that were needed, the utter horror of what had happened to this poor girl.

The male equivalent of Lesley Whittle would never have been described as an "heir," nor would his story have received quite the same measure of scrutiny. Far more recently, Ghislaine Maxwell, daughter of the disgraced newspaper tycoon Robert, charged in 2020 with sex trafficking crimes, was regularly referred to as an "heiress"; again true in only the loosest sense, but the term emphasized the heights from which she had tumbled. Back in 1974, meanwhile, the nineteen-year-old Patty Hearst—granddaughter of the newspaper magnate William Randolph Hearst—was abducted by a radical group calling itself the Symbionese Liberation Army, whom she later joined. A photograph of this young woman, holding a semiautomatic rifle in a bank raid, became the very image of anti-capitalist rebellion; and its symbolic power was multiplied to near infinity because Patty Hearst was a scion of privilege and wealth. A man of similar upbringing, doing such a thing, would have been remarkable enough. But a girl? Amazing! Incredible! Like it or not, female stories have an extra dash of piquancy. Even now (perhaps not for much longer) the norm is male. Therefore there is added value when a traditionally masculine "attribute"—gun-toting, great wealth—is filtered through the feminine. There is a twist, an added sharpness, a heightened level of window dressing; and along with all this comes a prurience, an excited desire to probe the space between the norm and the female assumption of it. Imagine the Hogarth tableaux with an heiress as their subject. Would we not peer at them all the more closely, with a still greater relish for the damning detail and the precipitous fall? Do we not do so, when these images step from the canvas and into real life: the stories of how Paris Hilton, the hotel heiress, collapsed and wailed as she was sentenced to a forty-five-day jail term in 2007; of how, in 2015, a man was convicted of "abuse of weakness" of the ninety-three-year-old Liliane Bettencourt, heiress to the L'Oréal fortune, from whom he had extracted some 1.3 billion euros' worth of gifts; of how Casey Johnson, pharmaceutical heiress and daughter of the future US ambassador in London, died in 2010 of diabetic complications aged thirty, her last tweet and self-destructive "party girl" behavior reported with due salacious gravity?

And yet. However much the heiress herself seems to buy into the troubled myth of her kind, it can also be viewed as just that: a myth. There have been those who had absolutely no time for it, and who in their various ways managed to thrive very happily upon their heiress status. This book will tell their stories, of course.

It will also, however, contain a unifying moral of Hogarthian bluntness: that it was better for a woman to have money, except when it wasn't.

PART I

UNPROTECTED

"Mr. *Cruickshank* stepped into three thousand a-year
By showing his leg to an heiress."

From *The New Monthly Magazine*, July 1823

MARY

LET US START with the story of Mary Davies.

Mary was born in London in 1665, the year of the Great Plague. At the age of twelve she was married, at the church of St. Clement Danes in the Strand, to a Cheshire landowner nine years her senior. Sir Thomas Grosvenor was a decent man, nothing like the horror husbands of fiction. Nevertheless the marriage was all about money: there was never an heiress, before or after, quite like Mary.

Mary was bought for some £9,000, which was both a huge sum and a bargain. Her dowry was a thousand-acre chunk of London: the Manor of Ebury, which in the seventeenth century was a marshy expanse of fields—enlivened by the occasional solitary mansion—separated by deep ditches and liable to be swamped. The manor was bordered to the north by what is now Bayswater Road and Oxford Street, and to the south by the River Thames. Its western edge was formed by the Westbourne: one of London's several lost rivers, which now runs beneath Knightsbridge, through a pipe above the tracks of Sloane Square Underground and down to Chelsea Bridge. The manor's eastern edge was another river, the Tybourne, whose main course—which then flowed under a bridge across Piccadilly, and was said to have been traversed by Queen Anne in a rowing boat—traces

Bond Street, underneath what is now Claridge's, across Green Park and through Victoria.

In other words, the twelve-year-old Mary Davies was heiress to what would become some of the most valuable land in the world. She was the winner in the real-life game of Monopoly. In 1723, seven years before she died, Grosvenor Square would be laid out on her acres, and a hundred years later Thomas Cubitt would raise upon them the ice-white glories of Belgravia: the squares and crescents that would become home to prime ministers, aristocrats, embassies, and oligarchs. Although Buckingham Palace itself is built within what was once James I's "Mulberry Garden," Mary owned the surrounding fields. Hyde Park had been annexed by Henry VIII, but the rest—save a few plots here and there—was hers.

On Mary's land the great traders' city was extended into a residential paradise. Order and money were created by speculators, developers, the kind of bold people who extend London still today. The marshes were drained, the rivers Tybourne and Westbourne were buried beneath the streets, the constant sound of water was silenced; the thieves and gypsies were driven from their colonies on what is now Belgrave Square, and the highwaymen from their lurking pitch at the Knight's Bridge on Hyde Park Corner; and the houses, first in dots upon the fields, then in irrefutable rows and squares, began to shape the modern city.

From Mary's inheritance, the well-to-do Grosvenor family became the supremely grand Westminsters, whose mansion on Park Lane (on the site of what is now the Grosvenor House hotel) stood at the heart of their empire. "It is customary to give place to the lady," wrote the reviewer of a 1921 book entitled *Mary Davies and the Manor of Ebury*, "but on this occasion all must feel that precedence is due to the land."[1]

Mary herself is an elusive figure—known only from a portrait, painted posthumously, which shows an unremarkable face; and from the things that happened to her, which were very remarkable indeed. Like Anne de Bourgh she has been depicted as her inheritance, nothing more. Yet clearly there *was* more, as her actions tell us; although what went on inside her head must mostly be guessed at, as her own voice is so rarely heard.

Legend has characterized Mary as a fresh-faced farmer's daughter, who lived in a fine, simple house off what is now Berkeley Square, and whose innocence beguiled the gallant young Grosvenor. Nothing of the kind, of course. The image of a prelapsarian London is potent, as is that of the carefree child roaming around her fields like a milkmaid in a Romney. In fact that land, which even in the seventeenth century was regarded as a great prize, had been acquired by a businessman, worldly to the point of notoriety and with scant feel for the pastoral.

Mary's great-great-uncle, Hugh Audley, was a lawyer by trade and made his fortune as a usurer. During the Civil War, when everybody needed money, Audley lent to both sides, on one occasion securing bonds of £10,000 for Charles I. When he died in 1662 a significant proportion of the gentry was in his debt, while he himself owned land all over England. His finest asset was the Ebury Manor, which—by way of "divers mesne assignments and acts in the law"—he acquired in 1626. He paid £9,400 for it, a meager percentage of his £400,000 fortune.

Hugh Audley had no children, and toward the end of his life he became whimsical in his bequests. Chance decreed that he should have died when the manor was left to his great-nephews, Thomas and Alexander Davies; although Alexander had cultivated Audley, and was in fact the first to realize the potential of this land. He built a mansion on Millbank, close to what was the the "horse ferry" (at the end of what is now Horseferry Road

whereby the animals crossed the Thames. When he died of the plague in 1665, six months after the birth of his daughter—the only child of the Davies family—he left a muddled inheritance of unfinished building works and debts, plus most of the Manor of Ebury.

His shrewd widow (who instantly remarried) cut straight to the essentials. Rather as the Duchess of Kent would later do with the future queen Victoria, Mary Tregonwell viewed her daughter with the cold obsessional passion of a gambler waiting to play an ace of trumps. Indeed Mrs. Tregonwell, a woman who had fought for what she had and recognized to the full its putative value, had all the steely common sense that Mary would lack; having never needed to acquire it.

Bluntly, an heiress was the card that everybody wanted to hold. Young women—girls—had always been barter. Margaret Beaufort, heiress to the fortune of the 1st Duke of Somerset, was married in 1450 to the son of her guardian, who (as was the way of guardians) wished to keep her money close. She was probably aged six at the time.* When the marriage was annulled she was married off again, in 1455, this time by Henry VI to his half-brother Edmund Tudor. A year later Margaret was a widowed mother, of the future King Henry VII: the Tudor dynasty had emerged, in extremes of agony, from her tiny twelve-year-old body.

Although that pregnancy was highly unusual, there was nothing odd—even a couple of centuries later—about the fact that Mary Davies was married at that age. The minimum age of sixteen was not enforced in law until 1929.

It was not just heiresses who were bartered, of course: Thomas Boleyn played his two daughters, Mary and Anne, like delicious

---

* Margaret is believed to have been born in 1443. The year 1441 is possible, but less likely.

pawns in front of King Henry VIII, and thereby achieved (before it all went wrong) rank and wealth. In other words, a daughter could be the means whereby a family made its way in the world and acquired its inheritance, which would then ordinarily go to a son. Not always, however. Before the king became a real possibility, Anne Boleyn had sought elevation through marriage into the noble Percy family, whose title dodged the apparently inviolable patrilineal principle when it died out—twice—in the male line. In 1679 the husband of Elizabeth Percy, sole surviving child of the 11th Earl of Northumberland, took *her* surname: the Percy title was simply too old and grand to be extinguished by nonsense, and Elizabeth was far too rich for any husband to object—her estates comprised Alnwick Castle, Petworth House, Syon House on the banks of the Thames and, in central London, Northumberland House. Aged twelve she married a son of the Duke of Newcastle, aged fourteen she married the MP Thomas Thynne, and by the age of fifteen she was twice a widow.

Thynne had been a victim of murder: he was shot five times in Pall Mall, on the orders of a Swedish count who had taken an interest in the Percy fortune. The heiress-chasing business was starting to get out of hand, in fact, and in a manner somehow typical of the brutally carefree Restoration era. It is unsurprising, for instance, that the Earl of Rochester—poet, libertine, friend of Charles II—should have absconded with an heiress in 1665. Pepys's diary recorded "a story of my Lord Rochester's running away on Friday night last with Mrs. Mallett [Malet], the great beauty and fortune of the North [in fact the West], who had supped at White Hall with Mrs. Stewart, and was going home to her lodgings with her grandfather, my Lord Haly [Hawley], by coach; and was at Charing Cross seized on by both horse and foot men, and forcibly taken from him, and put into a coach with six horses, and two women provided to receive her, and carried away. Upon immediate pursuit, my Lord of Rochester (for whom the King had spoke to the lady often, but with no successe) was taken at Uxbridge; but the lady is not yet heard of, and the King mighty angry, and the Lord sent to the Tower."

Elizabeth Malet was fourteen at the time of this forcible abduction, which had been well planned. Pepys—who is notably casual about the whole thing—went on to say that if Rochester did not manage to snare Elizabeth in the end, "my Lord Hinchingbroke stands fair, and is invited for her. She is worth, and will be at her mother's death (who keeps but a little from her), 2500l. per annum." Thus were heiresses traded and discussed: one can almost hear the chitchat in the club rooms and drawing rooms.

Such was Rochester's sexual attraction, however, that he did win the prize. In 1667 he staged a second abduction, this time with Elizabeth's consent (although not that of her father). The couple were married at Knightsbridge Chapel, one of the venues willing to stage what were known as "clandestine" ceremonies. In the first half of the eighteenth century, it was estimated that around 20 percent of weddings were clandestine. The most popular setting was the Fleet debtors' prison—of all places—and later the prison environs; ceremonies were conducted by clergymen who were already in jail, thus could not be threatened with imprisonment, and who turned a deeply irreligious blind eye to pregnancy, coercion, incest, and bigamy. Not that it was always the bride who had been hoodwinked. A brilliant coup was staged by a woman named Susan Forbes, who arranged a sham wedding as an act of revenge against her lover: he had managed to catch a rich wife, but the marriage was rendered invalid by Susan's inspired predating of the fake ceremony, in which an impostor had played the part of the lover. More usual, however, was the 1719 case of Anne Leigh, a minor heiress with some £6,000, dragged to the Fleet by a half-pay officer, who treated her so appallingly that, it was reported, "she now lies speechless."[2]

By contrast, a clandestine marriage that took place in Knightsbridge or Mayfair (young men about town would have known exactly where to go) was relatively acceptable, while at the same time a heaven-sent means to circumvent parental opposition.

For Rochester's seizing of Elizabeth was a noteworthy example of what had become an almost commonplace event. The "best man" was, originally, the one who helped facilitate the groom's seizure of the bride. Kidnapping was a live threat; it was also a deadly game. In a diary entry from 1690 John Evelyn recorded that: "One Johnson [sic], a Knight, was executed at Tyburn for being an accomplice with Campbell, brother to Lord Argyle, in stealing a young heiress." Mary Wharton, aged thirteen, rumored to be worth some £50,000, had been carried away from her relations in London's Great Queen Street and married off—clandestinely—to Captain James Campbell. Campbell had two accomplices, so why Sir John Johnston should have been the one executed for this crime is unclear, although the standing of the noble Argyll family with the new king, William III, was surely something to do with it. The Wharton family themselves petitioned the king for Johnston's reprieve, however, and an article (written more than a century later) asserted that, at the trial, "Miss Wharton had given evident proofs that the violence Captain Campbell used was not so much against her will, as her lawyers endeavored to make it."[3] The implication, that Mary Wharton was not wholly reluctant to be stolen by Campbell, is of course impossible to assess. To the modern eye it reads uncomfortably, like a date rape defense, but this attempt to shift blame onto a victim—still all too familiar—was then used with the utmost conscience-free abandon. The heiress, often characterized as a plain girl, was a willing elopee; the man who snatched her, usually a bit of a dasher, was her perverse salvation: thus went the argument, and the public—devouring the stories of female peril and male derring-do—tended to go along with it.

Nevertheless *l'affaire Wharton* caused a great scandal, which it was believed would hasten legislation to prevent clandestine marriages. For some years Parliament had been putting forward bills to that end, all of which failed to progress: ten such would founder between 1666 and 1718. The cited, somewhat progressive reason was that a young woman ought to be able to choose her own husband, rather than have to follow her parents' wishes. The actual, more deviant reason was that certain parliamentarians considered the reform to be against their own interest. In other words: MPs wanted to be in on their game, with rich wives of their own. Between 1660 and 1690 at least three of them—including the murdered Thomas Thynne—had married juvenile heiresses. Captain Campbell himself would become an MP when the Wharton scandal died down. Although an Act was passed in late 1690, rendering his marriage to Mary null and void (strictly speaking not Parliament's business), an active petitioner against it was his own brother, the 10th Earl of Argyll, who had surely fancied the prospect of that £50,000 flooding into his family's coffers. Marrying an heiress was the canniest move that a man could make, in fact, and the general feeling was that *qui voulait le fin voulait les moyens*: if the poor young thing had to be strong-armed into it, then such was life.

Given this lurid backdrop, Mary Davies—a potential rather than actual heiress, which was somehow even more desirable—was carted off to France to evade kidnap, although her mother was too ambitious to wait there long. From the age of seven Mary was paraded in a coach-and-six in Hyde Park, to be eyed by possible buyers, like a foal that promised to become a money-generating brood mare.

Lord Berkeley was the first to make a bid, on behalf of his ten-year-old son. He owned a palace in Piccadilly and a farm at what is now Hay Hill, which would have slotted like a very satisfying piece of jigsaw puzzle into Mary's land. He paid a deposit on her of £5,000, but when the time came could not raise the £3,000 of land demanded by that arch-negotiator, Mrs. Tregonwell. In the end it was the 3rd Baronet Grosvenor who faced down other suitors, paid off Berkeley (plus interest), and with his £9,000 took the prize. Mrs. Tregonwell did very well out of the deal. But Sir Thomas Grosvenor's purchase of Mary Davies has a fair claim to being the best property deal in history.

The Grosvenors achieved advancement—became marquesses, then dukes—in the main because they were so rich, and a large part of their stupendous wealth was acquired through that marriage to Mary. On the death of the 1st Marquess in 1845, *The Times* wrote (in an obituary tinged lightly with malice): "The world will inquire by what qualities the deceased was distinguished from other peers or other men . . . ? Wealth in every form happens to have been the great attribute by which the Most Hon. Robert Grosvenor, Marquis of Westminster, was distinguished, not only from mankind at large, but from the most eminent persons in the titled orders."

The obituary continued with an oblique nod to the role of the heiress—including an unnamed Mary Davies—in augmenting the fortunes of the aristocracy. It noted that "the honors of some of the most distinguished families in the country are *only* [my italics] derived from maternal ancestors. Paternally, the Earl of Clarendon is not a Hyde, the Duke of Northumberland is not a

Percy ... and even the Marquis, to whose life these columns have been devoted, derived several of his titular designations from the lands and manors of his ancestors in the female line."

You can say that again.

* * *

The life of Mary Davies spanned one of the most extraordinary periods in English history. When she was born—five years after the restoration of the monarchy—London was racked by plague, would soon be in flames, and was dealing with the chaotic aftermath of civil war, regicide, and the Cromwell interregnum. By the time she died in 1730, the country had—after the bloodless revolution of 1688—moved into a future that was mercantile and self-consciously rational, with a Bank of England and, in Sir Robert Walpole, a first prime minister.

Along with all this came property development: in a very big way. In the early seventeenth century monarchs had been nervous of too much building in London—the recurrent plague, the infamously volatile "mob"—yet at the same time they liked the money that it brought, and the always hard-up Charles I went against his "better" judgment to license the laying-out of the Piazza at Covent Garden. Residential at the time of its 1630s development (by the master Inigo Jones), it showed the way to a future of great London squares. It was built on land owned by the Russell family, soon to be the Dukes of Bedford, who in the noble tradition had supplemented their holdings by sage marriages to rich girls.

The man who would become the 1st Duke received £12,000 from his wife, Anne Carr, in 1637. The 2nd Duke, who married Elizabeth Howland in 1695—he aged fifteen, she thirteen—acquired a staggering £100,000. It all helped no end with the speculative building, which would later begin upon the family land at Bloomsbury: Russell Square, Bedford Square, and the rest.

It is astonishing to consider how much of London has been built upon, or with, heiress wealth. Elizabeth Sloane brought the 250 acres that would become Chelsea to her husband, Charles Cadogan, in 1717. Nine years earlier, the 1st Duke of Newcastle had bought the land that would become Marylebone. He died in 1711, leaving just one very rich child, Henrietta Holles. Her marriage to Lord Harley, son of the 1st Earl of Oxford, also produced an heiress: Margaret, born 1715, whose brother died when she was aged ten. She owned most of the land north of Oxford Street, which was developed properly after 1730, and which made her— "officially"—the richest woman in Britain.

Margaret was one of those heiresses who do not catch head-lines but are merely written about, whose money did not wreck her life but improved it. She put it to use both intellectual and charitable, and married (at the age of nineteen) a man of similar status—the 2nd Duke of Portland—with whom she was in love. Later their son would become prime minister. How simple it all sounds, put like this! How exactly like an heiress's life *ought* to be!

But Margaret had advantages over and above great wealth. Her upbringing, at Wimpole Hall in Cambridgeshire, was not merely the usual succession of days defined by different ways of filling one's leisure. It was stimulating, like the times in which she lived: the age of reason succeeding that of tu-mult. Her father Edward—son of Queen Anne's de facto prime minister—was a collector and artistic patron. Visitors to Wim-pole included Alexander Pope and Jonathan Swift. Margaret, quite unhampered by any sense that a woman should not en-gage with the prevailing climate of enlightenment, and with a mind that refused to be bored, began a natural history collec-tion as a child—starting with seashells—which by the time of her marriage had expanded into something serious, respected, and properly curated.

Margaret was a botanist, entomologist, and ornithologist, who also inherited her father's love of the arts. A polymath, in fact, whose wealth meant that she could attract the best specialists and create what became a notable museum, open to the public, housed at Bulstrode Hall in Buckinghamshire. Horace Walpole—diarist, aesthete, and fellow collector, not a man easy to impress—wrote of Margaret: "In an age of great collectors, she rivaled the greatest."

She was also a member of the Blue Stockings, a group in which one can discern the first tremulous stirrings of feminism, albeit within the hermetic circle of the well born and leisured. It was formed in the 1750s by a handful of women, including Margaret's close friend Elizabeth Montagu, who sought to create a proto-literary society. Men were also welcome—not least as they were of the caliber of Edmund Burke and Samuel Johnson—but this was, essentially, a setting in which women could talk freely about books and the arts, and encourage each other in scholarship and writing (Elizabeth Montagu wrote, in 1769, an essay on Shakespeare so good that people assumed its author to be male). Although female education was scant, and certainly did not extend to university level, there was nothing to prevent women from the moneyed classes pursuing knowledge. Nevertheless the norm, in high society, was unashamedly non-intellectual: gossip and gambling, needlework or watercolor-dabbling, ways to eat up the time rather than make use of it.

The Blue Stockings, therefore, were of some significance. Although the group's members did not talk about politics, they were—inevitably—political; although the society was rarefied, it represented an opening up, a shift within the lives of women. Its profound belief in the importance of education led the society to acquire a progressive aspect, and some of its members concerned themselves with philanthropy. Margaret herself was a strong supporter of Thomas Coram's campaign for a home for orphans and unwanted children (the Foundling Hospital, established in 1739). Today this has a slight air of the Lady Bountiful, but for this she can hardly be blamed: yes, it is easy for rich people to be charitable, but writing a check is not the same as genuine engagement.

So was it various accidents of birth that allowed this woman to lead a life of interest and fulfillment? The good brain, the cultured father, the intelligent husband, the upbringing that steeped her in a sense of what money could do, rather than how it could be wasted?

Unlike so many heiresses Margaret, 2nd Duchess of Portland, was protected in every way, but perhaps most importantly by her own nature. When the cultured father managed to overspend—it is possible to do so, even with such an income—and Wimpole Hall was sold to pay off his debts, it did not matter materially (plenty more where that came from); yet one also feels that, even if it *had* mattered, then Margaret would have remained in some measure immune. She had social position of a kind that was indestructible, but she also had inner resources. She had a curiosity that penetrated the blandness of privilege, and looked to a world beyond its gilded portals: in her intellectual outlook she was wholly a creature of her rational age, not of the late seventeenth century into which her sad counterpart, Mary Davies, was born, and whose schisms seemed to enter her very soul. The fifty years between them made a difference, certainly, just as they would between a woman born in 1940 and one born in 1990. But there were other factors at play. Margaret would always have been a rare type of heiress; and unlike Mary she belonged to a class—the ruling class—that was insulated against danger, as perhaps no other has ever been.

Two young women, so alike in their inheritances: the one north of Oxford Street, the other to its south; the one who controlled her fate, the other shoved and buffeted by it. Although the uncomfortable truth is that Mary Davies was doing quite well, on the surface at least, while her life was being controlled. The problems arose when she tried, at the age of thirty-five, to strike out and do what *she* wanted for a change. Having lived up to that point within a succession of luxury cages, it was her misguided quest for autonomy that eventually led her back inside one.

* * *

Although nobody knows if she saw it that way, Mary was lucky in her husband, Sir Thomas Grosvenor, with whom she was not obliged to live until the age of fifteen (another of her mother's negotiations). Handsome, to judge by his Lely likeness, a graduate of the Grand Tour, Thomas inherited his baronetcy in 1665 and built a large house at Eaton in Cheshire, which is still home to the Dukes of Westminster.

In 1680 Mary was sent up north to this house, where she spent twenty years with her husband and gave birth to eight children. Thomas became an MP and the local mayor, he owned horses that ran at Chester (where he had his own stand, and later a stud painted by Stubbs), he visited London occasionally with his wife. It was the prosperous, well-tended life of the country landowner family, at a time when England was regaining a stability that would have seemed unimaginable when the Grosvenor couple were born.

The 1688 "Glorious Revolution" ended forty years of the most extreme turbulence. The Dutch William of Orange was invited to take the throne, and the previous king—the Catholic James II—was booted into exile. England took a giant leap toward the modern era, establishing the primacy of Parliament and of Protestantism. All well and good: this seemed to be the way forward. Nevertheless the radical new status quo, with its reformed and tamed monarchy, was beleaguered for some seventy years by Jacobite rebellions. The deposed James II, languishing and plotting in France, had sizable support in his former country; among whose number, much to the embarrassment of her husband, was Lady Mary Grosvenor.

At precisely the most incendiary time, when her country had settled so firmly upon its course, Mary became a flagrant convert to Roman Catholicism. It was as seismic a choice as if the spouse of a prominent Jew had declared their support for Hitler. In the climate of the late seventeenth century—when popery was regarded as akin to devil worship—it was also an extraordinarily transgressive act, and one that could only cause immense damage to the Grosvenor family.

Was this a blow aimed directly at her husband, who—for all his decency—had bought her as if she were one of his racehorses, and thus symbolized the thraldom that accompanied her monumental inheritance? An exchange of letters between the Grosvenors implies that there *was* affection between them, for a time at least, although Thomas also wrote, apropos of who knows what: "Your unkindness to me sometimes strikes me to the heart." Meanwhile Mary's letters to female friends suggest a kind of torpid indifference: "Though Chester is so near I scarce ever see it, so can tell little what is done there, never inquiring after it."

She seems to have been ripe for something: a rebellion of her own. She certainly identified with the romantic Jacobite cause, rather than the money-centric future that her inheritance represented, although this may have been because the man who coached her in Catholicism was a fervent supporter and—it was inevitably rumored—Mary's lover. She may have been genuine in her faith. It was a perverse allegiance to proclaim, however, at a time when Catholics were being forced from public life. Thomas was strongly anti-popish and loyal to the new king William III, but now there were loud mutterings among the local gentry about the Catholic gatherings at Eaton Hall. The king—all too aware of the ongoing Jacobite threat—became coldly suspicious. Perhaps it all hastened Thomas to his death "of a feavour" in 1700, at the age of forty-four.

Whatever she had felt for her husband, without him Mary was lost. For the first time in her life, she was bereft of the protection that her wealth—and, perhaps, her nature—absolutely required. Nevertheless what happened to her was extreme, a story that might have been dreamed up by Samuel Richardson.

The book *Mary Davies and the Manor of Ebury* describes her at the start of the eighteenth century: "a young widow of thirty-five, willful in character, well-to-do, and therefore independent, at times unsettled in intellect, and liable to take extravagant notions into her head." The author seems fully to have accepted the contemporary view that Mary was weak-minded, mentally somewhat uncontrolled, and that her lack of understanding made her—to no small extent—the author of her own misfortunes.

And indeed it could be that the real difference between the two heiresses, Mary Davies and Margaret Portland, was very simple. One did not use her brain, or had not much of a brain to use, and the other delighted in its expansion. Mary saw only the limitations of being an heiress, and transcended them with the carelessness of a fugitive. Margaret saw no limitations, as her mind was free.

Yet one could take a slightly different view, and ask what chance had Mary to be otherwise? She was not raised among cultured people full of intellectual curiosity. From pretty much day one she was a commodity, bartered by her mother; married off to a man with whom she was probably always conscious of her origins (the notorious great-uncle who had appropriated a piece of London); and given no opportunity, at any point, to develop her own mind or interests. Mary *was* the Manor of Ebury. As far as she knew, therein lay her worth. So it might be said that her conversion was not—as it has been portrayed—a sign of stupidity, or obtuseness, or willfulness, but was instead the first moment in her life when she said: now I shall do something for and by myself. And because she had no notion of how to do this, because her independent judgment had never been exercised, because she was a woman of thirty-five who had never been let out of her playpen, it went more horribly wrong than anybody could have foreseen.

When Sir Thomas Grosvenor died, Mary was pregnant with the last child of the marriage. The day before her husband was buried (this timing has a vengeful air) she introduced into the domestic circle a Roman Catholic chaplain, a Benedictine monk named Father Lodowick Fenwick. After the birth of her daughter she announced her intention to travel to Europe with the Jacobite Father Fenwick and his sister, a Mrs. Turnour. Free, therefore, in every way.

But an heiress could never be free; as she was about to discover. Almost immediately after Thomas's death, control of Mary's inheritance began to be seized by trustees, her mother among them. They also sought to obtain guardianship of her children, including Richard, heir to the Grosvenor title. Then came the first, tentative suggestions that she might be confined to an asylum—that familiar method of dealing with an inconvenient woman, particularly with one who had money. The suggestion, of course, was for Mary's "own good." She was said to be showing increasing signs of mental instability—the religious conversion, the company she kept—why, one could almost smell the incense blowing through Eaton Hall! Yes, far better that she should be confined, if only for a time, before she did anything else of her own "free" will; especially anything that might involve money.

Again, the thing that should have been protecting her was putting her in jeopardy. To judge by a couple of her letters from this period—on the subject of her estate, which was being developed apace—there was nothing wrong with Mary's mind, beyond the fact that she wanted it to make its own decisions. For that reason, it would seem, she was being shoved out of the picture.

At the same time, the decisions that she made—the personal ones—were not good. It is not hard to understand why those around her, whose own heads were deliciously full of building prospects and lucrative leases, should have become alarmed, and why—more than two hundred years on—Charles Gatty's book took the view that Mary had become something of a liability. And there is some truth in that view. Because the fact of the matter is that the choices Mary was making, which she believed to be her own, were being powerfully directed by other people. Having never been anything but a pawn in other people's games, she had never learned the skill to play her own.

She thought that she was doing so. When she bustled off to her mother's house at Millbank—excitedly defying the advice of her trustees—and prepared for the journey to France, she was high on the spirit of adventure; and in Paris, where she stayed in a hotel close to the exiled court of James II, she acquired several suitors (no surprise there, a rich widow is scarcely less alluring than an heiress). This not being part of her companions' plan, she was persuaded by Father Fenwick to move on to Italy for the Papal Jubilee. When they returned to Paris in 1701, they were greeted by the chaplain's brother, Edward, who had been waiting for their return.

Mary had met Edward Fenwick before the trip to Europe. Later, Edward would say that she had been "wondrous taken" with him, and that because of this a cousin had encouraged him to court her. This makes him sound very much the passive party: the shy young man, who would never have dreamed of aspiring to Mary had she not fluttered her eyelashes, and who had to be persuaded into pursuit. Absolute nonsense, of course. It is obvious that from day one the Fenwicks had a well-worked plot to ensnare this woman. The priest played his careful part, and set the scene for the sexy brother. They were extremely well born, which no doubt both reassured and impressed, and they were Jacobite Catholics, those bold rebels whose spirit Mary sought pathetically to emulate.

Very likely she *was* attracted to Edward—activities like flirting were new to her, she was bound to be interested in the first personable man she had met since her husband's death—and this doubtless softened her up for what would happen. Nothing, however, could have prepared her. The events of early 1701 were sinister in the extreme, and for all their crude-colored melodrama have an uneasy contemporary resonance.

Soon after moving to the Hotel Castile in Paris with her entourage, Mary fell ill and was confined to her room. What took place inside that room would later be argued over, obsessively, in a London court case that lasted two years (with an intermission for war with France). The original illness was probably genuine. But there is little doubt that the Fenwicks—helped by a compliant doctor—used it as a highly convenient means to their own ends. Confined to her bed, pallid and powerless, Mary became the very embodiment of the victim-heiress: her vulnerability was absolute. The doctor administered emetics—suitable "for a horse," according to a witness—and repeatedly bled her with leeches. Then she was drugged with laudanum, which had been sprinkled into a dish of strawberries, and blacked out as if from an efficient dose of Rohypnol; this was date rape with a vengeance, and with one hell of a punch line. When at last she awoke from her semicoma, Mary was told—or "reminded"—that a ceremony of marriage had been conducted by Father Fenwick, and that she was now Edward's wife.

* * *

Mary would later suggest that the Fenwicks' ultimate plan was murder, which seems entirely possible. Had she expected love from her handsome Jacobite? Perhaps, although his avowal that she was deeply attracted to him—that in effect she "started it"—naturally cannot be trusted. He, meanwhile, was far easier to understand. He was born into a time and class that snatched women as casually as highwaymen did jewels, then for good measure dismissed them as mentally deficient when they flickered with protest.

Somehow, Mary managed to communicate with England. She escaped to her mother's house on Millbank. Once there she evinced hysteria, that definitively female complaint—a servant described her as "running up and down the house" all night—but the legitimacy of her distress was glided over. Instead it became evidence of lunacy. As in the worst nightmares, there was nothing that she could do to prove herself sane. She could not defend herself against what had become established fact. Only an unstable woman would have behaved as she had, and would say the things that she now said.

Soon Fenwick turned up, still smiling suavely, in pursuit of his conjugal rights, all set to take over her property and evict her tenants (which he actually began to do), demanding in his Chancery suit that he be paid £30,000, and what about her jewels, was she hiding them from him? Of course theirs was not a forced marriage! It was hardly his fault if the poor silly woman now wished it had never happened. Yes, she denied the marriage *now*, but that just showed how volatile, how whimsical she was! And indeed, many doubted her story of coercion. The more vehemently she protested, the madder she sounded. Such was the completeness of the case against her. Such, too, was the self-fulfilling nature of the decree that she was mentally ill. In the end, she became—at least in part—what she was said to be.

Not to be believed is terrible, but not to be believed when one is trying to prevent the seizure of one's inheritance—one's very self—is frightening beyond measure; not least because those who sought to protect Mary from Fenwick were only really doing so because they, too, sought control of what she owned. They wanted Fenwick out of the picture, but that didn't mean that they believed Mary's wild and incomplete recollections. She had gone to France in the company of these people, she had consorted with these reprehensible Jacobites; her history proclaimed her lack of good sense. Who, then, could prove that she had not wanted to marry Fenwick, and now said otherwise because she regretted having done so? But here is a response, which was not given at the time: so what if she did consider marriage to Fenwick? Was it not reasonable that this romantic dream—if it had bloomed for a while in her head—should have been exploded by what happened in the Paris hotel room: the confirmed details of bloodletting and laudanum, said to be "medicinal," conjuring the image of a woman so weakened that the man could take his brutal advantage?

However. Although Mary insisted that she was not married, Fenwick insisted otherwise, and given what was at stake there ensued a great lawyerly feast, a fandango of litigation "in all the courts of Law and Equity, for Fenwick claimed both the land and the lady."[4] But in every one of these courts the essential issue was the same, and it related to Mary's character. Was she a) an unstable woman who should never have been allowed onto the streets, such was her dangerous naivety; b) a lunatic woman who denied Fenwick because she had no memory of their marriage; or c) a devious woman who was *pretending* to be mad, in order to extricate herself from this inconvenient tie? Meanwhile the woman herself—forbidden to testify, as to be fair was Fenwick—sat in her great house at Eaton embroidering the intertwined initials of "M" and "T" (if only *he* were still alive, she surely now thought). In a voice both mournful and sane, she wrote to her mother: "I had rather come up to the trial and answer for myself." But that, of course, had never been permitted to her.

The Spiritual Court of the Dean and Chapter of Westminster dealt briskly with the marriage and pronounced it a sham with no canonical effect. This, however, was not the end of the matter. In 1703—contrary to the judge's instructions—a deeply stupid jury at Westminster Hall found in Fenwick's favor.

In the face of the testimony this seems incredible, but it really was not. It was a populist judgment, both typical of its time and easy to imagine today. Fenwick was the very image of the daredevil, the gallant Jacobite, the hero of the tale in fact; men almost always attracted the support in these cases—think Captain James Campbell versus Mary Wharton—but *this* Mary, plain and dull and outlandishly advantaged, had even less than usual to recommend her. Like Fenwick she could be reduced to a type, but in her case the images were frankly unappealing, as female stereotypes so often are: according to taste she was a hysteric, a ludicrous lovesick widow, a calculating Eve who had faked instability when it suited her and looked for pity where she deserved little. In the end she was simply too rich to command sympathy. And if the jury had felt that she had more money than was good for her, and that Fenwick had been obscurely entitled to a crack at it, their reaction of mingled envy and contempt is all too familiar.

So Fenwick won. But for some reason he never pursued a financial claim upon his "bride," nor did he seek to occupy any of her land. Perhaps, to use a twentieth-century phrase, somebody was employed to "put the frighteners" on him. One rather hopes so. In 1704 the Westminster judgment was overturned, and the so-called marriage annulled on the grounds that Mary had not been "compos mentis" at the time: another outrage, although with a better outcome. The gossip, in London society and coffee houses, may well be imagined. Mary's passage of torment should have been over, but there was no escaping the fallout from such an episode; which—in a twist that a dramaturge would reject as too absurd to be believed—acquired a blackly comedic subplot when a man in his sixties, Colonel Colepepper, a fantasist but one who knew exactly what he was doing, jumped smartly on the bandwagon and also claimed to have married Mary. An heiress-hunter out of Wycherley rather than Richardson, he proved far less troublesome than Fenwick. He was still, however, a deeply unwelcome reminder of the burden that Mary carried, along with the Manor of Ebury.

No matter. Her "protectors," led by her mother, were all too ready to relieve her of it. And now they had justifiable cause to hustle her from the scene, as they had tried to do after the death of her husband. The trauma of the intervening years had damaged her—how could it not have done? But how beautifully this played into the hands of those who had sought to have her put away four years earlier, who now could say that they had been right all along, that it was a kindness to confine this poor creature, and save her from the troubles that she would otherwise bring upon herself. Mrs. Tregonwell, that supremely nonmaternal woman, tried to regain the custody of the daughter whom she had ceded—or sold off—when Mary was twelve. The Grosvenor sons stepped in to prevent this, however, and gave their mother over to the care of their father's relations. "Dame Mary Grosvenor, Lunatick" lived with these perfectly nice people until her death, shielded within the somnolent calm of their Cheshire home, as the foundations of Grosvenor Square were laid out, brick by stately brick, upon her fields.

MARY, AGAIN

MARY DIED DURING the age of reason, having lost her own; or rather, having had it taken from her, first by stealth and then by force.

She was an uber-heiress, in what she owned and in what happened to her. Her story was extreme in every way. But because she was blamed for her own misfortunes—albeit in such a way that exonerated her; she had behaved like a madwoman because she *was* a madwoman—then that story, which should have been received with indignation, was absorbed into the narrative that portrayed the heiress as a mere item: wholly passive and there for the taking.

In other words, nothing changed.

Here is an example of the not uncommon fate that befell heiresses in the first half of the eighteenth century, that oh-so enlightened age, in which a handful of women were capable of studying the finer points of Shakespearean language or of a butterfly's wing, and thousands of others—both rich and poor—led lives dominated by injustice and fear. Naturally some of these moved to the dark side, and conspired with their men in the heiress-snatching trade.

As when, in 1728, the sixteen-year-old Sibble Morris was lured by two female acquaintances away from the bustle of

London, into a house off the Strand. There she found another woman—a Mrs. Hendron, again slightly known to her—and a man named Richard Russel, whom she believed to be a rich merchant. Although these people were familiar to her, the sight of them gathered together, in this unaccustomed way, rendered her fearful. Even the most innocent of wealthy young girls must have recognized something of the danger in which they walked. A clergyman appeared, and began to pronounce the marriage service, uniting Russel and Sibble in matrimony. The girl had to be helped to stand and refused to speak; it was a scene straight out of *The Handmaid's Tale*, with Mrs. Hendron in the role of an eighteenth-century Aunt Lydia, and evidence at the subsequent Old Bailey trial makes the parallels still more apt. "Hendron and others dragg'd her [Sibble] up Stairs to a Bed-Chamber, which was also shut up with Shutters, and Kitty Pendergrass and Peggy Johnson pulled off her Cloaths by Force, Hendron holding her Hands; and that one Mrs. Rigy was there present while all this was done, that they forc'd her into Bed, and that Hendron held her down in Bed." Then Russel, the new husband, joined his bride.

The girl could not bring herself to tell her father what had happened; only by chance did he find out almost immediately. A warrant was issued for Russel's arrest. He fled the country, which in itself was evidence enough to counter the usual defense, that Sibble Morris had married him willingly. Mrs. Hendron and Mrs. Pendergrass were sentenced to death. The stakes were high in this game, the chances of ultimate success slim, yet this did not deter the heiress-snatchers. The early eighteenth century was a gamblers' society. The instinct was to play all in the hope of the big win; or, in this case, a relatively small win. Mr. Morris testified that his daughter had been left a property in Southampton Street worth some £20 a year. He expected its value to increase; nevertheless, it was not a huge amount of money to die for. But heiress-snatching had become an activity almost for its own sake, a modish crime, backed by a whole network of dodgy priests, dubious venues, and accomplices for hire. There was, it seems, a sadistic adrenaline rush to be had from the planning, the seizure from the streets of London, the sudden forcible subjection of the rich to the will of the poor. At a time when about three-quarters of the population lived in squalor, and 2 percent had the vote, this was an irresistible inversion in the lives of those who had little, and in itself apparently worth the monumental risk.

Not all the snatches were so desperately serious. Some had an air of undergraduate japes. In 1725 the young Henry Fielding, future novelist and chief magistrate of London, was summoned to the Mayor's Court at Lyme Regis after a failed attempt to abduct an heiress named Sarah Andrews. Her guardian, Andrew Tucker, had made a complaint against him; Fielding, just down from Eton, rather splendidly refused to appear before a tribunal of "fat and greasy citizens" and sent his valet in his place. Indeed his stance throughout was that of the aggrieved party. So enraged was he about being thwarted in his desire for Sarah that, before fleeing Lyme, he affixed a note to a building in the town: "This is to give notice to all the World that Andrew Tucker and his Son John Tucker are clowns, and cowards." The girl was a cousin of Fielding, and in this case there had been a definite mutual attraction. Fielding, demonstrably, was not a savage. But his behavior, that reckless swagger of entitlement, was typical of the time.

Nor did things change as much as might have been expected after the passing of Lord Hardwicke's 1753 Marriage Act, which was nonetheless a giant leap forward: it "set the basic rules of marriage in England for nearly a century."[5] Essentially, it sought to halt the trade in clandestine ceremonies by rendering null and void any marriage not preceded by banns or a proper license, and by making any clergyman who conducted such a wedding guilty of a felony (there was an almighty rush to the Fleet in the weeks before the law was passed). As with previous similar legislation, it was fought ferociously by interested parties in the Commons—such as the secretary of state for war, Henry Fox, who had not long since eloped with an heiress. The MP Charles Townshend protested that the proposed law was an overreaction to a few highly publicized cases: "How rarely do such infamous marriages happen, especially with respect to those that are under age?" Not rarely enough, was the answer; but Townshend's was a quite widely held view. Another fear was that heiresses would now be sanctioned only to marry heirs, creating unions such as the one planned between Anne de Bourgh and Darcy, and collecting most of the country's wealth into a few large pockets rather than spreading it around a bit more liberally. An interesting interpretation of the redistribution principle; and one that was unsurprisingly rejected by the Lords, whose daughters these girls tended to be, and which was overwhelmingly in favor of the Hardwicke Act.

There were, however, large holes crocheted into the new law. Although consent was technically required for the marriage of a party under the age of twenty-one, those sufficiently determined would skip town, to a place where the banns could be read without anybody knowing about it, and the ensuing wedding would be perfectly legal. But perhaps the biggest get-out clause was that the new law did not apply offshore (Guernsey did a particularly good trade in clandestine marriages), nor in Scotland. Despite the country's union with England in 1707, marriages without registrar or clergy remained legal there until 1940. The result of this disparity can be summed up in two words: Gretna Green.

The clergy, whose less scrupulous members were impressively quick off the mark, were soon taking up positions at the little village just across the border from Carlisle, where the first "venue" one encountered was a smithy, and what were known as blacksmith weddings became instantly all the rage. Paintings of "runaway marriages" were a commonplace in even the best-ordered homes. Lydia Languish, the romantic young heiress in Sheridan's 1775 play *The Rivals*, longs to marry at Gretna and has a head full of elopement clichés ("so becoming a disguise—so amiable a ladder of ropes!"). In 1792 a real-life heiress, one Miss Goodfellow, absconded there with a young bombardier and his "best man"; by the time they reached their destination, however, Miss Goodfellow and her intended had fallen out, so she married the friend instead. Gretna Green was that kind of place. Las Vegas, but chillier.

It began as a craze, but the appeal of this marriage venue did not wane—its peak year was 1854, when 731 couples married there—and it served what many people regarded as a purpose. In 1782 John Fane, 10th Earl of Westmoreland, eloped to Gretna with Sarah, daughter of banker Robert Child, although this was the opposite of the usual heiress-snatch: far from being financially advantageous, it led to Sarah being cut straight out of her father's will (the old swine was unhappy about her marrying a man who would not take the Child surname*). Three Lord

---

* Such was Child's desperation to halt the marriage that he followed the couple on their way to Gretna Green, and was only stopped when one of his horses was shot by Westmoreland's men (so he was a bit of a swine too). Although Sarah inherited none of her father's money, she did have a life interest in his bank. This, plus Robert Child's vast estate, eventually passed to his only surviving grandchild: Sarah's daughter Lady Sarah Sophia Fane, later Countess of Jersey (see p. 125), whose husband was more than happy to adapt his family name to Child-Villiers.

Chancellors were married there, including the sixty-six-year-old Lord Erskine, who in 1820 eloped with his mistress while disguised as a woman, and found himself thus depicted in the eighteenth-century version of the internet meme: the cartoon.

There was, indeed, a comical aspect to all this. The term "Gretna Green," with its droll alliteration, entered the language and has never left. It became a signifier of larky licentiousness, of nudge-wink transgression—very English, despite the over-the-border setting.

"ELOPEMENT: On Saturday last, a young gentleman, the son of Mr. Allsop, surgeon, of Uttoxeter, contrived to escape with the grand-daughter and heiress of the late Thomas Bainbridge, Esq., of Wood Seat, in this county, and who has a fortune of 50,000l. The parties have bent their way to Gretna-green. A pursuit was attempted, but as the youthful pair had the start of *eleven hours*, with 'all appliances and means to boot,' it was considered as a hopeless affair."

This was a standard press snippet, conjuring a *Heat* magazine excitation, a semiconcealed sympathy with the daring young foxes who had eluded the heavy-footed hunt. Nevertheless the jokiness was only part of the story, its acceptable face; in truth, the life of the heiress remained horribly parlous, whatever Charles Townshend, MP, might have told the House.

Because of the Hardwicke Act, forced marriage naturally became less frequent, although it still happened often enough. In 1791, for instance, fourteen-year-old Clementina Clerke was seized by a man named Richard Perry, who pulled off the great gamble in what can only be called textbook fashion. He had overheard the girl's guardian talking indiscreetly in a Bristol tavern, showing off about her recent inheritance of sugar plantations in Jamaica (this compromised source of wealth was not, of course, unusual). Working at high speed Perry married

Clementina, but more to the point he managed to make her pregnant—twice—by the time he was brought to trial in 1794. Had he been executed, as was quite likely, the marriage would have been annulled and the children rendered illegitimate. Therefore Clementina, the stolen girl, was obliged to testify in Perry's defense, which was conducted by none other than the future eloper Thomas Erskine. The prosecutor was the son of that former would-be abductor, Henry Fielding. What a small world it was.

* * *

And then there was another problem, the one for which legislation could only do so much: those instances in which rich women freely chose to marry men from whom they should have run, screaming, before the real nightmare could begin.

Mary Bowes, a direct ancestor of Queen Elizabeth II, had no need whatever to wreck her own life.* She had every possible advantage—not just money—which makes her story all the more frustrating and perturbing. She was born in 1749, heiress to a coal magnate, and at the age of eighteen married the 9th Earl of Strathmore, who in the familiar British way (making a polite little bow to female financial dominance) took her surname as well as her wealth. She had both looks and learning. Like Margaret, Duchess of Portland, Mary was a Blue Stocking: an amateur botanist, a linguist, a patron. Unlike Margaret, however, she was also rather silly. A contemporary source wrote that

---

* The 14th Earl of Strathmore, Claude Bowes-Lyon, was the Queen's maternal grandfather. Lyon was the original family surname, before the 9th Earl became Bowes; his younger son, the 11th Earl, hyphenated the names.

"her judgment was weak, her prudence almost none, and her prejudice unbounded,"[6] and her house on Grosvenor Square was called a "Temple of Folly," filled with self-styled artists smarming their way toward handouts. For all her education, in fact, her susceptibility to a plausible man rivaled that of Mary Grosvenor.

At the age of twenty-seven, by then a mother of five, she was widowed and inherited the title of "richest woman in the country." Among the many suitors who began to buzz and hum around her was an Anglo-Irish officer, a couple of years her senior, named Andrew Robinson Stoney. Some three-quarters of a century later his liaison with Mary would become the inspiration for William Thackeray's 1844 novel, *The Luck of Barry Lyndon*, although that innately comic work lightens the gruesome truth no end.*

Like any top-of-the-range adventurer, Stoney naturally knew all about the widowed Countess of Strathmore, and had her firmly in his lethal sights. He had already got through one heiress. As an eighteen-year-old ensign he had targeted a naive Newcastle girl named Hannah Newton, whose fortune was at least £20,000. Interestingly, he decided against elopement; a man of his calculating type had realized that the odds of success were insufficiently favorable. Instead he simply pressed and insisted and manipulated until eventually the Newton family

---

* In 1841 William Thackeray, then an impoverished magazine hack, spent part of the summer at the home of a Cambridge friend, John Bowes. There he learned the story that he would develop into his novel. Bowes was the illegitimate son of the 10th Earl of Strathmore; although unable to take the title, he owned the family's English estates, with those in Scotland going to his uncle, the 11th Earl. His inheritance included a castle in Co. Durham and many thousands of acres in Yorkshire. It had come to him from his grandmother, Mary Bowes, the model for Thackeray's Countess of Lyndon, whose great misfortune it is to take Redmond Barry—the fictionalized Andrew Stoney—as her second husband.

agreed—a grave mistake—to the marriage. An example of Stoney's behavior, and surely a true story, was that he chucked his wife downstairs at a public assembly. He also tried to sell off her property, but in this he was forestalled. "She was a most wretched woman," it was written, "and brought no child alive into the world; which he much desired for his own sake." His monetary sake, that is to say. When Hannah died giving birth to a stillborn baby, Stoney was left, under the terms of his marriage settlement, with just £5,000. A fortune at the time, of course, but he was out for far more.

He spent the money in clubs, on women, at the races: normal behavior for a well-born young man of the late eighteenth century, in a milieu high on machismo, low on morality, which absorbed without much comment the decadent cruelty within Stoney's nature. He also attended evenings at Mary's "Temple of Folly" in Grosvenor Square. He must have had charisma, charm, sex appeal—all the usual—because her interest was aroused, and he came up with an astonishing ruse to pique it further. Mary had a slightly lurid reputation; there had been rumors, not entirely unfounded, of affairs throughout her marriage; she had become the target of a series of anonymous letters—clearly written by friends of her late husband—that were published in the *Morning Post*. Posing as the avenger of Lady Strathmore's honor, and having suborned the *Post*'s editor as an accomplice, he challenged this man to a fake duel in which he gave himself an injury, pronounced by a surgeon—another accomplice—to be near fatal. Then he laid his sword at the feet of the countess, who like an idiot placed it at the head of her bed, wrote Stoney a breathless love poem, and married him four days later. The groom was carried to the altar on a stretcher. One can almost see the amused glint of victory in his eye, as he stretched a feeble hand to his insanely rich and besotted bride.

What a coup! In a way one has to admire the man's skill and flair for detail, but then planning these things was much of the fun; as soon as he had caught Mary the game was over, and all that was left was the daily grind of sadism.

Like a good husband, Stoney took the name of Bowes. Then he became a very bad husband indeed. If even half of what was written about him was accurate—and there is no reason to believe otherwise—then he was a devil of a man, one of those who thrive on controlling a woman, in this case physically as well as mentally. He had, it was said, "a miserable sort of energy," which he deployed savagely: partly on the parliamentary career that he had acquired, partly on his old habits of gambling and mistresses, but also on making Mary's life hell. This came naturally to him, and thus began to bore him. What gave him an exciting challenge was when he discovered that she had created a safety net against her own infatuation.

Today, the inability to escape an abusive partner is usually (not always) associated with lack of means. Then—as has been said—it was a problem more likely to afflict a rich woman: unless careful provision had been made, she could not walk out without losing everything to her abuser. In Mary's case, provision *had* been made. As a precaution against a previous suitor, she had executed a deed securing to herself exclusive control over her property. When Stoney discovered this, his rage contained an element of delight at the fact that he had a new project to occupy his mind; and within four months, by a grotesquely inventive mixture of violence and humiliation, he had succeeded in forcing Mary to revoke the deed. His cleverest trick—reminiscent of the contemporary threat of holding compromising images on a smartphone—was to oblige his wife to write her "Confessions," a grim little memoir of indiscretions, which he then held as a blackmailing tool.

Once Mary had signed away everything, she was in very big trouble indeed. What she now believed was that the monstrous marriage would go on forever, because she could not afford to leave. There were two children with Stoney, whom he would surely use as weapons. There was also, undoubtedly, a risk to her life. Nevertheless, after eight years with this maniac she reached the end of the line; helped by a few loyal servants she fled the marital home—her own house at Grosvenor Square, now of course lost to her—to begin the long fight for restitution. The great society gossip Horace Walpole recorded that she had "eloped," which was then the usual interpretation when a person took flight, although he was perplexed by the fact that she was not known to have a "swain." Swains, indeed, were very much off the agenda. Mary presented herself at the Court of the King's Bench and protested against her husband "for ill-treatment of her person." Quick as a flash Stoney produced the Confessions; look what he had had to put up with, shackled to this scarlet woman for so many years! This worked less well than anticipated. It was perfectly clear that his wife had written the document under duress, and anyway the love affairs it recorded had taken place before the marriage to Stoney. So his pose as deceived husband failed to stand up—in court, at least.

Mary began divorce proceedings, and at first public sympathy was dutifully with her. As with Mary Grosvenor, however, this was not where sympathy *naturally* lay. There was this irrepressible urge to side with the man: the chancer, the dasher, the adventurer that so many longed to be, if they only had the chutzpah. When the sixteen-year-old Maria Glenn, a Somerset girl with expectations from two sugar plantations, was abducted and married off to a local farmer, James Bowditch, in 1817, the bells rang out in Taunton after Bowditch was absolved—on appeal—of all blame and Maria found guilty of perjury. She was deemed a shy, unprepossessing girl. He was very handsome. There was a powerful assumption that Maria had been all too eager to marry him in the first instance, then had lied about this in panic when her guardian stepped in.

These fearless fortune hunters had a rock-star gleam. And Stoney, who was only too aware of this, began to play the advantage. *Now* those painstakingly extracted Confessions revealed their worth: Stoney bought a newspaper—with his wife's money—for the express purpose of having them published, and commissioned cartoons that plucked fiercely at the vulnerable spot of Mary's racy past. Public opinion turned, as it had longed to do, and massed behind him like a chorus. He was the good guy, the wronged party. Had he only left it there, he might have kept hold of his wife's money.

But Stoney was the sort of man who could *not* leave things; the thought of Mary on the London streets, plotting with lawyers to have that vastly precious deed overturned, was too much for him to stand. He had his wife abducted by a gaggle of henchmen and taken off to be imprisoned at Durham (her own house again), where she was subjected to renewed horrors before being helped to escape, again by her servants. Walpole, his "my *dear!*" tone never less appropriate, wrote to a friend about the return to court of the "veteran madwoman"—as Mary had become, to the society that she once commanded—"and the enormous barbarities of her husband who beat her six days and six nights . . . for which the myrmidons of the King's Bench have knocked his brains out—almost."

Yes: justice, coming rather too late for Mary, was nonetheless imminent. In 1787 Stoney was sentenced to three years in jail, and the following year the deed that gave him control over Mary's property was invalidated. Divorce, which then required an Act of Parliament, brought the marriage to an end. Stoney spent the remaining twenty-three years of his life within the rules of the King's Bench prison for debt, where he continued much as before—had five children by the daughter of a fellow prisoner—and remained something of a curiosity. Thackeray's friend Leigh Hunt recalled being struck by Stoney's appearance, "much of a gentleman" in his cocked hat, and how inconsistent this was with a man who had "run a needle through his wife's tongue."

Mary Stoney Bowes died in 1800, ten years before the man whom she had fought and conquered, at a price that even an heiress struggled to pay. She was buried in Westminster Abbey, wearing—it was said—a "superb bridal dress."

* * *

Why had she married him? This was the question that would go on being asked of heiresses, even as the circumstances of these marriages changed. Why, when one had the power of near limitless choice, would one choose so badly?

Mary Bowes was not Mary Grosvenor, who had been as horribly easy a target as a pheasant emerging dazed from a rearing pen. She was a woman of the world, of sexual experience. Nevertheless, she was duped. One could say that she was effectively forced into a reciprocal gesture, after Stoney had apparently fought a duel on her behalf. Yet the fervid poem that she wrote in his praise suggests that she really did fall for this man.

Well: the brute fact is that only an attractive, confident man would attempt to become a fortune hunter in the first place. It was no good trying to seduce an heiress if one looked like a Georgian king. A kidnapper could be any old ruffian, but a con man had to look like Callum Turner in the 2020 film adaptation of *Emma* and deploy bucketloads of slightly elusive charm. Elizabeth Bennet, one of the least silly girls in fiction, is temporarily bulldozed by Wickham's cultivated brand of boldness. Here one sees the type in action, the gallant officer with his air of slight danger, telling lies with ardent smoothness, unable to resist Elizabeth's credulous response—it is much more fun, after all, to dupe a woman like her—but always with an eye elsewhere, to the main chance.

Pride and Prejudice was published during the peacocking Regency period (1811–20), when the concept of the heiress and her hunter was as much a fixture of popular culture as mother-in-law jokes in the mid-twentieth century. Bath—a city that Jane Austen knew very well—was alight with highly sexualized flirtation, rather like an early nineteenth-century Ibiza, and an important venue for traders in the marriage market. As always, the cartoonists knew exactly what was going on. That great visual chronicler Thomas Rowlandson created masterpieces such as "The Successful Fortune Hunter, or Captain Shelalee Leading Miss Marrowfat to the Temple of Hymen," in which a prancing Wickham leads an heiress with a face like a pig through the Bath crescents. Not kind, but (as it were) on the money.

The cartoonists were also alert to the situations of real-life heiresses, familiar with every detail of the runners and riders in breathless pursuit of the prize. The next girl to inherit the title of "richest heiress in the kingdom" would provide them with a veritable cornucopia of material—although satire, in the end, would prove an inappropriate response to her story.

CATHERINE

THE YOUNG WOMAN in question, who inherited her spectacular fortune at the age of sixteen, was born in 1789—the year of revolution—and herself represented something that felt attractively fresh. Catherine Tylney Long was a bright, savvy heiress, clued up as to the implications of her inheritance, whose origins in "trade" (in fact the East India Company) meant that the money, too, was very much new money. She was pretty, sweet, and immensely popular: a Regency It girl. Had she been born 200 years later, she would have had a Kardashian-level following on Instagram and not impossibly a cameo role on *Made in Chelsea*. As it was, she had a Cruickshank cartoon entitled "Worshippers at Wanstead"—Wanstead House was her property in Essex—in which she was depicted, perched upon a throne, with a gang of drooling admirers at her feet. She also may have had a nod from Jane Austen, who in around 1816 revised the early novel *Susan*—turning it into *Northanger Abbey*—and changed the name of its lead character to Catherine; or, as she became after marriage, Catherine Tilney.

The real Catherine was the eldest child of Sir James Tylney, who in turn was the sole heir of a rich uncle, known as "the Bachelor Earl" after being found in bed with a manservant. When Sir James died in 1794, and his only son in 1805, Catherine inherited the lot.

And it really was a lot. Wanstead, now a park on the outer reaches of northeast London, was then a serious estate: the Palladian mansion at its heart had cost £360,000 when it was built in the early eighteenth century. She also acquired thousands of acres over six counties, a huge chunk of cash, beautiful Draycot House in Wiltshire, and an income of at least £40,000 a year, which was about four times that of the average peer.

The dire fates suffered by earlier heiresses served as a warning, a guide to what not to do, and ensured that Catherine was better prepared for what was coming her way: the men, the hangers-on, the need to keep her wits in the face of luscious flattery and smiling thieves. She was moved to Grosvenor Square (where else), taught the workings of society and how to deal with begging letters. "Establish that character of *a lady of business*," she was told, advice that any heiress should heed and rarely does. Yet Catherine started very well indeed. She took an interest in what her trustees were up to, and dealt smartly with the Duc de Bourbon, who had fled France for the safety of Wanstead and showed no signs of wanting to leave. A gambler would have put good money on this young woman coping beautifully with her situation, and becoming a Margaret rather than a Mary.

In 1811 she was invited to the Grand Summer Fete held by the new Prince Regent, the future George IV, who with his free-spending habits (the ball cost £120,000) could certainly have done with some of Catherine's inheritance. Meanwhile his brother, the Duke of Clarence—later King William IV—was entranced with the money but also, quite sincerely, with Catherine herself. Despite being twice the girl's age and with a long-standing mistress, he fully intended to propose.

He was a fortune hunter, in fact, albeit one who in no way resembled a Regency buck (like all the Hanoverians, he was resplendently plain); but who may well have expected his social position to carry the day. On account of her relatively *nouveau* inheritance, Catherine was called by some "an ill-born mushroom." Of course this was jealousy, the usual cross borne by rich girls, especially pretty ones; nevertheless, a number of heiresses have been immensely keen to climb away from what they regard as ignoble origins (hence Barbara Hutton's predilection for spurious European "princes"), and the fact of the matter was that William was a royal duke. In that society, it was quite a card to hold. Although there was no thought at the time that he would become king, had Catherine married him she would, in 1830, have become queen consort. Furthermore—quite a thought—a child of the marriage would have ascended the throne instead of Queen Victoria.

Catherine's mother very much wanted her to marry William, and in this she was wise. An older man, of unimpeachable standing, would have guaranteed his wife's protection. He would also have been grateful to her, which is never a bad thing in a marriage; cynical perhaps, but cynicism was very much needed with a situation like Catherine Tylney Long's. Whom to trust? It was very hard to know. It was back to the familiar question: how was an heiress ever to be valued *for herself*? How could she tell a Morris Townsend, gracefully pledging his love while internally counting the millions, from a man who was happy to have the money but at least as happy to have the girl?

She could not. But with a man like the Duke of Clarence she could be sure of something still more important, in that era of blistering inequality: that he would not behave like an Andrew Stoney.

It might have seemed, however, that a nephew of Viscount Wellington—later the 1st Duke, the hero of Waterloo—could also be trusted on that score. In any event that is what Catherine would have wanted to believe, given William Wellesley Pole's vastly superior attractions. This was what an A-list fortune hunter *should* be like. "Mr. Pole"—a year older than Catherine, son of the 3rd Earl of Mornington—was well traveled, a superb horseman, the very glass of fashion, a dandy friend of Beau Brummell and immensely sexy; he turned the daring new fashion for waltzing into something like dirty dancing. And he was determined to knock to one side the other William, the waddling old duke who represented stodgy German safety.

Unsurprisingly, Catherine fell for Pole, just as the more experienced Mary Bowes had fallen for Stoney; yet she kept her cool and held off from marriage. Pole left her unsure, stirred but nervous. His short history was undeniably checkered—he had, for instance, both excelled and disgraced himself as his uncle's aide-de-camp in the Peninsular War. Wellington, who at the time dismissed Pole as "lamentably ignorant and idle," later admitted a kind of admiring bafflement when he wrote: "He is the most extraordinary person altogether I have ever seen. There is a mixture of steadiness and extreme levity, of sense and folly in his composition such as I have never met with in any other instance."

As a young man Pole had debts for the usual reasons—horses, clubs—and had lived with a woman (a seamstress in Ipswich), which was a little more out of the ordinary. The difficulty was how to judge whether his behavior was that of a young man who would eventually get it out of his system, or that of a man who would simply get older and possibly worse.

Like Stoney, he tried the trick of fighting duels on Catherine's behalf (one of these, on Wimbledon Common, never actually reached the point of exchanging blows) but her reaction was nothing like that of Mary Bowes. In a burst of good sense she instead switched allegiance to the Duke of Clarence, who informed his poor ill-used mistress, the actress Mrs. Jordan, that her services were no longer required.

If only she had kept to her decision, and to the advice of her mother and two sisters (as well as to the anonymous letter writer who asked: "Is it possible that the amiable, the virtuous and good Miss Long is going to bestow her hand upon that reptile Pole?"). But love—or lust—will out, even against royalty, as those devilish cartoonists were all too aware: "Miss Long-ing for a Pole," was one caption. Catherine knew about his past, yet found herself willing to believe that he would change—the reasoning generally used by somebody unable to resist marrying the wrong person. Meanwhile her family was won over by the immense charm of the Wellesley family, which after all contained the revered figure of Wellington, and thus was surely safe? "She is a very pretty likeable creature," wrote Pole's mother to her son, in a tone both lightly reassuring and not reassuring at all, "and if ever you make her unhappy *I shall hate you my dear!*"

Naturally there was a prenup: Regency style, which meant that it was heavily weighted against the woman. Pole refused to bring any of the estate to which he was heir, and took a lifetime interest in Catherine's. In fact he could have seized the lot. He was entitled to his wife's property and her earnings (in this case, her hugely valuable rents). The trustees—one of whom discerned in Pole scarcely "a squeeze of cordiality"—did their best, however, managing the rents themselves and handing them directly to Catherine, with the express command that Pole was forbidden to "intermeddle therewith." They also protected Catherine against "his debts or engagements," which, given his past, was extremely important.

Nevertheless Pole, in a concession surely made by Catherine's side with the utmost reluctance, was handed the magnificent Wanstead House and its 300 acres of parkland. That was the early nineteenth century for you. It makes one long to reach back in time and hiss dire warnings into the ears of this young girl, whose trustees doubtless had to restrain themselves from doing exactly that. Yes, the Duke of Clarence was fat and plain, but glamor is not everything, and Catherine's best option would have been to marry him and take lovers (as so many wives did). At that time, twenty years after Mary Wollstonecraft's *Vindication of the Rights of Women* but almost sixty years before the first Married Women's Property Act, there was simply too much money around to take risks. And too many men *were*—potentially—a risk. Only a very lucky woman like Margaret, Duchess of Portland, whose class protected her like an additional shield—she was doubly glazed, as it were, against the fortune hunter—and whose husband stood as her equal, could escape a marriage market that all too often resembled a horror film in periwigs.

Or Catherine could have remained single. This was the safest course of all. It was arguable, moreover, that there was no more desirable life than that of an unmarried woman with means and independence. As the campaigner Barbara Leigh Smith would write some forty years later, a spinster had the same rights to property as a man; she could act as a trustee or executrix, which a wife could not; and, if she had an illegitimate child, it would "belong" to her rather than to its father. Here, then, was the solution—the way to keep these oh-so vulnerable heiresses out of harm's way—yet it was never really contemplated. Marriage was a risk, but it was also the journey's end. "Being married gives one one's position, which nothing else can," as Queen Victoria put it, apparently without irony.

Accordingly, in 1812, Catherine Tylney Long took William Wellesley Pole to have and to hold at St. James's, Piccadilly, with the bride in a thousand-guinea white ensemble and with a break midway so that somebody could send out for a ring, which the groom had neglected to obtain. If Catherine had a qualm at that moment, it was too late. The *commedia* was about to begin.

So was this an example of the mysterious masochism that can be discerned in the heiress—the subliminal guilt about her undeserved good fortune, and the consequent desire to create a situation in which she might lose it all? To the modern eye, it might look that way. And the possibility does lurk; although that tendency really belongs to the later heiresses, whose wealth bloomed in a world so much more alert to the concept of inequality (Catherine, through no fault of her own, would not have known that the cost of her wedding outfit would have paid the average annual wages of twenty manual workers).

The heiresses unprotected by law had no "need" for masochism, as sadism so often awaited them. Yet there must have been a psychological element to their all-too-frequent recklessness. Perhaps their wealth—so strikingly rare at a time when an heiress was only created by default, in the absence of men—made them feel that they were insulated against reality, even though they knew at the same time that they were not. Perhaps, rather like a woman in possession of extreme beauty, they felt that the rules of the game were theirs to bend. Nor was it entirely clear what the rules were. This was a world that liked to arrange its marriages, yet ran alive with people who thumbed their noses at any such notion: as Austen's novels show, elopement and fortune hunting and general romantic chaos were the jagged fault lines in a society that strove for order, regulation, relationships like the one in which Marianne Dashwood—whose heart had yearned for the Pole-like Willoughby—finds contentment with the older, solvent, majestically reliable Colonel Brandon. A girl like Catherine Tylney Long was not obliged, as was Marianne, to marry for money. Therefore she could marry for "love," and her heiress's sense of entitlement—which she must have had, despite her sweetness of character—made her hell-bent upon doing so. And here, again, is the irony that runs through so much of this story: that the girl who could not afford a free choice of husband often got the far better deal.

Catherine knew that her marriage was risky, otherwise she would not have hesitated. She was twenty-three, no child at that time (it is the age at which Jane Bennet—in *Pride and Prejudice*—threatens to become unmarriageable). She seems to have calculated that she could introduce a rogue element into her life, because that life was so much her own to command. But of course it was not a calculation at all; it was a chasm leaped because she deemed Pole worth the jump.

One could simply say that she "fell in love," just as Mary Bowes did before her, but is this ever really so simple? It is a choice—and the theme of *Sense and Sensibility*—to follow one's emotions, rather than allow rationality to question them. Anyway Pole was not lovable; he was fanciable. His sexual prowess was the stuff of excitable gossip. To be frank about it, the most likely explanation for Catherine's decision to marry him is that they had slept together—she was rumored to have sneaked him into Draycot, the Wiltshire family home—and that she became unwilling to relinquish this beguiling new experience (also, perhaps, less than keen to undertake it with the Duke of Clarence). She was known to be pregnant just a couple of months after her wedding, although as she miscarried it is impossible to know when conception took place.

And, for a time, it seemed as though Catherine's daring might be rewarded. Her husband united her names with his own— became William Pole-Tylney-Long-Wellesley—and the pair were seen, and saw themselves, as what today would be called a power couple: written about, envied, imitated, followed by a perpetual spotlight. Pole did the usual thing of becoming an MP. Catherine —

now the It wife, famed for changing her outfits three times a day—sought to advance his career by turning Wanstead into a latter-day Holland House, a place where politics met society and had the time of its life. Her husband, meanwhile, focused on the acquisition for Wanstead of luxury adjuncts: stables, a whole pack of old-fashioned staghounds, a carriage drawn by four gray Arabians who flourished plumes in the Wellesley blue. That kind of spending—marked by a perfectionist obsession with detail—is common among the extremely rich, who are capable of demanding the replacement of an entire bathroom because they dislike the soap dish. In this case, however, the cash was not Pole's to spend.

Then it became clear that there was not quite as much money as had been thought. There was plenty, but Pole had been spending as if there were an infinity.

Instead of easing up—behaving rationally—he did the opposite. In a show of petty rage he withheld the £15,000 that was owed to each of Catherine's sisters under their father's will. He also became far more careless of his wife's feelings. If she had ever believed that her husband wanted her *for herself*, she was being quickly disabused of the idea. Pole respected her less with every diminution of her income, and resented the fact that she expected him to love her—the unfortunate truth being that romantic love tends to thrive upon starvation. "She devours him with her eyes, and she is desperately in love" was the observation of one of Catherine's sisters, whose concern was by no means solely for her own inheritance.

* * *

In 1813 Catherine had a son. "For my part I think it an ugly little wretch," Pole wrote to his mother, "but Mrs. Wellesley makes a great to-do about it." The marriage was just a year old, but from this point onward it would be a swift descent into the grossest kind of Hogarthian tableaux.

Pole spent huge amounts, mainly on clothes and on Wanstead, and when he asked for top-ups from his wife's own protected income, she very stupidly agreed. So much for "that character of *a lady of business*," Catherine's former self-respecting guise, which had been lost somewhere on the dizzy road to St. James's, Piccadilly. Clearly—very Barbara Hutton—she hoped that giving Pole more money would make him love her more. In fact he began to despise her. His infidelities were such that by his midthirties he would claim to have slept with "a thousand and three women" (that "three" giving an air of verisimilitude to the boast). Then, in 1815, when Catherine was pregnant again, he asked her to sign a will that would give him £50,000 if she died in childbirth. Even more foolishly, she signed it.

What rage there was in these husbands, who seem to have been possessed with a churning resentment of their wives' money: their desire to take it over was impelled by greed—obviously—but also by a sense of profound masculine grievance, that it *ought* to be theirs, and that "any means necessary" was entirely justifiable in their quest to restore what they saw as the natural order. And the law, of course, backed them every step of the way. It gave a husband absolute power over his wife, as if her body were a domain that he ruled. It is a familiar fact that there was no concept of rape within a marriage (perhaps less known is that this anachronism was not formally abolished until 1991). In 1832, the legal tract *Bacon's Abridgment* stated that "the husband hath by law the power and dominion over his wife, and may beat her, but not in a violent and cruel manner," a pronouncement that fourteen years earlier had been endorsed by an upper-class wife who remarked: "I maintain there is but one crime a woman could never forgive her husband, and that is a kicking." The quasi-dictatorial powers conferred by marriage also allowed a man to forcibly seize and confine his wife. In 1716 a woman was kidnapped by the husband from whom she was separated, and coerced into signing a document that gave him an income for life; she sued in Chancery and took the case to the Lords, but both courts found against her. Only in 1891 was the practice of seizure declared unequivocally illegal. In 1735 an anonymous woman protested in print about the practice of "wife-confinement," citing the story of a wife who killed herself by jumping from the window of the garret in which her husband had imprisoned her; the man was prosecuted for manslaughter, but acquitted. Wives were also locked up, sometimes in chains, in private asylums. This threat was the most terrifying of all. Escape was impossible, unless one's whereabouts were somehow discovered. Then a wife could be discharged by a court if doctors pronounced her to be of sound mind. Again, there were rarely repercussions for a husband. This particular practice was largely prevented by changes to the law in 1774, which made it far more difficult to have a woman committed, but it could still be done if one were clever about it (as in the case that inspired Wilkie Collins's *The Woman in White*). And as late as 1840 a judge upheld a husband's right to confine an "errant" wife in his own home.

It hardly needs saying that everybody connected with the law was male. Judges, lawyers, juries: not a woman among them to see the other side, to shout for justice, to proclaim—for instance—the shattering double standard whereby male adultery was an accepted norm, and an unfaithful wife could be stripped, like a prisoner of marital war, of every conceivable human right. In fairness, the politician Charles James Fox had made exactly that last point in Parliament in 1779. Attitudes *were* changing, although this would only gradually become apparent.

As long as marriage was defined as the subsuming of the wife into the entity of the husband, then the law, logically, would be the means whereby that concept was preserved. One can see why women like Mary Bowes and Catherine Tylney Long ended up signing away their money under pressure, and why the men who forced them felt so confident that they would get their way. The law did find for Mary in the end; yet she had endured a terrible purgatory before it did so, and had surely doubted that any sort of redress against her husband would be possible.

The belief that a wife could be dominated was so powerful in men like Andrew Stoney and William Pole because it was, in effect, statute. Yes, the law expressed this notion of male dominance in cool and dispassionate form. With splendid magnanimity it required any violence to be kept within limits, and it would only approve of locking a wife permanently in her bedroom if she had truly transgressed; but none of this expunged the notion itself, nor mitigated its effect upon a husband's psyche. If a man were decent, like Thomas Grosvenor, he would not be tempted to use the inherent imbalance within marriage for his own ends. A less honorable man, however, knew that he held a legally permitted weapon in his hands.

So Catherine signed, as her husband asked her to do, and for a short time was rewarded with a for-old-times'-sake blast of his extraordinary charm, before learning in 1818—around the time that she gave birth to a daughter—that another woman had also, that year, had a baby by William Pole.

* * *

As Pole doubtless told his wife, in the unanswerably casual manner of the posh boy pulling rank, this was common enough within the class to which he belonged. But Catherine was not an

Anglo-Irish aristocrat closely related to the Duke of Wellington. She was a nice girl from the new gentry who had won the equivalent of the lottery, and she was horribly out of her depth in these dirty, decadent waters. Striving for the requisite bitter sophistication, she agreed to pay her husband's mistress £500 a year, on condition that the woman and child lived in France. Naturally they returned almost immediately, and the affair with Pole resumed.

Once the façade of his marriage had been defaced, the devil in him was let wholly loose (he would not be the first person to evince guilt about their behavior by behaving even worse). His spending became deranged: in the two years up to 1820 he spent £300,000. This was financial incontinence in the style of certain twentieth-century heiresses, although the motive here was different. Of course there was straightforward pleasure in throwing money around: Pole loved creating a superb stage set at Wanstead upon which he—the Regency dreamboat—could play a leading part. But there was also, again, that dark male rage against the wife. Wasting her money was like an obscure act of revenge. For even though the law gave him access to all that she owned, he still had to circumvent trustees and settlements and pettifogging stops upon his rights of possession. The money was his because he had married her, but it was not *his*. And if he could not have it for himself—to do with whatever he wanted, without having to answer to anybody—then he could at least prevent *her* from having it. Frittering away all her thousands was a version of the "if I can't have you, nobody will" motive for murder, a mad rationale for destruction.

So Pole spent upward of £30,000 on his political career, whose early promise fizzled out in the manner of his brief tenure as his uncle's aide-de-camp. He ran an establishment with his mistress, and he continued with his favored pastimes of racing, hunting, and gambling. His debts, as they had been when he was a young man, were astronomical, although as an MP he was exempt from prosecution. When he resigned his position in 1820, he was declared bankrupt and became liable for arrest at any moment. Therefore he hotfooted it to France (lodging at first with his old friend Beau Brummell), and from that place of safety arranged for some of the contents at Wanstead House to be held as security, while he paid off what he owed.

At this point, Catherine—who thanks to the prudence of her trustees was not liable for these debts—could have escaped. She could have thrown up her hands and said: enough. Instead of which she traveled to Paris with the couple's three children, from where she wrote: "I have never been happier in my life."

From a modern standpoint, indeed perhaps from any standpoint, this seems frustratingly inexplicable. Masochistic, indeed. True, the marriage tie had been made in the sight of God and all that, and divorce was a near impossibility: "a woman should never part from her husband while she can remain with him," as Lord Melbourne would later put it—dreadful advice, but adhered to by most wives, indeed until quite recently. Yet in circles such as the Poles' it was not unusual—even in the early nineteenth century—for a couple to separate. This divorce-lite was pretty much the best available solution to the problem of one's spouse.

Catherine's explanation of her behavior would have been, presumably, that she loved her husband. Certainly he had known exactly how to make her fall for him, and how to keep her in that state of thralldom. He was kind, then cruel, then repentant, then viler than ever, keeping Catherine alert with hope and in perpetual search of ways to bring out his better side (perhaps the worst thing about Pole was that he had good qualities, assiduously repressed). Before accepting his proposal she had been clear-eyed, down-to-earth, ready to put sense before sensibility. Now not a trace of that detachment remained. It was as though she had made a pact, of a kind that could only have arisen between an heiress and a fortune hunter: she had granted her husband power over her emotions, in exchange for the power that she still wielded over his finances.

It is very dangerous to place one's happiness in the hands of another person. There is no painless exit route, should they prove unworthy of that act of trust. When Pole went to Paris, Catherine had a very tough choice: to bite the bullet, cut him out of her life and wait for her heart to recover; or to follow, forgive, and pray for things to improve. Of course anybody reading this story will think that she should have done the first of these, and of course they would be right. But romantic love is such an odd one. It is perhaps the hardest sensation of all for another person to empathize with—not being in love with the chosen object, one will simply think "why him?"—yet there is no doubt that Catherine felt it for her husband. As her sister put it, she was "desperately" in love with him; it is perhaps love's greatest mystery that it should have so little correlation with whether or not the recipient deserves it.

The security on the contents of Wanstead was doubled to £60,000, meaning that things had to be sold. Then it became clear that the house itself would have to be sold. This was entirely and solely the fault of Pole; accordingly a report on the 1822 auction at Wanstead flowed with sympathy for a woman "whose husband has, in some dozen years only, dissipated the accumulated riches of ages, without dignity, and sunk into comparative poverty, without pity."[6] The sale was a wildly popular sightseeing event, although nobody spent much money: an exquisite Buhl armoire went for less than £20, and less than half of Pole's debts were cleared. Therefore he conceived a plan of demolishing Wanstead and selling the bricks and timber. That beautiful, magical house, with its ceiling frescoes by William Kent, was effectively turned into scrap, which fetched £10,000. Also sold was another of Catherine's lovely homes, Tylney Park in Hampshire. Yet from Italy, where she and Pole were now living, and where she received news of the death of her mother (who had been more right than she knew when she tried to prevent this marriage), she wrote: "I have received the greatest kindness and affection from Mr. Long Wellesley."

His profligacy, it should be noted, was not of an uncommon order. Vast sums were regularly squandered in that age of gambling and high living, when men spent so much of their time showing off to each other in clubs and at race meetings. Reactions, on the part of the squanderer, varied. Charles James Fox was discovered calmly reading Herodotus—"what would you have me do?"—after losing thousands in a single night of cards. George Payne, who lost £40,000 on two rolls of the dice in the early nineteenth century, cried merrily: "It's a pleasure to lose it, by God!" The Hon. Henry Augustus Berkeley Craven shot himself after losing "only" £8,000 on the 1836 Derby.

Had the thousands that he wasted belonged to him, William Pole would probably have absorbed the event and moved on, having behaved in a manner deemed foolish but acceptable. But the money was his wife's, and public excoriation of his behavior was being voiced as far away as America (where, it was smoothly reported, he had "unfortunately been so simple as to lose at sport the trifling estate of £60,000 per annum"). Therefore there was an element of shame, a hovering charge of ungentlemanliness. Although he would never have admitted it, this infected Pole like a sickness and, knowing himself to be a pariah, he decided to inhabit the role wholeheartedly. He was not an Andrew Stoney; he was a fatally charming lightweight whose class arrogance acted as ballast to his personality. But the last remnants of good in him were driven out during his years in exile, where his behavior took on the hyperactive lunacy of a man with nothing to lose.

* * *

In Italy he took up with a new woman, his cousin Helena Bligh, also married and who today would be called a piece of work. The relationship began in typically unlovely style: Mrs. Bligh fell pregnant, an abortion was procured, and she left her husband for Pole. Mr. Bligh wrote to Catherine, informing her of the facts, but Pole had got in first with a story about how Mrs. Bligh had fled her awful marriage, and perhaps the two women would become friends? They did. Indeed Catherine was so filled with pity for this poor creature, that she encouraged Mrs. Bligh to travel with herself and Pole to Florence, where they attended the opera *à trois*.

Could she really have been so naive? Did she not entertain just the smallest suspicion that her own marriage was in fact the awful one? Apparently not. Her reaction when she was confronted with the truth (which servants had tried to hide from her) suggests that she had suspected absolutely nothing. "I have always thought that the term broken-hearted was just an expression," she said to her doctor, "but I have such a pain in my chest it genuinely feels like my heart is breaking."

She roused herself to force Mrs. Bligh from the hotel. Such a middle-class attitude, she was informed by Pole—a well-born wife would have had no problem with this imaginatively enlarged ménage. The couple returned to Paris, where Mrs. Bligh was waiting.

"I had hoped"—Catherine wrote to her father-in-law, the Earl of Mornington—"by a silent submission to the wrongs I have experienced and conduct above reproach that I might yet reclaim my husband . . . In this hope I have been painfully deceived, and I have reached the moment when a patient exercise of every measure calculated to produce such a result serves only to mark me out as a victim for further insult and degradation . . .

"My dear Lord, this must end . . . I have borne it till I can bear it no longer. There is a point where submission becomes a weakness, and resistance is felt a duty. I have reached it."

It was touching, impressive, almost saintly in its passive strength. Or was it?

"You damned bitch," was Pole's reaction, when his parents turned up in the hope of discussing the situation. "You have set my own father and mother against me."

Not quite; but it may have been that Catherine's letter did, at last, mark the start of her fightback, and that its nobly suffering tone was both genuine and displayed to the gallery, setting out her case—as it were—for any future battle. Who could blame her for doing so, except her husband?

Her health was now affected. The broken heart was a poetical abstraction, but the racking chest spasms were grimly physical. It is not impossible that these were caused in the first instance by Mrs. Bligh. The lock on Catherine's medicine chest had been broken, and a remark made by Pole suggested that he knew who had done it. "We must get rid of this damned dangerous bitch," he said of his mistress (one must allow him this: he was evenhanded in his insults). But the moment passed, and he kept her on.

Whether or not Mrs. Bligh did attempt an actual poisoning, the chest pains were ongoing and exacerbated by acute stress; they sound much like what today would be called panic attacks, and can only have intensified still more when Pole opened an inevitable new front in the war. He began to use the children as weapons, which legally he had every right to do. Just as a husband had control of his wife, so a father had control of his and her offspring.

And indeed, when Catherine left Paris at last and returned to the house at Draycot, she was "allowed" to take the children on condition that she paid her husband £4,000 a year in alimony.

Unbelievably—it *was* unbelievable—she still hoped that he would join her, and to that end offered money to pay off Mrs. Bligh. Catherine was addicted to a belief that things would change: the hopelessly lovestruck part of her could not break free of her husband. Yet at the same time she was being advised to do exactly that. It was suggested by her solicitors—and the self-preserving part of her was listening—that she should seek a Bill of Divorce to end the marriage and reclaim what was left of her property. She should also seek to prove that Pole was unfit to have custody of the children. Attempting both these things together was, at the time, the legal equivalent of climbing Everest in pointe shoes.

Divorce is still immeasurably more complicated when there are children: they almost always become the most valuable of bargaining chips. Two hundred years ago, when just seventy-five divorce petitions were granted between 1800 and 1830 (overwhelmingly to men); when, in 1804, a separated husband had been defended for snatching a baby literally from its mother's breast; and when, in 1820, it had been expressly stated that the inherent power of a father over his children could not be abrogated by any private agreement—such as Catherine had entered into with Pole—it was clear that she had one hell of a fight on her hands.

Again, slowly, attitudes were shifting. The Court of Chancery was reluctant to interfere with a father's rights, yet more enlightened minds knew that sometimes they should. Prejudice against adulterous wives remained strong, as they were deemed so threatening to the status quo, but Catherine's virtue was un-impeachable. How could anybody have thought that Pole—now a syphilitic, soon to be taken to court by Mrs. Bligh's husband for the crime of adultery—would be a better parent than his wife? Nobody did, in fact; the problem was forcing the great behemoth of the law to admit it.

Apparently heedless now of public opinion—Bligh had won £6,000 in damages, which were never paid—Pole occupied his time in dreaming up new ways to terrify Catherine, saying for instance that he wanted to send his ten-year-old son to sea, which she could not have prevented, and sending letters that she dreaded opening. "Rely upon it," he wrote, "neither God nor the devil shall interfere between me and my children." Then he took the very bold step of returning to England with a now-pregnant Mrs. Bligh. His debts still followed him like a pack of his old staghounds, but he was too possessed to care. However much he wanted money, his real desire was to win against his wife: to emerge from that marriage, in which almost everything had been laid waste, as the "victor."

* * *

Yet it was Catherine who did so. Her triumph could scarcely have been more equivocal, however, as she was dead by the time it happened.

Her last year of life was quite ghastly. She spent it dodging Pole when he broke into her London home, moving the children to places where she hoped they would be safe from ab-duction, bracing herself to read his horrible letters. Meanwhile her health worsened, and the tightening spasms in her chest grew agonizing. Quite possibly she still loved this man who had wrecked her life, even as she served him with the suit that would end their marriage, and revoked the old will that would give him £50,000 when she died. "I have shown patience and forbearance enough," she told her doctor, "it is full time that I should assert my rights; I am resolved to do so, they will find me firm." It is somehow clear that this was not her nature, that she was steeling herself. Then, as now, women can find it hard to proceed against abusive partners; because of residual affection, because there are children, because they are unsure that the law will be on their side. Catherine *knew* the law was not on her side, yet she carried on. It might be said that there was scant alternative. It would have been far easier, however, simply to separate and let the rest go. The situation was not that of Mary Bowes, who was escaping physical cruelty and had the evidence to put her husband in jail. Catherine was taking on a man who had been cruel in ways that the law—as she well knew—might deem permissible, and who would stalk her freely for the rest of her life, as vengeful ex-partners sometimes do. It was extremely brave to provoke Pole when she had no guarantee of resolution, and the strain on this mild, passive woman was frankly too great.

She asked to see her children, from whom she had separated for their protection, and in September 1825 they arrived at the house in Richmond where she was living with her sisters. Her face was painted, so as not to alarm them with its sickly whiteness. Into that sad and tremulous peace came the horseman, bearing another of those dreaded envelopes: "I feel persuaded that, if I were to attempt reading the letter, my spasms would return, and I might be dead in a few hours." Her prophecy was entirely accurate. She died the following day, aged thirty-six.

The cause, according to her doctor, was the broken heart cited by Catherine herself (or, more prosaically, the cumulation of years of anguish). However: given that Pole believed he would inherit £50,000 on her death, murder has to be a possibility.

Catherine's weakened state and stomach cramps are certainly compatible with poisoning. It would seem that Pole had not approved when he suspected Mrs. Bligh of dabbling in such things, but who knows?—perhaps it had given him ideas. He did have a servant who he boasted had killed "nine persons." Had some poisoned item been introduced to the house at Richmond? Had a resident servant been paid to do the deed? It is highly unlikely, and just about possible. Whatever the truth about Catherine's death, it was one thing above all else: unnecessary.

News of it caused shock and grief in the public that had once followed Catherine's joyful, beribboned progress to the altar. She was loudly mourned and, as would later be done for Diana, Princess of Wales, people lined the streets to salute her coffin as it journeyed to Draycot. Blame, too, was in the air: everybody knew about Pole. "The premature death of an amiable lady," wrote one newspaper, "furnishes a lasting lesson to the heartlessness of too many of the men of the present age." Yet men were about to take up her case, and with a vigor that one wishes had benefited her when she was alive. Lord Chancellor Eldon—who in a former life had eloped to Gretna Green, but now was doggedly upholding the established order—found himself so shocked by Catherine's story that he declared: "I should deserve to be hunted out of society if I were to hesitate one moment whether I should permit these children to go to a father who had the slightest connection with so abandoned and infamous a woman as Mrs. Bligh has proved herself to be." And if this rather threw the blame at the wrong person, at least it brought Lord Eldon to the right conclusion.

For the first time in legal history, a father was deprived of his children on the grounds of unfitness: a complete vindication of Catherine's willingness to pursue this action. The children became Wards in Chancery, day-to-day care was given to their aunts, and their official guardian was none other than the Duke of Wellington, soon to become prime minister, one of the thousands who had watched the progress of Catherine's coffin to Wiltshire.

For Pole, it was as though his own kind—his family, indeed—had turned on him. Being the man he was, the kind who could bear to lose only at cards, he appealed Eldon's judgment. Again playing to type, he accused Catherine's sisters of being a pair of incestuous lesbians, then in a supreme burst of tantrum threatened to assassinate the Duke of Wellington. Unsurprisingly, the custody appeal failed; nevertheless Pole did win his case against the revocation of Catherine's will. Almost as a consolation prize, he was awarded the £50,000 that his wife had signed away under duress, and this ridiculous decision meant that he had the means with which to continue his fight. Their mother being gone, he took out his anger on his offspring: squeezed his eldest son continually for money and kidnapped his daughter, who was held captive for a short time by Mrs. Bligh. The adult lives of the Pole children were not happy—the second son became a prizefighter and none of them married—which suggests that the damage went too deep for eradication.

Had Catherine not died, might things have been better? Yet it is debatable whether, had she lived, custody would actually have been given to her. Despite the seismic judgment that took the children from their father, the fact is that they were then handed to a male guardian; and no ordinary guardian at that. Giving them into the ultimate care of the Duke of Wellington was an act that could not be gainsaid, as if today one were to entrust something to the Queen. There was no risk involved at all. To have granted the children to Catherine, outright, might well have been a step too far in the 1820s, when the Custody of Infants Act—which gave mothers of "unblemished character" custody of their children up to the age of seven, and access thereafter—was still more than ten years away.

That legislation was passed by men, but the hand that had forced it through Parliament belonged to a woman: Caroline Norton, who had intellect and influence, and who had suffered in a way that made her determined to amend the system. In 1836 she left her husband, a drunk, who had failed as an MP but was ingenious in the pursuit of revenge. He made claims upon Caroline's earnings as a writer—as the law allowed—although she cleverly turned this back upon him, by running up debts for which—as the law demanded—he was responsible. Then he abducted their three children, justifying the act by launching an action against the then prime minister, Viscount Melbourne, whom he accused of adultery with Caroline. This was almost certainly a lie, against which she was disbarred from defending herself in court: "a woman is made a helpless wretch by these laws of men." The jury found for Melbourne, but Norton had done the harm that he intended. Caroline did not even know where her children were. She was allowed to visit them in Scotland only when her youngest son was dying, arriving at his bedside too late. She wrote fiercely: "what I suffered respecting those children, God knows . . . under the evil law which suffered any man, for vengeance or for interest, to take baby children from the mother."

Her absolute determination to change that law was a thing of beauty, born of monstrosity. She was strong in a way that Catherine was not, although the danger of identifying Caroline too closely with modern mores is shown up by this statement: "The natural position of woman is inferiority to man. Amen!" It seems amazing that such a woman could have believed such a thing, but then Mary Wollstonecraft wrote in 1792: "Marriage is the cement of society . . . the only way for a woman to rise in the world." A person is of their age, however much they also transcend it.

And this was an age in which men worshipped women as the "fair sex" and were capable of treating their wives far worse than their horses. At times, however, the sexes could be allies. Caroline would never have effected any reform without the backing of her friend Lord Lyndhurst, the three-times Lord Chancellor, who hustled the 1839 Custody of Infants Act across the line. Catherine had been protected by her trustees (as far as she would allow them)—although the greatest male support had come after her death. One wonders what would have happened had Caroline Norton been conducting her campaign for mothers' rights a decade earlier, and whether the knowledge of that powerful female sympathy might have helped Catherine's story to end more happily. Because one does rather feel that she gave up, not the fight, but the life that it had exhausted.

After her death, Pole's own life dissolved into a meaningless, murky shambles. He married then abandoned Mrs. Bligh, and died in 1857. His disgrace was complete, his thoughts on the subject a mystery. "Redeemed by no single virtue," wrote the *Morning Chronicle*, "adorned by no single grace, his life has gone out without even a flicker of repentance."

And Catherine Tylney Long would scarcely have noticed his passing if she had married the Duke of Clarence, later King William IV, as her mother had advised.

ELLEN

WHENEVER NEW LEGISLATION is brought in, those sufficiently determined will instantly try to find ways around it. Thus it was that the 1753 Marriage Act, which had sought so sincerely to regulate marriage, in fact helped to generate the unruly mania for elopements. Furthermore, although these rushed events were all too often about money, their caution-to-the-winds aspect put a heady emphasis upon love, reinforced by the growing fashion for emotion-centric literature.

Love, indeed, was all the rage. Jane Austen cast a wise, cool eye upon this tendency—*her* Catherine Tilney's marriage was rooted in a realism that her namesake chose to ignore—although she also occasionally endorsed it. Indeed she expressed the view (in a letter) that it was dishonorable to marry "without Affection," but then thanks to family support she could afford to believe this. Similarly Sarah Child, cut off by her super-rich father when she married John Fane, Earl of Westmoreland, remained easily wealthy enough to live by the Romantic creed. Which in itself was subverted, of course, if one party were marrying for love, and the other for a more venal reason.

Nevertheless—and needless to say—the 1753 Act had been necessary. So, too, was the revised Marriage Act of 1823, which sounded last orders on the snatching of underage heiresses, by specifying that a man who married a minor (under twenty-one) without consent would have no access to her money. Well: better late than never.

Not that young men didn't still try their luck. In 1832, it was reported that inhabitants of Stamford were delighted when an underage heiress took up residence in the town, together with a female friend. "The young ladies were extremely attached to each other, and their affection was such as to invite at last some suspicion." What people suspected was not lesbianism (not in early nineteenth-century Lincolnshire) but that one of the women was, in fact, a man. As indeed, he was: "a modern Don Juan locating with his lady love in the fens," as the newspaper expressed it, benevolently assuming that the lady love's money was not the real object of this escapade.

So such incidents remained newsworthy, and elopements continued. The peak year for marriages at Gretna Green was still some thirty years away.* Nevertheless by the end of the Georgian era, in 1830, the culture was moving on from the days when any young man with good looks and/or a military uniform was almost honor-bound to prove that he could hook a wife worth at least £10,000 a year, in between riding in a match race across Newmarket Heath and picking up a new mistress at Drury Lane.

There was, however, one big story to go. And what a story.

In March 1826, a report in *The Sun* newspaper began thus: "An extraordinary case of elopement, or rather of abduction, has lately taken place at Liverpool, which has occasioned no trifling sensation in the counties of Lancaster and Chester." The girl in question was Ellen Turner, "a young lady of about sixteen years

---

* Not until 1856 did Scottish law change to require twenty-one days' residency before a wedding could take place.

of age, and of more than ordinary attractions both of purse and person." Actually she was fifteen—a child—although her serene, rather exotic looks and remarkable self-possession gave her an air of maturity. *The Times*, smitten by her demeanor, would later write: "altogether there is something . . . fascinating about her"; what seems to have impressed the newspapers was how little she resembled their idea of a victim.

Nor did her abductor, thirty-year-old Edward Gibbon Wakefield—"a gentlemanly man . . . what the French would call a *bel homme*"—fit the popular image of an heiress-snatcher. Perhaps uniquely among these men, he was neither a desperado nor an upper-class oaf. Born into a distinguished Quaker family,* he was extremely clever, a trained lawyer and a subsequent high achiever. He shared with other heiress-snatchers that mind-warping sense of entitlement, yet conducted himself with an air of rationality; his confidence derived not from the usual auda-cious sex appeal but from his personality, which was powerful in the extreme, and from the slippery eloquence so typical of an advocate. He was an immensely complex man, infinitely more so than Andrew Stoney, and considerably more than William Pole. In other words, this last great story was characterized by the highly unusual casting of its two lead roles.

Wakefield had, in fact, already tried his luck with an heiress. A restless and wayward young man, bored with the law and longing for a career in politics (where slippery eloquence would go down even better), he had taken the swift old route to advancement and, in 1816, eloped with a Ward in Chancery. There was affection

---

* Wakefield's father was a statistician and practical philanthropist, a friend of the reformer Francis Place. His grandmother, Priscilla, was an early feminist writer as well as a children's author; in 1798 she set up a "frugality bank" that was, effectively, the first savings bank.

between Wakefield and his bride, but the union was rendered still happier (for him) when he received the highest settlement that Chancery ever made to a ward's husband. His mother-in-law, the surviving parent, had been in violent opposition to the marriage; yet Wakefield persuaded her to cave in. When his wife died in childbirth, he was left with an income of some £2,000 a year. His grief was genuine but his ambition stronger than ever, as was his desire for more money: in those days it was impossible to be too rich when launching a Parliamentary career.

Ellen Turner represented the most tempting of prizes. Her father was a mill owner and High Sheriff of Chester, and she herself "the possessor of property, if general report is at all to be relied on, to the amount of more than a million sterling." In fact she was the new holder of that supreme title for the female commoner, "the richest heiress in the kingdom," which after Catherine Tylney's death was an uneasy crown to wear.

Tales of heiress-stealing had acquired a folkloric quality, but that did not mean that the crime was no longer a reality. Ellen's fabulous wealth made her a kidnapping target, as her father was all too aware, and accordingly she was safely stowed at a genteel seminary in Liverpool; therefore there had to be a plan for her removal. It was highly detailed, as plots of this kind often were, so much so that one wonders why their perpetrators did not use the same gifts to pursue honest careers. In the 1817 Maria Glenn case, for instance, "evidence" was given that the girl had frequently been seen with her alleged abductor, thus casting doubt upon her claim to have been seized against her will. In fact these sightings were faked by female accomplices. Clever.

The Ellen Turner abduction was carried out by Edward Wakefield and his brother William, but the idea originated with a woman: Frances Davis, one of nature's adventuresses, who was of a similar age to the brothers but very soon to become their stepmother. Her father lived close to the Turners' home—glorious Shrigley Hall—at the edge of the Peak District. So she knew all about the rich Miss Turner, and saw possibilities in her. Women beware women . . . Her idea, probably quite vague at the start, was that one of the Wakefields should court this girl and try to bring her fortune into the family. In early 1826 the brothers were living in Paris, where Frances visited them and the subject of Ellen began to be discussed. Gradually this developed into a full-blown scheme for kidnap and forcible marriage.

Frances returned to her father's home forthwith. She bustled off on a visit to the Turners, from whom she learned Ellen's whereabouts. Back came the Wakefield brothers, primed for action. As the prosecuting counsel at their trial would ask, with hefty irony: "Did the jury believe that they had quitted their gay circle in Paris to sojourn on a visit with a schoolmaster in Macclesfield?" Indeed they had not. With start-up money loaned by Frances, they launched their plan: step one of which was to buy a secondhand carriage.

On 7 March this carriage was driven by the Wakefields' servant to Ellen's school. A letter was delivered to the girl, saying that her mother was seriously ill, and that she should hurry home in the waiting transport. Although she had enough of her wits about her to protest that the servant in the carriage was not her father's, both she and her school were reassured that he had been commissioned to look after her.

She was then taken to a hotel in Manchester, where Wakefield himself—whom she had never seen before in her life—told her that in fact, not to worry, her mother wasn't ill at all; what had actually happened was that a bank had collapsed, her father had lost most of his money and had run away to Kendal to escape his creditors, he had not wanted the school to know this, hence the earlier falsehood, blah blah blah, and now they were going to see him. *The Times* suggested that Ellen was "buoyed up with the assurance of seeing her papa," but when the carriage reached Kendal and there was no papa, Wakefield's story became elaborate. Chief among the creditors—he explained—was his own uncle, who was owed £60,000 and, who having demanded Shrigley as security, "could turn her father out of doors." So her father's solicitor had come up with a plan whereby Ellen should marry Wakefield, thus regaining Shrigley and allowing her father to stay in it. He, Wakefield, had protested at the idea—surely there was some other solution?—but no, there it was, their marriage was the only option. With an air of great reasonableness, he informed Ellen that—in the words of *The Times*—"it now remained for her to determine whether she would accede, or her papa would be turned out of doors!"

Anybody reading this story will surely wish that Ellen had, at that point, punched Wakefield in the mouth and told him to stop with his farrago of lies before hotfooting it back to Shrigley. But she was fifteen. She had been plunged into a situation in which people she had never seen before were telling her terrifying things; they had behaved decently so far, but how did she know that they would continue to do so? She was fearful for her father. The unkindness of the plot was that it played upon Ellen's closeness to her parents, used her anxiety about them against her. "I believed what they had told me," she later said in court. How could she have dared to do otherwise? And one senses the conspirators' delight in the various pantomimes designed to achieve verisimilitude; as when William Wakefield suddenly appeared, saying that he had just met Mr. Turner, who was hiding at an inn at Carlisle. Ellen was told of her father's desperate request that she should marry at nearby Gretna Green—the destination to which the carriage had been trundling ever closer—and bring the marriage certificate to the inn: "he entreated her not to hesitate, for if she did there would be an execution in the house at Shrigley, and they would all be ruined."

Meanwhile Mr. Turner, who of course was in no financial difficulties whatsoever, was instead in a state of the utmost bewildered anguish. News had come from Ellen's school that she had disappeared in an unknown carriage, but nothing more was known until March 11, when a letter was received, signed by Wakefield, informing the Turners that their daughter was married. "The distress occasioned to Mr. Turner and his lady," ran *The Times* report, "by the announcement of this worse than death of their only child, may be readily conceived."

Would the Turner parents really have preferred Ellen to be dead rather than married to an abductor? Naturally not: but this form of words was designed to indicate something else, a fear that the marriage had not actually happened. It was a similar situation to the one in *Pride and Prejudice*, when the youngest Bennet sister, Lydia, absconds with Wickham, and the great terror is not that they have eloped, but that they haven't: "they are certainly not gone to Scotland," Elizabeth says, when she confesses all to Darcy, meaning that they have bypassed Gretna Green and are living in sin—a dire and irremediable circumstance. Virtue, at that time, was the prize above rubies. Its loss was truly calamitous. Lydia Bennet has no money, so it is reasonable to think that Wickham would not want to marry her. Ellen had all too much money; therefore the concern was that she had been taken, with a ruined reputation, to be married "on the Continent" (which, in this context, had a "here be dragons" aspect); and was thus doubly lost.

She was, indeed, traced to Calais—the disembarkation port in France—and two of her uncles were tasked with sailing across and bringing her back. The Turner connections went into overdrive:

The Times reported that "applications were immediately made to the higher departments of His Majesty's government," including the foreign secretary George Canning. However, Wakefield was sufficiently well born to have connections of his own. He had been waiting at Calais for his friend, "the Ambassador to the Swiss Cantons," whose protection would have allowed him and Ellen to travel to Paris; "and, clothed with such patronage, evade any attempt to take him or his prize." In a near incredible coincidence, the ambassador arrived on the same boat as the Turner party. Wakefield hailed his friend, and at almost the exact same moment Ellen spied her two uncles. But for that, the coup might have become unstoppable.

Things were not as bad as the Turners had dreaded. Ellen *had* married Wakefield, at Gretna Green. Then she had traveled south with her new husband and his brother: "they had," *The Times* reassured its readers, "three separate beds." Naturally she had expected to see her father after the ceremony, but was told that he had returned immediately to Shrigley, where Wakefield's brother then pretended to go. Meanwhile Wakefield himself suddenly remembered an urgent appointment in Paris (as one does) and suggested that Ellen might be reunited with her father at Calais. Again, one wonders what she could have been thinking, during these long bumpy journeys and uneasy nights in a succession of coaching inns. She later told the court that, at her captor's request, she had written a letter to her mother from Calais, in which she signed her name as "Wakefield." Could she have refused? Hardly. Wakefield was twice her age, he had the backing of his brother, and every time she was about to be released from her ordeal something happened to prolong it. Compliance would have seemed the safest route to freedom, right up to the moment—on March 15, eight days after this all began—when she saw her relations disembark from the boat.

Even then, Wakefield refused to throw in his hand; the scenes at Calais were the strangest of the lot. He hustled Ellen back to their hotel, and with apparent calm—such was his faith in his persuasive tongue—faced her uncles: "after some preliminary stipulations, which were rejected, [he] consented to produce Miss Turner; but he expressed a hope that nothing would be said to make her hate him, or prejudice her mind against him, or words to that effect." Which sounds like an attempt to suggest that Ellen had not been an unwilling partner to this marriage, but would say otherwise if led to do so.

At the hotel, Wakefield continued to bar her uncles from sight of Ellen. A ludicrous argument ensued with Mr. Turner's solicitor, who had turned up with a Bow Street officer* in the hope that Wakefield would give himself up. He declined to do so. He had reached the sanctuary of France and, for the time being, that was where he was staying. He asked if there was an intention to prosecute, then declared: "If it is a marriage, I must keep her; if it is not, I can have no claim on her." The reply, that in the solicitor's view the marriage was illegal and prosecution inevitable, bounced off this incalculable man, who merely said: "She may think favorably of me, but nothing compared to the unbounded affection she has for her parents; I dare say she will fly from me to you when she sees you." Again he was suggesting that Ellen was quite happy with him, or would be, if her family would only leave them alone together.

When, however—having finally run out of arguments—Wakefield finally consented to deliver her up, Ellen's reaction was perhaps not quite as ambiguous as he had hoped. Told that the marriage was not lawful, she replied: "Thank God for it."

---

* Bow Street Runners, as they were known to the public, were London's first professional police force. They were formed in 1749 by Henry Fielding, who in a previous life had himself attempted an abduction.

She was now safe with her relations, and very soon would be back in England, although the horrors of newspaper publicity and a horribly intrusive court case lay before her: the all too familiar plight of the female victim.

* * *

On April 4, 1826, beneath the regular newspaper update on the "Shrigley abduction," there was a report in *The Times* from Ireland, about the kidnap of a farmer's daughter—heiress to about £100—whose captor was encouraged, by one of his co-conspirators, to "insure the prize." Despite his reluctance to commit this act of rape, the man was hanged.

Wakefield's crime, however, was no longer a capital offense. The 1823 Judgment of Death Act had removed the automatic death sentence from most felonies. Furthermore he believed that he would be charged only with a "misdemeanor," and thus avoid a possible sentence of transportation; when his lawyers' attempt at plea bargaining failed, he was reported to be "considerably agitated."

For he had, in his controlled way, been very careful with Ellen. Within his act of incaution, he was cautious. Ellen's analysis of his behavior, as quoted at the hearing, was admirably succinct: her abductor had treated her as a gentleman would, yet his conduct had been that of a brute. Blithely ignoring the last part of this statement Wakefield wrote repeatedly to Mr. Turner, deploying his familiar tone of anxiety, self-justification, and petulant defiance: "I cannot allow your daughter to be made to dislike me, however wrong my conduct may have been. I have taken religious care to treat her as a sister, and though she was lawfully my wife, I never enforced the rights of a husband."

But what a strange plan this was! It fell into two parts: the plotting, instigated by Frances and carried out by the brothers, and the aftermath, handled by Wakefield alone. The abduction itself seems recklessly retrograde, now that the laws around underage heiresses had tightened. The image of this little gang of people, huddled together in the salons of French society, pondering how to pull off a forced marriage, is frankly bizarre. True, the newlyweds might have gotten safe passage to Paris (and what was that ambassador thinking of—his percentage?). But then what? Did Wakefield expect to return, in due course, and become the Honourable Member for Macclesfield?

The answer, apparently, is yes. And much of his confidence derived from the fact that he had done something of the kind before. He had absconded with a girl and his mother-in-law had taken the course of least resistance, deciding that it was simpler to let him get away with what was, effectively, an act of blackmail: the fact that her daughter had been complicit in the elopement meant that Wakefield held a very powerful bargaining chip.

The seizure of Ellen Turner, however, was so different a circumstance as to make it scarcely believable that Wakefield—and his co-conspirators—had hoped for a similar outcome. Could they really have thought that the Turners would condone the theft of their fifteen-year-old daughter, would hand her (plus gigantic fortune) to a man whom she had never met and tell her to make the best of it? It sounds deranged. Even at the height of the heiress-snatching madness, families had always called a halt to those forced alliances if they were able. That man of the world, the industrialist Mr. Turner, was the last person on earth to have accepted Wakefield's crude attempt to best him in a deal. Where, indeed, was the leverage over Ellen's family, given that the girl herself did not want to be married?

It is possible that the plotters had not, as they say, thought it through. Or did they have a more obvious kind of blackmail in mind? Once caught, Wakefield sought to minimize his offense, but had he made it to France who knows what would have happened; Ellen's unviolated return might have been his price.

That was one option, certainly, but there was another. There had been a fabulous effrontery in the choice of *this* girl to steal—so rich, so covetable—yet perhaps that had been the very point. It was all very well for the Turners to refuse to back down, but proceeding against Wakefield meant a court case; and here, indeed, was his ace of trumps. The "scandal" that would ensue from such an intensely public event had been more than his first wife's mother could face. With Ellen Turner—that great and luminous prize—the publicity would be magnified tenfold at least, and the threat to her reputation potentially immense. When Wakefield asked Mr. Turner's solicitor if there was an intention to prosecute, he was also inquiring as to whether Mr. Turner was ready for whatever a defense lawyer might come up with.

With his Gray's Inn training, he knew what he was dealing with. He appreciated the complexities of a case such as the one in which he figured, which involved both English and Scottish law: Ellen was abducted in one country and married in another. Because the laws on marriage differed in Scotland (this, of course, being the point of Gretna Green), he therefore held out a not wholly forlorn hope that the strange union might be decreed valid, whether the Turners liked it or not.

And he always spoke as if Ellen *would* like it. Did he actually believe that? Impossible to say, with such an unaccountable man. Impossible to know what Wakefield himself thought of the case put forward by his defense counsel, Mr. Scarlett, whose opening speech was a classic of its victim-blaming kind, and precisely what he would have gambled on the Turners seeking to avoid.

"She [Ellen] has been described to be a clever girl, a person of quick apprehension and sagacity. Could such a person have been deceived in the manner which it was attempted to be shown she had been?" The marriage, said Scarlett, was legal, because Ellen had "concurred" in it. He would bring witnesses to show that she had been "full of gaiety and alacrity, and that she had never ceased expressing her pleasure and satisfaction. Those who saw her would tell them, that they had never witnessed in any person a greater degree of cheerfulness and joy."

These witnesses included the "blacksmith" who had married the couple at Gretna Green, and a succession of chambermaids and coachmen. None of them said that Ellen was the most joyful person whom they had ever seen—that was a bombastic lie—but they did testify that they heard her laugh, that she seemed in good spirits, and that she was under no restraint. Their testimony was reminiscent of the appeal hearing in the Maria Glenn trial, at which it was "proved" that the girl herself had been a willing abductee. It was, in fact, the defense that had been produced in so many of these cases, and that a book of "Law Quibbles" had grappled with back in 1724, alighting upon the decisive conclusion that if a woman were seen to get into a carriage *first*, before it took her away to who-knows-what fate, this meant that she had *chosen* to go. "If a man steal an Heiress, it is Felony . . . But if she carries him to the Place appointed for Marriage, he will not be Criminal." Although presumably if she had climbed in because she had a pistol—real or metaphorical—aimed at her back, the logic of the quibble would disintegrate.

Contemporary trials are frequent reminders of the fact that the question of consent does not go away; no more does the still trickier question of whether, if yes later turns into no, this means that it was no all along. As men had done before him, and would do after him, Wakefield sought to suggest that Ellen had been happy in his company until she was confronted with reality—in this case, her family—and girlish excitement turned to guilty regret.

Yet how could he hope to get away with this, given the nature of the abduction? Well: there is always, in courtrooms, the unaccountable factor of prejudice. Juries had found for Edward Fenwick and against Maria Glenn. The defense had cobbled together enough witnesses to hope that, when taken all together, their sketchy recollections would cast doubt upon Ellen's whole story.

On the other hand, there were witnesses who did not recall Ellen as being cheerful at all. A woman who owned an inn at Carlisle described how the Wakefields had kept the girl in the carriage for some time after their arrival; the implication being that she was not in a fit condition to be seen. The innkeeper, glimpsing her within, said that she looked "dispirited." Another woman described her as "the very picture of despair." A waiter in London recalled that she was crying. There was also a mass of evidence about the lead-up to the plot—Frances Davis's withdrawal of money, the purchase of a carriage under a false name—while Ellen's boarding school confirmed her account of how she was lured into said carriage on the seventh.

Nevertheless counsel for the defense sought to imply that the girl had been complicit in it all, and that her relief at the sight of her uncles simply meant that she had had enough. And his speech was clever, because it plucked at the collective folk-knowledge of Gretna Green, romantic elopements, young heiresses who longed for nothing more than to break free with a fortune hunter but who were sadly susceptible to remorse... So yes, people might have asked themselves: how *could* this self-possessed girl have been deceived by such a tale? Why *did* she laugh and smile? Assuming that she did, incidentally, and that Wakefield had not been running round the northwest on a bribery spree.

It is impossible to know what it was like for Ellen during that surreal week, spent with two men at a succession of coaching inns, on the journey that took her interminably from Liverpool to Gretna Green to Dover (long enough today, but 200 years ago?). It may well have been that she sought to be friendly, as victims of kidnapping are known to do. There was the crucial consideration that she believed she was doing this for her father, whom she adored. The evidence that she was free to go at any time was meaningless, if one assumes that she was staying for Mr. Turner's sake. And then there was the figure of Wakefield, with his peculiar will and mesmerist's charm: it is not hard to believe that he could convince this girl of any story that he chose to invent, nor that he was able at times to amuse and relax her.

He may, in the course of that week, have persuaded himself that she would—eventually—accept him as her husband. He certainly did not lack confidence in his own attributes; nor were these negligible. He had brains and ambition, he was not un-attractive to women, and he had what was then called "breed-ing," which he would surely have factored into his calculations. His father was a gentleman; Mr. Turner was an industrialist. Ridiculous though this sounds, it would have signified. Much later in the nineteenth century, the heiress—and countess— Daisy Warwick would still feel able to pronounce: "Anyone engaged in the arts, the stage, trade or commerce, no matter how well connected, cannot be asked to the house at all." Of course the snobbery that old money displayed toward new was utterly absurd (as if old money hadn't done exactly the same things, but longer ago! The Spencer family had been wool merchants; the earldom—later dukedom—of Bedford was first acquired because John Russell could speak Spanish and Henry VII had needed exactly that skill). Nevertheless Wakefield would have been bolstered by his "superior" background, and quite possibly by the belief that it sufficed to make him good enough for the girl whom he had decided to claim. Although not quite a fantasist, he frequently behaved like one. To Ellen's uncles he had confided, with a slightly lunatic pride, that "he never started anything that he did not accomplish." A telling remark; not least for its supreme disregard for the rights and feelings of the girl whom he had seized, stolen, as if she were worth no more than her inheritance.

* * *

The trial of Edward Wakefield was awaited with as much excitement as if a murder had been committed. It was not quite as great a cause célèbre as the quasi-trial of George IV's loathed wife, Queen Caroline of Brunswick, who six years earlier had been accused in the House of Commons of adultery. But people were intensely compelled: by the enigmatic personalities of Wakefield and Ellen, by the sheer oddity of the event that brought them together and, perhaps, by the fact that the crime harked back to those legendary abductions of an earlier era (the past being always and illogically more glamorous than the present).

Proceedings were on a scale that seems disproportionate to the issue at hand. The stakes had already been lowered by reports that Wakefield was likely to be charged with a misdemeanor, although this did not lessen anticipation. By way of an aperitif, *The Times* wrote that "the briefs for the prosecution are of an enormous size, occupying more than 200 sheets" (one wonders that there was so much to say) and that some seventy (seventy!) witnesses had been subpoenaed, including the Bishop of Gretna, who was reported to have gotten drunk on the journey to Lancaster Assizes.

And Wakefield was still putting up a fight, which was impressive, albeit in a wholly contemptible way. He managed to get the trial delayed, thereby creating an interim period that he filled in characteristic fashion. At Christmas 1826 he sent Ellen a book, with his portrait drawn on the flyleaf and a love poem inscribed beneath. He also took to wandering about the lanes by Shrigley Hall. He was behaving like a rejected lover, as if to create the impression that there had been a real relationship that he desperately wished to rekindle. Possibly a part of him had come to believe this, although at the same time he was deliberately trying to unnerve: in modern parlance he had become a stalker, and there are few things more distressing to a woman.

By March 1827, however, he had run out of road. The trial was at last ready to proceed, with Wakefield's brother also indicted (Frances—the woman who was now their stepmother, and whose idea this had been in the first place—had the case against her dismissed on grounds of insufficient evidence). And, instantly, an intriguing legal conundrum arose. If Ellen Turner were Wakefield's wife in law, she could not testify for the prosecution. Only if force had been used could a wife give evidence against her husband. The defense counsel put up its case for the validity of the marriage, which of course was what Wakefield had wanted all along; the prosecution counterclaimed that there had been intimidation, which meant that Ellen would be both able and required to testify, and this argument prevailed. But what an outrage, really, that having been kidnapped, lied to, terrorized, driven from pillar to post without a clue as to what might happen next, this girl of just sixteen was obliged to prove her story in front of a breathlessly packed courtroom.

Her actual testimony was short, a recollection of the various intricate stories that had got her to Calais with a ring on her finger—too large a ring, as it happened, so Wakefield bought another one in France. She had believed, she said, that she was his lawful wife.

* * *

Defense counsel Mr. Scarlett, in that morally superior way beloved of certain lawyers, conceded handsomely that Wakefield had done wrong—"it was admitted by Mr. Wakefield himself"—but shook his head over the attitude of Mr. Turner: "he wished that those who had been instrumental in getting up the prosecution had shown less disposition to vengeance." Then Scarlett turned to Ellen Turner, and launched an attack of quite breathtaking cruelty.

Having dealt with the witnesses who recounted a smile here and a laugh there, and in doing so chipped little pieces out of her reputation, he went all out to destroy it entirely. This is textbook stuff today, in cases where a woman has made an accusation of rape. Two hundred years ago it was so shocking—such a sudden and complete assault upon the teenage victim—that one wonders what conversations had gone on beforehand between Scarlett and Wakefield, and whether the counsel had attempted to dissuade his client from taking this path.

What made Wakefield so reckless, after so much caution? The best guess is that he had, in his narcissistic way, believed that he would eventually win the day; that up until the last moment he had been convinced that there would not be a trial, that his tactics of delay and pester, pester and delay, would cause Mr. Turner to back down; and that by default he would claim Ellen as the victor's spoils. When this did not happen—when he realized that he was not in control of these events—he became, as narcissists do, uncontrollably angry. So he sent his counsel out to win Ellen for himself, by the simple expedient of ensuring that nobody else would want her. It was a high-stakes gamble, with almost no chance of success, and had it come off it would have been a second abduction of a truly vicious kind.

Thus it was that Mr. Turner's desire for "vengeance," as the defense put it, provoked the same urge in Wakefield; and the father's desire to protect his daughter led, most ironically, to her exposure to calumny in court.

All along, Wakefield had insisted that he and Ellen had slept in separate beds. He actually signed a document to that effect, as did his brother. Ellen also stated that the "marriage" had been unconsummated, and her emotional condition when rescued by her uncles—furious rather than distraught—wholly supported this, as did the overwhelming substance of the prosecution evidence. A servant at Penrith recalled Wakefield saying: "I must see where you sleep, my dear," which sounds wholly typical of his desire at that time to keep the situation nuanced, to render Ellen slightly compromised without ever going too far.

Then came the testimony for the defense of M. Quillac, owner of the inn where Ellen and Wakefield stayed in Calais.

"They remained five or six days at the hotel," he said, "where they passed all the while as man and wife, and she went by the name of Madame Wakefield.

"They rented a saloon and two chambers with two beds; they were apartments both opening to the saloon as well as to each other, and were those frequently used by married people; the rooms formed one connected set."

The court was shown a plan of the hotel, with its inconvenient and damning arrangement of rooms.

One further point emerged from questioning: that this hotel had not been selected by chance. M. Quillac told the court that he had known Wakefield "for several years." You bet he had.

Prosecuting counsel Mr. Sergeant Cross—who had known about this line of defense, but had not expected it to be used—saw his chance. He seized the evidence by the horns and shook them with sorrowing violence throughout his closing speech, lamenting like a preacher "the base hardihood of the defense which had been made by these parties [the three defendants]. That daring defense was no less than this—that they had in law committed no crime, because they had, in fact, fully perpetrated their detestable act, under circumstances of singular atrocity. Had they not, in bare-faced and profligate defiance of their own deliberate and solemn declaration in hand-writing, infamously and falsely insinuated, by their plan of the sleeping-rooms, that this infant was defiled by the robber who had stolen her?"

Reminding the jury that M. Quillac's testimony was the outlier—all the other inns had given evidence that the parties slept in separate beds—Cross brought his speech to a conclusion that, if somewhat hyperbolic, undoubtedly reflected the views of the majority in the courtroom. Such a defense, he thundered, was one that he himself hoped never to have to conduct. "To stain forever the condition of the victim of their perfidy—to wound through all life the dearest feelings of her already sufficiently afflicted family—to belie their own letter, which declared that the parties had lived as 'brother and sister,' was a consummation of infamy that had never been surpassed."

The jury retired for twenty minutes and returned verdicts of "Guilty."

* * *

Whatever the reasoning—or lack of it—that led to this decision, that it proved the correct one is shown, indubitably, by the full text of a letter that had been referenced briefly at the trial, and was published in *The Times* on March 29, 1827. It had been sent to William Wakefield the previous year by a Miss Bathurst, who had been in Paris at the time that this fateful scheme was dreamed into life.

Her epistolary prose style was worthy of Jane Austen's *Lady Susan*, although her powers of prediction were poor.

"My dearest little Willy O,—Now for your brother's marriage; I hope the old people will forgive." There followed references to several of these people—their names tactfully replaced with dashes—and to their "bitter-tongued gossip" about the abduction, which one can well imagine. "However, Edward is on the right side of the hedge, for he has the girl, and if he get the money, let them laugh that win. But I want to know, if when of age, she has anything independent? Well as I like him, and much as I rejoice, for more reasons than one, that he is married—*bona fide* married; and moreover to a young creature whose education, mental and corporal, will occupy and attach him sooner or later; yet I am fair to confess, a more audacious rape of a second Helen, no Paris ever undertook . . . Little did I think when we laughed with Miss Davis about Miss Turner, and I desired to get her for you or him, that Edward would, in two or three days' time, woo, wed, and carry her off; but he is born for odd adventures . . . If this poor child should die, he will be forbidden every house where a young girl is to be found; but I hope she will live to couple him with riches."

Extraordinary! If Miss Bathurst had been writing this letter about the theft of a budgerigar, it would have seemed callous in the extreme. Not a thought for the "young creature," nor for her parents; it was the old amorality again, the one that backed the fortune hunter, except that in this case the man could not even plead that he needed money; in fact what one detects here is an intriguing bass note of class superiority, as if with this bold act of theft—of reclamation—the upper echelons had put the mill-owning *nouveaux* back in their box, and restored the natural order.

The expressed belief that this was a "bona fide" marriage is interesting; that must have been what they all assumed. Interesting, too, is the casual use of the word "rape," for which *The Times* apologized on Miss Bathurst's behalf. It may have been a sophisticate's synonym for "abduction," or it may have represented another assumption: that the marriage—to which Ellen had not consented—had in the nature of things been consummated, also without her consent.

This, then, was how the venture was viewed. It was a decadent joke played for deadly serious reasons, for a reward that would be shared among the plotters; it was a gentleman's wager, part-designed by women, as these abductions so often were; it was a dare, which Wakefield felt challenged to complete. Once he had done so, as the inimitable Miss Bathurst deliriously proclaimed, the prize was his.

And the heiress, as so often, was the mute guest at the party.

* * *

At least in this case she had all the sympathy. "Their act forms an era in the history of crime," wrote *The Times* of the Wakefield brothers; "to plot and execute the fraudulent abduction of a child, who had neither ever beheld, nor ever been beheld by, the villain who withdrew her from her asylum . . . is an act which we believe was never known to occur till now in the history of civilized man." As with the prosecution's concluding speech, this was something of an exaggeration; also a sign that society had turned against a crime at which it had, formerly, turned a blind eye.

Yet in May, at the hearing to determine sentence held at the Court of King's Bench, Wakefield was back to his old petulant tricks. Having authorized a defense that sought to ruin Ellen's future he now, in an attempt to mitigate his prison term, made this amazing statement: "I claim credit for my forbearance—nay, even for my solicitude toward my wife."

"My wife" was a nice touch. Wakefield repeated it throughout, in case the court had not gotten the message. He also whinged eloquently about how much money he had lost in the past year. He really had not learned that remorse would work better in this situation than defiance; perhaps he could not bear to display it, given that he seemed scarcely to feel it. Nor had he grasped that stealing a girl was one thing—a very bad thing—but trying to steal her lifelong reputation was immeasurably worse.

Accordingly Mr. Sergeant Cross, in reply, stormed on to the attack.

"When we came to the trial, I was petrified with horror to find that the defendant was prepared with evidence of contamination. We cautioned them to abstain from that course . . . They brought the keeper of the hotel at Calais to prove facility of intercourse; and to carry the insinuation further, they put themselves to the expense of procuring a plan of the house, for no other purpose than to cast a stigma that should last for life, upon the honor of that young lady."

Wakefield's shapely, legalistic speech in his own defense had the twin effect of rubbing the entire court up the wrong way and earning him three years in Newgate. His plea for his brother to have a shorter sentence—a hint at the finer qualities that he did possess, beneath the murky tangle of arrogance—similarly failed. William would also serve three years, albeit in the more pleasant confinement of Lancaster Castle. The marriage to Ellen Turner, the status of which nobody quite seemed able to decide upon, was dissolved by Act of Parliament; to be on the safe side, as it were.

The Times, making its comfortable and righteous conclusion on the subject of Edward Wakefield, pronounced: "We will now leave him to that ignominy and infamy which will render him an outcast, and follow him through life,—a far severer punishment than any the laws can inflict upon him."

And yet. The mysterious Wakefield spent his time in Newgate readying himself for a surprise second act, and upon his release became the man that he had always threatened to be—difficult, clever, inspired, highly successful. On the face of it he had emerged a transformed character, a living tribute to the ideals of his prison reformer cousin, Elizabeth Fry. More likely he had been clear-minded enough to see where he had gone wrong, and intelligent enough to put it right; he put his conclusions to use both altruistic and self-advancing, which is generally as good as it gets.

In Newgate he observed—as had his cousin—the stupidity and waste of the prison system, but also of the then prevalent sentence, which he himself might have received, of transporting criminals to the colonies. He conceived a new theory of colonization, publishing his first book on the subject while still in jail, in which emigrants were ordinary citizens rather than convicts; this was transportation as social engineering, an attempt to help the problem of poverty in Britain as well as to improve the condition of her dominions. Whatever one might think of such "reforms" today, in Wakefield's time they were quickly accepted and admired. They influenced the development of South Australia, and led to the establishment in 1836 of the "free city" of Adelaide. For the rest of his life these colonies would be Wakefield's home, and he himself a testament to his own theory. There was no possibility now of the treasured political career in Britain, but he found it in Canada—where he was advisor to the

Governor-General—then in New Zealand, where he became a member of the General Assembly.

He had been, as Miss Bathurst brightly put it, born for odd adventures: one of the few accurate predictions in her letter. Yet nobody could quite have imagined this future for the man who tried to dodge a Bow Street officer in a hotel room in Calais, and chucked infamy at a young girl across a courtroom in Lancaster. He became distinguished and influential, although in the end he overplayed his hand—as was his way—and precipitated his own fall from favor within the New Zealand administration. He died at his house in Wellington, in 1862, by all accounts still yearning for England. One of his rivals in the General Assembly, who reluctantly conceded the force of Wakefield's brain and, when he chose to deploy it, his astonishing charm, pronounced a suitably intriguing epitaph: that "the only security against him was to hate him intensely."

As for the heiress whom he had abducted, and whom his trial had both sullied and vindicated, she not long afterward married Thomas Legh, a member of the prosecution team. "If this poor child should die . . . ," the terrible Miss Bathurst had lazily postulated in her letter; she got that right as well. Ellen Turner died in childbirth, aged nineteen.

SUNDRIES

WITH THE ASCENSION of Queen Victoria in 1837, stories such as these became steadily erased from the social landscape. Marriage was acknowledged to be about romantic love, but not in the sense of dashing off to Gretna Green and sticking two fingers to the established order. Look at the queen herself, and her adored Albert! Through them, love and marriage were presented as a union all of their own, which in turn stood at the heart of family: a splendid metaphor for a stable nation.

That, at any rate, was the PR. But the Victorian era was famously an age of concealment. It draped furniture legs in cloth and swamped female legs in crinolines (garments in which nobody could possibly have eloped; how could a woman dash anywhere in that mad ballooning skirt?). Essentially what it sought to conceal were the visible signs of mayhem, caused by the usual suspects—sex and money—to which the Georgian era had allowed free, if high-risk, expression. And which, of course, continued much as before, behind the façade of God-fearing decorum.

Indeed the very first year of Victoria's reign produced the case of Henry Brooks, who was charged with an interesting variant on the crime of heiress-abduction: he *pretended* to abduct an heiress, in order to gain an impressive amount of credit on the strength of it.

Calling himself Henry Beauclerk, representing himself as a relation of the Duke of St. Albans, or sometimes of the Marquess of Waterford, he traveled about Kent gathering money from people duped by this irreproachable persona. He then rolled up at an inn in a splendid carriage-and-four, accompanied by a girl-friend. There, in the words of *The Times*, "it was intimated to the persons about the inn that his lordship had run away with a rich heiress"—that is to say, his female accomplice. "This affair of gallantry of the *soi-disant* noble lord spread like wildfire along the line of route, and when the carriage arrived at the Rose Inn, Canterbury, between three and four hundred persons assembled to catch a glimpse of the runaway pair."

What a fascinating snapshot of the way in which people re-acted to the very *idea* of an elopement, lining up to watch it as if the roads were so many red carpets: Henry Brooks/Beauclerk must have relished every disreputable moment. Off he and his heiress went to Dover, where they put up at a hotel and enjoyed a glorious champagne-fueled spree, which came to a halt only when Brooks was arrested while trying to cash a Coutts check for £50. In his possession were duplicates of some valuable items of plate, which he had handled in his guise as aristocratic heiress-catcher. Meanwhile his accomplice, having handed over to the law some money acquired by her boyfriend, hotfooted it back to London, immeasurably less damaged by her adventure than a real heiress would have been.

This crime sub-genre—in which the word "heiress" was flour-ished like a posy, in an attempt to dazzle and deceive—was not uncommon in the mid-nineteenth century. In 1843 a Scottish woman named Frazer was charged with having fraudulently at-tempted to obtain goods—a huge quantity of men's clothing—from a West End shop. In the go-for-it spirit of Henry Brooks, she was calling herself Lady Elizabeth Charlotte Berkeley Craven, and had ordered twelve dozen shirts at a cost of a guinea each. The shop assistant, who was neither dazzled nor deceived, called for the police.

The mysterious Miss Frazer had worn the guise of Lady Elizabeth for some time; the shirt-buying extravaganza was in the nature of a climactic event. Preceding it was a tale in which a woman, living in a wretched slum off Long Acre in Covent Garden, had masqueraded as an heiress to the Earl of Berkeley and to some £17,000 a year, with a sum of £70,000 promised as her dowry. How did she pull this off? Her dupe was a gentleman's valet, considerably younger than she and foreign-born, with the residual trappings of family wealth. Somehow Miss Frazer had persuaded him that she was an earl's daughter. Clearly the valet's English was not good enough to pick up on any betraying solecisms of speech or manner, which after all the shop assistant had perceived within five minutes. In any event he asked "Lady Elizabeth" to marry him; *The Times* called him "the simpleton on whom she was to bestow her fair hand." Why she would have wanted to marry him is another question that he seems to have overlooked.

It is entirely possible, of course, that the dupe was in fact planning to be the duper, and that these two were deceiving each other. If so, the valet was not very good at it. Miss Frazer relieved him of his watch, saying that she would exchange it for her own ancestral timepiece, which naturally never materialized. Then the man handed over £5, to be spent on searching out his ancestral arms and quartering them with those of the Berkeley family. Again he probably saw this as a valuable future investment—Miss Frazer had actually named a date on which they would attend an entertainment held by her friend, the Duke of Cambridge— although the long-term plan, the valet testified, was that they should live in Corfu, "as the air of that island peculiarly suited her constitution, rendered delicate as it now was by sumptuous living among her noble relations."

What a very good talker Miss Frazer must have been; although she was merely winging it when compared with the unnamed woman who, in 1860, chose as her mark a rich widower from Lincoln named Taylor. Telling him that she, too, had been recently widowed, she disclosed that she was heiress to an immense property in Scotland, but that—alas!—she lacked the few hundred pounds needed for "preliminaries" before she could take it on. Not to worry, announced Mr. Taylor; he had £1,000 at his disposal, and it was hers if she wanted it. "Notwithstanding the cautions of intimate friends," wrote the *Manchester Guardian*, "they were married."

Hustling him away from these friends, the new Mrs. Taylor induced her husband to move a few miles away to Boston, where "everyone was congratulating the husband of a millionaire." After a few months even this fool of a man, who was obviously cross-eyed with lust, began to wonder when they might visit the fabled estate in Scotland. Thereupon his wife disappeared to London—"Chancery"—for the day and returned with a document, stamped with what she claimed to be the Lord Chancellor's seal, proclaiming that she was indeed heiress to "the Gordon property": a nice, generic, aristocratic-sounding Scottish name. The seal was in fact the impression of a half-crown coin.

Not until most of Mr. Taylor's money was gone did he demand of his wife that she visit her solicitors, to request an advance on her fortune. Not until the couple went to London, for a mythical appointment with Mrs. Taylor's mythical legal team, did he realize what had been going on. By some means his wife managed to elude him and stay in the city (there to give birth to his son), leaving behind belongings that included a trunk, supposedly full of valuable plate, actually a box of rocks.

No question about it: the chutzpah of the fake heiress stood comparison with that of the fortune hunter, and quite possibly exceeded it. These women were real-life Becky Sharps (*Vanity Fair* was published in 1848), brimful of bravura and sharp of wits, gloriously active in a way that actual heiresses were so rarely able to be. They were creatures of their age, one so hierarchical that people swooned before an earl's daughter, yet those with nothing to lose were offered a perverse, picaresque freedom to morph and reinvent. At the same time they were sisters beneath the skin of a young woman who, almost 200 years later, bamboozled smart Manhattan by—again—assuming the persona of an heiress. That golden word, still sounding its aeolian tune . . . Anna Sorokin, "Anna Delvey," Russian-born and raised in Germany, arrived in New York City in the mid-2010s and presented herself as the soon-to-be recipient of $60 million from a sustainable energy firm (good pick). As with those earlier bold fakes, she was seen through by shrewd staff members—bellhops, restaurant workers—whose suspicions she placated with $100 bills, acquired Henry Brooks–style by the cashing of dodgy checks. Yet a staggering number of people were convinced by her, despite the fact that the kind of lies she told should not really be possible in the age of Google: potential investors in her "plans" for a chain of clubs, à la Soho House, who pledged some $50 million in business loans; PR firms who offered flights on private jets; and young New Yorkers panicked by the FOMO that she was able to instill with her casual deployment of trigger words ("inheritance"), her cleverly drab European *chic* and elusive, low-key air of being at the center of events. Her equivalent of the "Lady Elizabeth" card was to claim intimacy with the international art world, a sphere so innately baffling—and awash with money—that it was again a superb choice on her part. What a girl! She ended up with a jail sentence of four to twelve years, of which she served less than three, although her failure to self-deport from the US led her almost immediately back to prison in 2021. Nevertheless, in a world where celebrity has infinitely more power than morality she is likely to profit from her crime, albeit not quite in the way that she intended: a payday of $320,000 from Netflix for her story[7] will surely not be her only reward.

Meanwhile her remark—"resilience is hard to come by, but capital is not"[8]—could stand as the creed of the fake heiress. Nor would it have been a bad thought for the heiress herself to have kept in mind.

* * *

And what of those heiresses, the real ones, back in the genteel pre-feminist bear pit of the nineteenth century?

Well: things continued to improve, not least because there were now ways around the law that handed a woman's property to her husband. When Catherine Tylney Long married the dreaded William Pole, her trustees had tied up as much as they could; under duress she signed most of it back to him but, as the century progressed, marriage settlements became much firmer, thanks to the development of equity law. By the middle of the century, around 10 percent of society—the "top" 10 percent, the ones who had money worth protecting—was marrying under the settlement arrangement, whereby a wife kept control of her property through the use of trusts. There was even such a thing as a "constructive" trust, which a woman could handle (shock horror) without her trustees. Marriage settlements laid down conditions, and husbands knew the deal before they got into it. It was becoming possible for a wife to have a private income, one that did not depend upon her husband being the kind of man who allowed this.

So a giant step forward for heiresses; yet a mass of womanhood remained unprotected, and in many ways even the "10 percent" belonged to that majority. For instance it was still the case that a wife's body belonged to her husband, however rich she was. She still required him not to seize, abuse or confine her; as was now far less frequent, but still just about legal. There was also the issue of what happened in the event of a separation. The 1839 Custody of Infants Act had improved the situation with regard to children, but a husband was still able to take unannounced possession of a wife's money.

As he did, in fact, during most marriages: Elizabeth Gaskell described how her husband "composedly buttoned up in his pocket" a check that she had earned through her writing. In 1856 she wrote, in some anguish, that "a husband can coax, wheedle, beat or tyrannize his wife out of something and no law whatever will help that I can see." A woman named Frances Elliot, also a writer although far less celebrated, could have told her as much from firsthand knowledge.

Frances, born in Berkshire in 1820, was heiress to a sizable fortune that brought her some £5,000 a year. In the 1850s she became a successful journalist, then an author. She was a close friend of Wilkie Collins (some of her anonymous pieces in *The Art Journal* were assumed to have been written by him), and had an affectionate relationship with Charles Dickens, acting occasionally in his theater company. In 1863 she married a much older man, the Very Reverend Gilbert Elliot, from whom she soon separated. Her strategy for ensuring that Mr. Elliot received none of her money verged upon the disreputable; but given the legal situation at the time—given, moreover, what she had gone through with her previous marriage—it was more than justified. In fact, it was to be applauded.

Her first husband, John Geils, was an impoverished Scottish cavalry officer, whose estate near Glasgow was heavily mortgaged. He was yet another of these dire and dreadful fortune hunters, who were so much alike in the fundamentals, while exhibiting their own kinky peculiarities: Geils's first variation on the sadism theme was played on his honeymoon, when he employed his mistress in the capacity of Frances's personal maid.

As usual this was just a taster of what was to come, in a marriage that lasted seven years and produced four daughters. Frances, according to her own account—which there is no reason to doubt—"lived most wretchedly: Mr. Geils enjoyed her money, treated her with humiliation and neglect, bestowed his favors on servant girls, used rough and violent language, threatened physical cruelty, and himself invaded the conjugal couch at times and in ways the most nefarious." Such was the evidence that she gave to the ecclesiastical Arches Court in 1847. She had left her husband and thrown herself on the fickle mercy of the law; Geils had accordingly summoned her to Canterbury, where he claimed that she had contrived the story with her mother, who had tried to seduce him before his marriage. Unlikely, yes. But the sort of claim that would have gotten a serious hearing.

The real problem, however, was the nature of this close-knit arena, and "the position in which justice is placed by the family connexions of the Court itself." In other words, Geils was related to most of the people in the room, including the judge.

Frances's own counsel—about the only person to whom Geils was *not* related—had called this out, but was doing so to the very people contained within his accusation. "I see a phalanx against me which quite oppresses me," he said. How much more frightening this must have been for Frances—like a piece of terrible absurdist theater—although eventually she was granted a judicial separation. She then sought a divorce. In England this still required an Act of Parliament; in Scotland the law was more progressive, and in 1849 she brought an action that was promptly contested by her husband, citing the English judgment.

The enigmatic Mary Davies, upon whose fields Belgravia was raised, in a posthumous portrait by Dorofield Hardy.

The heiress who got it right: Margaret, 2nd Duchess of Portland, in an enamel by Christian Friedrich Zincke.

An engraving of Mary Bowes, Countess of Strathmore, whose encounter with a sadistic fortune hunter was unfortunate indeed.

The cartoonists always knew what was going on: here, in the lubricious 1811 work "The Disconsolate Sailor," Catherine Tylney Long stands between her future husband, William Wellesley Pole (left), and the future king William IV, then the Duke of Clarence.

Ellen Turner, the victim at the heart of the last great Georgian heiress-snatch, in a portrait by Henry Wyatt.

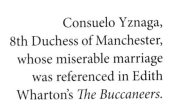

Consuelo Yznaga, 8th Duchess of Manchester, whose miserable marriage was referenced in Edith Wharton's *The Buccaneers*.

Sexy Jennie Jerome, the first and most gorgeous of the American dollar princesses, who took London by storm and became Lady Randolph Churchill.

Jennie with her sons, John (left) and Winston.

May Goelet, who found happiness as the 8th Duchess of Roxburghe.

Minnie Stevens: her marriage to Sir Arthur Paget was encouraged by the Prince of Wales.

The formidable Grace, second wife of Lord Curzon of Kedleston, photographed in her marchioness's finery by Bassano.

Consuelo Vanderbilt, 9th Duchess of Marlborough, dressed for the coronation of Edward VII in 1902. The tiara gave her a headache, she later wrote, and the "dog collar" chafed her neck.

Alva Vanderbilt's "summer cottage"—Marble House in Newport, Rhode Island—where Consuelo was confined before her marriage to the Duke of Marlborough.

The object of the exercise: Blenheim Palace, which would be restored to glory by the Vanderbilt millions.

La Grande Mécène: the young Winnaretta Singer.

Winnaretta's house at 43 Avenue Georges Mandel, now home to the Fondation Singer-Polignac, where the drawing room could seat 200 people.

The Palazzo Contarini Polignac, on the Dorsoduro in Venice. At the house today are four pianos that belonged to Winnaretta.

His argument was dismissed, but this did not stop him. He had no intention of stopping. Like Stoney and Pole before him, he was energized with the rage of the thwarted, and he took himself off to the House of Lords to appeal; not until 1855 did Frances achieve her Scottish divorce. She had suffered the social stigma of separation—which only really affected a wife—and for a time was prevented from seeing her children. Like Edward Wakefield, Frances had the capacity to create for herself a worthwhile second act, and to absorb the fact that she had spent seven years with a bad man, then ten years getting rid of him. But Wilkie Collins—a friend to women in general, and to Frances in particular—exploded with indignation on her behalf in a short story written in 1859:

> England stood disgracefully alone as the one civilized country having a divorce-law for the husband which was not also a divorce-law for the wife . . . She was indebted to the accident of having been married in Scotland, and to her subsequent right of appeal to the Scotch tribunals, for a full and final release from the tie which bound her to the vilest of husbands which the English law . . . would have mercilessly refused.

* * *

By the time that Collins wrote this, Frances had her English divorce. She had obtained it after an absurdly overdue change in the law, contained in the 1857 Matrimonial Causes Act, which took divorce out of the hands of ecclesiastical courts and placed it within the sphere of common law. Yet it was in this legalistic shift that she found a weapon against her second husband: a means to warn him off should he even think about pursuing her inheritance and her earnings. She threatened to "reveal" what was in fact a lie, that her marriage to Geils had *not* been rendered null, and that therefore the Very Reverend Mr. Elliot was a bigamist.

Charles Dickens disliked what she had done. He thought it tantamount to blackmail. He had a point, of course. Yet what did he really know—despite his extraordinary imaginative empathy—of what Frances had endured, and what vengefulness might seethe inside her? The victim of her righteous rage was the wrong man—poor Mr. Elliot!—but that is often the way of it. Anyway she was not just fighting for herself; this was about more than just one woman. Around seventy petitions, signed by thousands (including Mrs. Gaskell), had been presented to Parliament demanding the kind of changes that lay within the 1857 Act, and other changes that would soon follow. The *Saturday Review* asked plaintively: "Is there a plague in England or Egypt worse than the strong-minded woman?" It was, as the phrase has it, on the wrong side of history.

Henceforth there would be no more horror stories like those of Mary Davies, Mary Bowes, Catherine Tylney, Ellen Turner, and Frances Elliot. There would be other stories, and they would not always be edifying; but certain principles were being established that would remove forever the injustices suffered by those earlier heiresses, whose lives had been afflicted by their great good fortune.

That said, there were heiresses who did *not* suffer. The determining factor—as is so frequently the case in Britain—was class. Being indisputably aristocratic meant that one's life was encircled by an untouchable golden rope, composed of twin strands of social position and wealth, which were fused in a manner impossible either to disentangle or to breach.

Being female was no drawback to such women. Quite the opposite. One simply had to have the luck of being the right kind of heiress, the kind that nobody would ever dare summon into a court (except that of Queen Victoria): like, for instance, Frances Vane-Tempest, who as an only child acquired the fortunes of both her parents, and whose husband Lord Londonderry—whom she married in 1819—took the name of Vane,* or Lady Mary Douglas-Hamilton, who in 1895 would inherit an income of £35,000 a year from the 12th Duke of Hamilton. Had she been male, she would have also had ten British and two Scottish titles; but what, in such circumstances, did that matter?

These women, who were supremely protected in the manner of Margaret, Duchess of Portland, were not blessed with her Enlightenment curiosity. They liked the world as it was too much to ponder its mysteries. Although not necessarily lightweights—they were often political hostesses, and sometimes cared about the arts—they were generally unperturbed by abstract concepts such as equality. While members of the upper-middle classes fretted over the issue of women's rights, those who inhabited the celestial world of Piccadilly mansions and stately homes were really not too bothered, because their power was so delicious and unassailable. Their husbands comprised the ruling class: owned pretty much everything, from land to coal mines to Derby winners, and at the same time governed the country. Their wives, meanwhile, ruled society, or rather Society, which was the part of society that mattered to them.

Lady Jersey, for instance, who had inherited the money that her mother—Sarah Fane—gave up when she eloped with the Earl of Westmoreland, led a life of absolute gilded freedom, with a house on Berkeley Square and a superb estate at Osterley. She was a patroness at Almack's Assembly Rooms (the most exclusive

---

* The couple's eldest daughter, Lady Frances Vane, married the 7th Duke of Marlborough and was Winston Churchill's grandmother.

arena of the Regency era), and had so many affairs—possibly including Lord Palmerston—that her husband, when asked why he did not fight her lovers in a duel, replied that he would have to take on every man in London. She was vaguely engaged with the Tory cause, cried when told that the Duke of Wellington was no longer prime minister, and tried to exert her influence against the Reform Bill of 1832; a damning thing, today, to have opposed that first great broadening of the suffrage, but it would not have occurred to her to think in such terms. If she preferred the system as it was, one can hardly blame her.

And at least she enjoyed herself. She delighted in the inheritance that made her lovely life possible, and which was so immense that she could give away £80,000 to family members and scarcely notice. Although nothing like Margaret Portland in character, like her she inhabited a world that did not require her to feel guilt, and within which she was wholly invulnerable. There has perhaps never been a creature as lucky—undeservedly so, but then luck usually is undeserved—as the highborn heiress at the height of the Victorian era. Her creed was pronounced by the Hanoverian-born 7th Duchess of Manchester, who later married the 8th Duke of Devonshire, and who in the 1860s uttered a sentence worthy of Oscar Wilde: "I hear much of women's rights, but I only know that I have no wrongs."

* * *

In fraught contrast was this, from the social reformer Caroline Norton in 1855: "I do not ask for my rights. I have no rights. I have only wrongs."

Her particular cause, after the passing of the 1839 Custody of Infants Act, was the secondary monstrosity that had afflicted her life, and that Frances Elliot had sought to forestall: the fact that an estranged husband could at any time lay claim to his wife's money. Caroline's urgent influence was at work in the long lead-up to the 1857 legislation, as was that of an efficient group of women led by Barbara Leigh Smith, who were not impelled to campaign by grim experience—who indeed sought to distance themselves from Caroline's scarred reputation—but who were, nonetheless, bent toward similar ends. They were aware that the megarich had what was effectively their own system of private law, which enabled wives to maintain control of their inheritance. Quite simply, they wanted the same law for all women. They also wanted equal access to divorce, and a reform of the law with regard to adultery.

Resistance was strong. Prominent among the bill's opponents was William Gladstone, who said that it would "lead to the degradation of women." He opposed divorce on religious principle, and feared that men would be high on the excitement of sexual novelty were it too easy to obtain. There was also, always, a concern about the legitimacy of children. However Prime Minister Palmerston, an altogether worldlier character, was determined to get something through.

The hero on the front line was Caroline's friend, the former Lord Chancellor Lyndhurst, who at the age of eighty-four was still protesting from his wheelchair against "the system of hardship and cruelty as regards to women." He spoke about Caroline's specific grievance, asking: "Is that fair? Is that honest? Can it be vindicated upon any principle of justice, of mercy, or of common humanity?" Pressing his case, he moved on to the issue of discrimination against women with respect to divorce. The new bill proposed that a man could divorce his wife for adultery, whereas she needed to prove some additional affront such as cruelty, bigamy, or desertion. Lyndhurst must have known that he had no chance of getting rid of this anomaly (it was not removed until 1923). It confronted the sexual double standards that still, in fact, exist; there is only so much that legislation can do. Nevertheless, he had done a truly brilliant job of hijacking a bill that was designed simply to move divorce into the realm of common law. He had made it about so much more. In doing so he forced legislators to confront the wider concerns that women had been eloquently expressing, and that men—increasingly, if often reluctantly—were acknowledging to be valid.

The Victorian era was beginning, dimly, to understand that its definition of marriage was untenable, although there was still a long way to go. Divorce remained rare, expensive, and generally socially disastrous, even into the twentieth century (for instance, not until 1955 were divorcees allowed to enter the sacred Royal Enclosure at Ascot), and of course this was far truer for women than men. The decision as to whether it was better to stay or go remained a very difficult one for an unhappy wife. So traumatic was a divorce suit that it seems no exaggeration to compare it with the present-day dilemma of whether or not to proceed against a rapist. In 1884, for instance, Lady Colin Campbell was granted a judicial separation from her husband on the grounds that he had knowingly infected her with a venereal disease. Both parties filed for divorce; Lady Colin was accused of adultery, which his lordship had been committing all over London. She lost her suit.

Nor did the 1857 act concede on the key issue: that a wife should retain control of what she owned. Although the rich spouses of parliamentarians were doing exactly that, knowledge of their own hypocrisy rarely troubles those in public life, and they preferred to stick to the convention that—for the sake of its powerful symbolic stability—marriage should be seen to hold the equivalent of a joint bank account. Which was all very nice, very Victoria and Albert. The problem, however, was as immaculately expressed by the writer Caroline Cornwallis in the

Westminster Review: "No law can be good or wholesome which gives a bad man the liberty to do with impunity what a good man's conscience would prevent him from attempting."

Time was running out for those who sought to argue with this logic. In 1870—as had become inevitable—the first Married Women's Property Act was passed. It equivocated somewhat, and did not trespass too far upon the sacred notion that a wife had no independent legal identity; thus Millicent Fawcett could, even after the law was enacted, be robbed of her purse, and be amazed to hear it described in court as belonging to her husband. The 1882 legislation put an end to this nonsense, however, and enabled a wife to hold "all real and personal property" that she owned at the time of her marriage, or subsequently acquired. It was over, as soon would be a husband's right to control his wife physically: to own her body. It may have been pushing it slightly to write, as a legal commentator did in 1897, that "woman was born in chains and, behold, now on every side she is free." But there is no doubt that the slogging quest for justice—for a semblance of equality—had gained a momentum that would roll on at speed into the new century, bringing with it the vote, the right to enter the professions, the evolution of feminism; and that the nature of the heiresses's stories would start to change.

Which does not mean that they would not have benefited from reading this, preferably every day of their lives, from a letter written in 1849 by the novelist Geraldine Jewsbury to Jane Carlyle:

I believe we are touching on better days, when women will have a genuine normal life of their own to lead. There perhaps will not be so many marriages, and women will be taught not to feel their destiny *manqué* if they remain single.

PART II

AMERICAN DREAMS

"You are now free, and the best thing you can do is marry an heiress; there are heaps of them in New York."

From a letter written in 1887 by a wife requesting a separation from her husband, then on business in the United States

DOLLARS AND CORONETS

THEN: A CHANGE, as signaled by the publication of a story in *The Strand Magazine* entitled "The Great Californian Heiress."

The story appeared in 1895, the year that Lady Mary Douglas-Hamilton inherited her immense fortune. For British aristocrats at the top of the tree, life appeared to be continuing in much the same old way: in sequestered ballrooms and clubs, on grouse moors and at Goodwood, with the bon vivant Prince of Wales at the heart of society, and the rebarbative, reassuring figure of his stout little mother at the heart of the nation.

Yet popular culture had seen the way the wind was blowing—financially, sociologically—and what it saw was the veritable tempest that had hurtled toward Britain from across the Atlantic. In 1880 the prolific Mrs. Oliphant had written a novel entitled, bluntly, *The Greatest Heiress in England*. Eleven years later, Sara Jeannette Duncan was telling the story of *An American Girl in London*, the "emancipated" daughter of a baking-powder magnate, whose "crowning exploit"—according to the review in *The Times*—"is the acme of originality in an American heiress. She refuses an offer from a scion of the nobility!"

By then, the plot of Dollar Princess marries Son of Duke had become as fashionable and familiar as that of the Gretna Green elopement of a century earlier. New York electrifies Wiltshire, railroad money saves ancestral pile: these were the tropes, the images, replacing those of heiress-seizures and flights to "the Continent." This was the new reality, as wealth grew exponentially in the hands of bold men like Cornelius Vanderbilt—who died in New York City in 1877 worth an estimated $105 million—and as the air of infinity, which had once bloomed around the income of the British landowner class, began to close in.

At the time of Vanderbilt's death, 7,000 families owned four-fifths of the British Isles, and 250 families had 30,000 acres or more. From the 1880s onward, the slow decline of the landowning class began. It was propelled by the forces of democracy—the doubling of the size of the electorate meant that the social status quo simply could not hold—and by more basic events, like a succession of bad harvests; the fact is, however, that when change is ready to happen it will always find its way, its trigger, and this shift of power from landowners to wealth-creators was becoming as unstoppable as greater rights for women.

Men who understood money were now the source of true power. The Prince of Wales—whose friends included the Rothschilds, and who relished the company of rich Americans—knew this all too well. Untrammeled though it was, the life of the aristocrat had been an insular one, in which a country house, filled with the accretions of generations, was the center of the known universe. Now the world was suddenly bigger. The country house still held its sway—as it does today, even for rock stars and oligarchs—but the time had come to open its doors wider. Those outside the magic circle had to be invited in (not just Americans, incidentally; the giant dowry of Alfred de Rothschild's illegitimate daughter enabled her to become the 5th Countess of Carnarvon in 1895, although that was not quite as widely broadcast).

Land, the basis of the aristocrat's wealth, had suffered from increased international trade and its effect upon agricultural prices; then it suffered from taxation, as proposed in the 1909 "People's Budget." When the House of Lords opposed this measure, Lloyd George simply scythed away at their powers. Having refused to vote for their own impoverishment, they found themselves hastening their obsolescence; and the First World War— which killed more aristocrats than any conflict since the Wars of the Roses—almost finished the job. In the years around the war, a quarter of British land was sold. In London, the Bedford family sold its entire Covent Garden estate for £2 million in 1913, and within a decade or so almost everybody had disposed of their money-eating town houses: "It will be interesting to see what the pictures look like in a small house," said the Duchess of Devonshire, after the sale of the family mansion on Piccadilly (these things are relative; the "small house" was in Carlton Gardens). Even the Grosvenor family succumbed. In 1886 the 1st Duke of Westminster had held a tea party at his Park Lane mansion to celebrate the Derby win of his horse, Ormonde, who was guest of honor and ate all the flowers: this was the aristocracy in its oddly innocent, seemingly eternal pomp, but in 1924 the family sold Grosvenor House to Lord Leverhulme, who had acquired his peerage through business (soap) and who unceremoniously demolished the place.

Aristocrats are survivors, on the whole, willing to do whatever it takes. Perhaps that is their greatest gift. In the seventeenth century, the Grosvenors had snapped up Mary Davies and her marshy acres; in the twentieth, the Bedfords opened up Woburn Abbey and turned its once monastic grounds into a safari park. In the twenty-first century, age of the meta, the Carnarvon family's Highclere Castle would be used as the setting for *Downton Abbey*, whose plot references the very societal shifts (including a countess born in America) that made it possible to film inside a stately home. Throughout much of the nineteenth century, these houses had been as impregnable as bank vaults to all but the two thousand or so interrelated families that comprised Society. By the end of that century a Rothschild could buy an earl, and the Manchesters and Marlboroughs, the Curzons and Roxburghes and Angleseys, were looking speculatively to the United States for funds and fresh blood. A sure sign of the times came in a 1907 newspaper report of a man accused of fraud, who—as guarantee of his gentlemanly creditworthiness—had offered the reassurance that he was "married to an American heiress."

Between 1870 and the outbreak of war, 102 American girls* married members of the British aristocracy. It was an exchange, as surely as the dynastic marriages of old had been: the *nouveaux* bought their way into the aristocracy and the stately home got its roof fixed. And it was a good joke—one the public would have relished—that the heroine of *An American Girl in London* should turn down a nobleman and marry the boy next door from Yale. The culture clash was also presented on the stage, with a flurry of plays such as *The White Chrysanthemum*, first staged at the Criterion in 1905, in which a young man is forced by his father to become engaged to a New York heiress named Cornelia Vanderdecken, even though he really loves a poor English girl named Sybil Cunningham . . .

In truth, however, the old New York families were as outlandishly select as any in Britain. The label of the "Four Hundred"—for the number of people who comprised high

---

* To give a wider statistic, it is estimated that a total of 454 American girls married titled Europeans within this time period. The figure is cited in *The Husband Hunters: Social Climbing in London and New York* by Anne de Courcy (W & N, 2017).

society—was a perfect symbol of exclusivity, the American version of the elect who congregated every June at the Royal Enclosure at Ascot.

Edith Wharton, née Jones, born in 1862, was a member of this world (the phrase "keeping up with the Joneses" is said to refer to her family). She was also able to cast a cool eye upon it. Indeed she called its inhabitants "a group of bourgeois colonials," who had transformed themselves "into a sort of social aristocracy." An intelligent artist will look critically upon their own class and country, and Wharton certainly did so in her novel *The Age of Innocence*, published in 1920 but set some fifty years earlier. Its central theme characterized the complex relationship between America and Europe, what these two worlds are deemed to represent to each other; opinions that are of course highly subjective. The Prince of Wales, later Edward VII, visited New York in 1860 and adored it as a place of freedom. Yet Wharton's novel casts Europe in that role, as a broad-minded and cultured place that New York replicates but does not really understand. She contrasts the sophisticated figure of the Countess Olenska—American-born, wholly Europeanized—with a society of astonishing conformity: Washington Square is home to a *haute bourgeoisie*, as fanatically alert to class nuance as the inhabitants of E. F. Benson's Tilling.* More English than the English, in fact.

For instance the countess, who is scandalously separated from her rich Polish husband, has an open, relaxed friendship with the visiting Duke of St. Austrey. He takes her to a party—"You

---

* E. F. Benson's exquisitely hilarious *Mapp and Lucia* series (six novels and two short stories) is set mainly in the fictional town of "Tilling," based on Rye in East Sussex. Benson lived there from 1919 in the very beautiful Lamb House, previously the home of Henry James and incarnated in the books as the town's foremost residence, the much coveted "Mallards."

know what these English grandees are"—and this causes its own, minor frisson: "I thought the shortest way was to go straight to Countess Olenska and explain—by the merest hint, you know—how we feel in New York about certain things."

"New York society is a very small world compared with the one you've lived in," the countess is reminded. "And it's ruled, in spite of appearances, by a few people with—well, rather old-fashioned ideas."

It was ruled, in reality, by Caroline Schermerhorn, wife of William Backhouse Astor Jr., whose dominance of this arena was absolute, and whose ballroom at Newport was built to contain precisely 400 people. If Mrs. Astor did not want to know you, she did not know you: it was that simple. The story went that her nephew-by-marriage, William Waldorf, left New York for England in 1891 because he and his wife Mamie could not stand living in Caroline's shadow, socially speaking (ironically, by so doing he acquired a title, which was the one thing that Mrs. Astor could not have). Caroline was a descendant of one of the original Dutch settlers—whose English equivalent was the families who had "come over with the Conqueror"—and the Astors had made their money three generations ago, the equivalent of being an aristocrat whose mercantile ancestry was long forgotten. The taint of trade had long been absorbed, and the air smelled only of leisure (bay rum, Floris scent, thoroughbred horseflesh).

A man like Cornelius Vanderbilt, however, still reeked of what he was, a businessman of genius, who controlled shipping, then railroads, and had started life as a Staten Island ferryman, whose money was all a bit rugged and recent for Mrs. Astor's ballroom. Nevertheless his grandchildren were allowed in: another irresistible change. Their acceptance was marked by a legendary evening in March 1883, a kind of belle époque Met Ball at which 1,200 guests dressed themselves as old-style European aristocrats (what else); an era-defining party thrown by Cornelius's granddaughter-in-law, Alva, at her astonishing Fifth Avenue mansion-cum-chateau, at a cost of $250,000. Talked about for weeks beforehand, previewed constantly in the newspapers to whom Alva threw a succession of delicious little bones, it was graced by the imperial presence of Caroline Astor, who wore blue velvet and a priceless cache of diamonds on every available part of her body, and who had metaphorically bowed her head to the inevitable.

What a moment that must have been, when Mrs. Astor walked in! The old order bestowing its blessing upon the new, welcoming it with who knows what feelings: not just Vanderbilts but Rockefellers, Goulds, and Carnegies, the "swells," the names upon which New York rose and became the foremost city in the world, the people who shook up and shaped Manhattan with their ruthless drive, their grand civic philanthropy, and their fabulous Beaux Arts houses, so unlike the determinedly discreet downtown brownstones whose "uniform hue"—according to Wharton's *The Age of Innocence*—"coated New York like a cold chocolate sauce." The real rulers of America, who were said to possess more money than was in their country's Treasury; and, from the turn of the century, when Grace Vanderbilt acceded to the throne vacated by Caroline Astor, the rulers of New York society.

* * *

Why did these dynamos want poor old Britain, one might wonder, when they were so clearly the future? It is amazing, really. Theirs was the New World, which for one hundred years had proclaimed its belief in equality. But the society run by Mrs. Astor had a symbiotic bond with the Old World, whose legitimate child it was. European culture and customs were its collective lodestar: Crown Derby, riding to hounds, and a Gainsborough in the drawing room. And the "new" New Yorkers—many of whom wanted to live within Mrs. Astor's magic circle, because apparently there was nowhere else that signified—perceived that a European title had a supreme cachet, that it could be bought with their near-infinite millions, and that it would constitute an entry pass that could not be gainsaid.

Instead of remaking society entirely in their own image, therefore, they created a facsimile aristocracy, a blend of money and breeding in which a Miss Vanderbilt became the Duchess of Marlborough, a Miss Goelet the Duchess of Roxburghe, and a Miss Jerome—daughter of a brilliant Wall Street speculator—the mother of Winston Churchill. This, then, was the Gilded Age: Versailles on Fifth Avenue. And the mystique of a title endured long past that era, as for instance when Barbara Hutton married Alexis Mdivani, who was descended from minor Georgian nobility and (stretching a point) called himself a prince. Heritage notwithstanding, he would surely not have cut it in Mrs. Astor's ballroom; although oddly enough his first wife, Louise Astor Van Alen, was Caroline's great-granddaughter.*

The visiting aristocrat was a familiar figure in upper-class New York. *The Age of Innocence* addresses the subject with its usual satiric delicacy, identifying a careful code of conduct, an assumed indifference that is—aptly enough—very English. "New York took stray noblemen calmly . . . but when they presented such credentials as these [the Duke of St. Austrey's] they were received with an old-fashioned cordiality that they would have been greatly mistaken in ascribing solely to their standing in

---

* James Van Alen II married Caroline's daughter Emily, who died giving birth to Louise's father in 1881.

Debrett." Despite this determined refusal to be overawed by a peerage, when a dinner is held for the duke there is a tremendous pulling out of all the stops: the "du Lac *Sèvres* and the Trevenna George II plate were out . . ."

In other words people *were* impressed, because a title of the unassailably grand variety was the supreme symbol of what this society sought to attain.

And—ridiculous though it may be—it signifies even now, else presumably the Californian-born Meghan Markle would not have wanted to become the Duchess of Sussex and Jeff Bezos would not have commissioned a coat of arms.[1] Back in the late nineteenth century, meanwhile, clever Alva Vanderbilt played a title—twice—as a trump card with which to clinch a social game that had been loaded against her.

First there was her 1883 ball, which she held in nominal honor of her good friend Consuelo Yznaga, an American-Cuban heiress from Louisiana, who seven years earlier had married the heir to the dukedom of Manchester. At the time of the ball Consuelo was merely Lady Mandeville. She was also very unhappily married, and visiting New York with her husband as a means to delay confronting his creditors. But hardly anybody knew that, whereas everybody knew that she would one day be a duchess, and this was an almighty attraction—even to Caroline Astor.

Alva's husband, Willie K. Vanderbilt, was attracted to Lady Mandeville in a more straightforward way, or so it was strongly rumored. He was a dedicated philanderer, most flagrantly with a beautiful courtesan from Kansas, whom he kept in high style in Paris. Quite usual behavior, of course. William Backhouse Astor was rumored to behave similarly on his yacht. Wives generally put up with it, in the knowledge that they could do much the same thing as long as the rules were observed; a husband was only given up on if he was truly too dreadful to bear. Alva, however, was not a usual woman. For her, the Kansas courtesan was the last in a haystack of straws. Possibly Willie had guessed that this would be the case, and provoked his wife into ending a marriage that he too wanted over. In any event, and against the advice of her lawyers, Alva plunged in and filed for divorce, generating what today would be called a tabloid frenzy: pages and pages of detail printed and pored over in the press. Indeed the suit was described as "the biggest divorce case that America has ever known. It is, in fact, the biggest ever known in The World" (take that, Henry VIII).

Alva's divorce came through in early 1895, the year her eighteen-year-old daughter Consuelo—named for her erstwhile dearest friend—was launched upon society: not the best timing. In typical fighting fashion, Alva tried to use the newspapers for her own ends and syndicated the story of Consuelo's coming-out ball. As so often, she was way ahead of the curve—anticipating the days when people would queue up to sell their weddings to *Hello!*—but, at the time, the move was interpreted as evidence of her innate vulgarity. Since her divorce she had not exactly become persona non grata, as she was still invited to parties, but when she attended nobody except her hostess would speak to her. When she went to church—the Vanderbilts favored St. Bartholomew's on Park Avenue—she was cut as completely as if she were under suspicion of murder. Like the Countess Olenska in *The Age of Innocence*, she was viewed with fear and suspicion, as a disruptive element, but unlike the countess she had never been part of the innermost social circle, and the outrage of her divorce meant that she could be rejected with relief.

In America, as in Britain, divorce was possible but unacceptable. It is hard to comprehend, but that was how it was. The land of the free was the land of the puritan; it was also, when it came to high society, the land of the impossibly correct (women would leave the room if the word "divorce" were uttered). Nevertheless most states had granted property rights to wives, some twenty years before the passing of the 1870 Married Women's Property Act. Whereas in Europe the patrilineal principle was akin to an eleventh commandment, and a woman only inherited when there was no man available to do so, an American fortune would likely be parceled equally between children regardless of sex. May Goelet, who married the Duke of Roxburghe in 1903, was left $20 million when her father died, the same sum as her brother. A couple of territories had even given women the vote in the 1870s, although the fight for national suffrage would take another fifty years. On the whole, therefore, it was better to be an American female than her British counterpart. And these greater freedoms would—one might think—have generated a different outlook, a less passive approach, an innate understanding of the equality principle.

Not, however, within the sacred purlieus of society as portrayed in *The Age of Innocence*. Newland Archer, the central character, is a correct but imaginative young man who finds himself perturbed, then helpless, in the face of Countess Olenska ("It frightened him to think what must have gone to the making of her eyes"). May Welland, his fiancée, is a very different creature, who observes conventions to which the countess is oblivious and is apparently happy to be treated like a porcelain doll. Archer tries delicately to prod her into life but—as he says to himself— "There was no use in trying to emancipate a wife who had not the dimmest notion that she was not free; and he had long since discovered that May's only use of the liberty she supposed herself to possess would be to lay it on the altar of her wifely adoration."

In fact May, that sweetly blushing Dresden figure, is strong as steel; but one would not know it to look at her, and that is the point. She would have fitted very well into late Victorian England, which worshipped the demure and pure—or at least the semblance of those traits—and which, in so many ways, set the code of conduct for upper-class New York.

Although he tries not to be, Newland is dismayed by May's dutiful parroting of received opinion; "he wondered at what age 'nice' women began to speak for themselves." There was no such concern, however, with the American girls who arrived in England from the 1870s onward, and who did indeed bring enlivening air into Victorian drawing rooms. But then they had never belonged to the world inhabited by May Welland. The three Jerome sisters, for instance—the first to hit London—were the daughters of a man who, at the height of his wayward fortunes, owned a Madison Avenue mansion with its own opera house, but who was nevertheless deemed not up to the social mark (the great entrée of the *nouveaux* into the Four Hundred was still some fifteen years away). Their mother Clara, understandably vexed with the situation, accordingly set sail with her beautiful daughters for Europe.

A comparable move would happen some fifty years later, when Ohio steel magnate James W. Corrigan set up in Europe because New York would not accept his wife, Laura (she was known to have once been a waitress in Cleveland). James returned to America in 1925, where he died three years later, but Laura Corrigan remained in London and became a successful social hostess. She rented immense houses that their owners could scarcely afford, and spent her summers in Venice, where she was said to be "holding most of the palaces in fee."[2] She was mocked for her eccentricity—her party trick was to stand on her head, mindful presumably of her wig—and for her malapropisms, as when she told the Duke of Devonshire: "My doctor said to me, if you want to avoid indigestion, you must masturbate, masturbate!"

But she was *in*, as she had never been in her own country. This
was not really because Europe was less snobbish than New York.
Of course it was not. It was because an *émigrée*—especially one
so rich and generous with their hospitality—had an added fascination, a novelty value. This wore off, as novelties do, but by
then Mrs. Corrigan had become part of the social furniture: one
of many Americans who had, since that first wave of husband-
hunting girls, gravitated to Europe and given its tired old ways
a vital shot in the arm. Indeed Maud Burke of San Francisco,
who married a country baronet, left him to his Leicestershire
hunt, and transformed herself into "Emerald Cunard," became
the gleaming lodestar of London society between the wars. "Bertie and I were never chic enough for Lady Cunard," said Queen
Elizabeth, in reference to herself and the future George VI.

During that same interwar period an enclave of Americans—
notably Hemingway and Gertrude Stein—was establishing itself in Paris; albeit for artistic reasons rather than in order to
dine with dukes. Back in the nineteenth century, however, Paris
was very much part of the social Grand Tour. Alva Vanderbilt
visited in the 1860s, when she was Miss Smith of Alabama, as
did the Jerome women. They would have been far from indifferent to French culture—it profoundly infused Alva's aesthetic
sensibility—but this was the era of the Second Empire, and a
more worldly kind of education was on offer. The court led by
Napoleon III was fun, in a demanding, high-toned, peculiarly
Parisian way, and extravagant to a degree to have made Robes-
pierre wonder why he had bothered. Moreover, its extreme sexual sophistication surely played its part in honing these young
American women for the British marriage market: any lingering
trace of puritanism was purged, coquetry replaced winsomeness,
and the bed-hopping high jinks that they would later encounter
in stately homes had scant power to shock.

In London, meanwhile, society was dominated by the Prince of Wales and his easygoing "Marlborough House" set. Positively Parisian in his frank love of women, unabashed in his liking for the rich, Bertie—as he too was known—was an easy nut to crack for American heiresses. He found them direct and unstuffy and no doubt wonderfully unlike his mother. Deference was so familiar as to be something of a bore: these girls had what he called "snap." They also had a clean-limbed, confident elegance, which came partly from their more liberal upbringing, partly from the fact that they could afford to be dressed by Worth, the first male couturier, whose clothes fitted like dreams; no miserable drooping bodices of the kind seen in British country houses, no inverted snobbery about grooming one's horse better than oneself. These attributes soon caused the better class of American heiress to have European suitors hurling themselves at her. "How I should hate to be May Goelet," as the Princess of Pless later put it, "all those odious little Frenchmen and dozens of others crowding around her millions." (The princess, incidentally, was an impoverished British beauty, a Miss Cornwallis-West, who had married a vastly rich German.) She then added graciously: "An English duke does not crowd around—he merely accepts a millionairess."

True enough. But twenty years before May Goelet was "accepted" by the Duke of Roxburghe, the American girls in Europe had to be accepted en masse, and there was no better social sponsor than the Prince of Wales.

* * *

Jennie Jerome, first of the Americans to marry an English aristocrat—Lord Randolph Churchill in 1874, when she was aged twenty—would later be the prince's mistress. It was a casual affair, as hers tended to be; even in this uber-worldly milieu, Jennie's sex life was noteworthy. She had an estimated couple of hundred lovers, who as she got older tended to get younger (in 1900 she would marry George Cornwallis-West, brother to the Princess of Pless, who was the same age as her elder son). It was also suggested—on not much evidence—that her second child, John, was not Lord Randolph's. Her first, Winston, was probably conceived before marriage: his premature appearance was tactfully attributed to Jennie having "a fall."

Her dark prettiness was piquant, both ingénue innocent and deeply sexy. She was described as having "more of the panther than the woman in her look." Small wonder that Lord Randolph succumbed so instantly. He was the third son of the 7th Duke of Marlborough, and proposed after three days. Negotiations were entered to ensure that both sets of parents were happy—neither was, at the start; not least because Randolph had asked Jennie to marry him before securing permission to do so, an astonishing breach of social protocol. Moreover this was the first of these transatlantic marriages, the template indeed. The terms had to be right. Essentially what was needed was a lot of money from the American side, and the promise of non-disreputable behavior from the other, which meant that Randolph agreed to enter Parliament. Nevertheless, there was ongoing resentment from the Marlborough end. Jennie refused to play the American tourist, awestruck and humble in the face of the ducal palace at Blenheim; in fact with her accomplishments (she was a talented pianist), her amusing, informed conversation, and her gorgeous clothes, she felt more than a match for her new family. Naturally she ruffled some ostrich feathers. "It is no use disguising it," Jennie wrote to her mother, in the unworried tones of the irresistible female, "the Duchess hates me simply for what I am."

A succession of deaths and daughters meant that, for a time, Jennie's son looked set to inherit the title. When Consuelo Vanderbilt married the 9th Duke in 1895, her new mother-in-law instructed her: "Your first duty is to have a child and it must be a son, because it is intolerable to have that little upstart Winston become Duke."

Later still, Jennie would write: "In England, as on the Continent, the American woman was looked upon as a strange and abnormal creature, with habits and manners something between a Red Indian and a Gaiety Girl. Anything of an outlandish nature might be expected of her." This, again, sounds a lot like jealousy on the part of the English, expressed in the usual way by pulling up the metaphorical drawbridge and leaving these girls to freeze outside in their Worth. The "buccaneers," as they became known, were deemed a threat. They *were* a threat. The fact that they were prey, at least as much as predators, was overlooked: the female tendency to blame other females was very much to the fore. How—went the thinking—could the Hon. Leonora receive her proposal from Lord Right when these luscious, good-humored creatures wrapped in supple satin were opening their checkbooks left, right, and center? And how, once American women had set themselves up as social hostesses, were their British counterparts to compete? The Prince of Wales was the very embodiment of the bon vivant—"is there no cheese?" he once queried plaintively after a six-course dinner—and he frankly preferred the company of people whose finances could take the strain of entertaining him.

A group of female aristocrats was sufficiently concerned to visit the Archbishop of Canterbury and ask him to hold devotional meetings, attended by women like themselves, in which they would pray for a return to the old order. Their argument—apparently delivered in all seriousness—was that the incomers were having a deleterious moral effect upon the Prince of Wales. What a scene this must have been: the barely contained agitation of their ladyships, the trapped clergyman striving for emollience. Of course he had no intention of doing what they asked, not even when things got still worse for them, and a terrible vista began to emerge in which every eligible man in the country got married to an American. Not even when, in 1876, twenty-three-year-old Consuelo Yznaga went one better than Jennie Jerome, and nabbed a future duke.

Some sixty years later, Consuelo would become the model for a character in another of Edith Wharton's novels, the unfinished—and posthumous—1938 work *The Buccaneers*. It depicts this very phenomenon, of the rich American girls who tried their luck in Europe when the *Age of Innocence* society refused to accept them. Although the book has no ending, it does not promise one of unequivocal happiness; this was the story told from the other side, of the displaced girls who were shaking up London society. The Consuelo figure, Conchita Closson, marries the English Lord Richard Marabel, who offers nothing except his good name. He is a loose-living gambler, who takes his wife's money then effectively abandons her. This, pretty much, is what happened to Consuelo Mandeville. After attending the 1883 ball thrown in her honor by Alva Vanderbilt, she returned to London with her husband, Kim, who thereafter led his own life. Consuelo wrote helplessly to a friend: "his movements are so erratic that I think I had better say he won't come with me on Sunday. He so often disappoints me that I generally make up my mind to go without him." Eventually Kim went to live with a music hall performer, a male impersonator named Bessie Bellwood, leaving his wife to try and sue him for the return of her own money.

"These awful English marriages . . . strangle you in a noose when you try to pull away from them," wrote Edith Wharton in

The Buccaneers. Consuelo, the duke-snatcher, was indeed much to be pitied. She had married Kim in good faith, and having been sold out of her homeland she wanted to stay in England after her marriage foundered. But the position of a deserted wife—especially one without family backing—remained problematic, and divorce still too bold a step. Nor was the status of duchess, acquired when Kim inherited in 1890, much use to her. The title brought with it a heavy weight of debt, which her money had been designed to alleviate but which her husband was blithely spending upon himself.

The 7th Duchess of Manchester—whose husband inherited in the very different world of 1855—had no wrongs. The 8th had little else. The sense of disillusionment, if the alluring Miss Yznaga had believed that an aristocrat would also be a gentleman, must have been stark. Her husband had seemed to fall in love, and not merely with Consuelo's £200,000 dowry, yet within a few years he was treating her as if she had no worth beyond her money. The heiress's burden; which incidentally was repeated in the next generation when the Manchesters' son, the 9th Duke, married a rich girl from Cincinnati and blew her money on the kind of pleasures favored by his father. He was declared bankrupt in the 1920s, and in 1935—aged fifty-eight—sent to jail for obtaining money on false pretenses.

Back in the late nineteenth century, what mostly saved the 8th Duchess was the friendship of the Prince of Wales (and of his wife, the forebearing Alexandra). Consuelo entertained him, sang literally for her supper in between drags on a cigar, read his palm, and taught him to play the banjo; one can imagine how much fun this was, compared with the usual drawling chat about who was expected at Cowes and what was going to win the Stewards' Cup. When her money began to run out, she kept her end up with the prince by asking friends to bring a course each for the monumental dinners that he took as his royal due. Then, most enterprisingly, she started a sideline for her fellow Americans. She taught the young women who were arriving in London in numbers how to succeed in its society; those who came up to the mark would, for a sizable fee, be invited to a dinner attended by the prince and (if required) introduced to a potential husband. The passing of the 1882 Married Women's Property Act meant that Consuelo's earnings from these activities were entirely her own, untouched by Kim's light fingers.

Other American women followed her example in making money out of social networking: not a bad business idea at all, and another example of the innovatory spirit that caused some spluttering into the kedgeree. Mary "Minnie" Paget, a friend of Consuelo's, also helped new arrivals for a consideration, although it was suggested by the *New York Times* that her patronage might sometimes be more of a hindrance; Minnie Stevens, as was, had been a little too honest about her social ambitions when she first came to London in 1872, and was embarrassingly ditched by a suitor who discovered that she was not—despite her nickname of "The Great Heiress"—quite as fabulously rich as he had believed. Furthermore her mother, Marietta, was no elegant Clara Jerome. She was a chambermaid who had married her hotelier boss, Paran Stevens; origins that inevitably excluded her from the Four Hundred, and were not wholly overlooked by England either.

The Stevens women were made of fine stuff, however, and were not the sort to be daunted. As the future Duchess of Cambridge and her mother would do in the early twenty-first century, they rose calmly above sneers about their origins (such as the infamous "doors to manual" joke, made by some of Prince William's less lovely friends, in reference to Carole Middleton's former job as an air hostess). The Stevenses also held a valuable card. On his visit to New York in 1860, the Prince of Wales had stayed at Paran's Fifth Avenue hotel, a tenuous connection but, given Bertie's liking for Americans, invaluable. After six years in London, Minnie was encouraged by him to marry his good friend Arthur Paget, soldier, racing man, and grandson of the Marquess of Anglesey. Paget—who had already proposed and been rejected—seems to have been sincerely fond of Minnie and she, who had taken a few too many turns on the society round-about, needed a husband. Naturally Bertie was thinking of his friend's finances, but also of Minnie's amour propre: as a marriage broker, the future king showed kindly good sense.

Seventeen years later, in 1895, Paget's younger brother Almeric would also marry an American heiress, Pauline Payne Whitney. This was a showier alliance. Almeric was a dynamic individual, a businessman and MP, who acquired his own title as the 1st Baron Queenborough (and lived to be an admirer of Hitler). Pauline's father was the US Secretary of the Navy under Grover Cleveland, who attended the wedding. Her brother, Harry, married a Vanderbilt—like the European aristocracy of old, its Gilded Age counterpart was clever at keeping its privilege close.

Minnie Paget had surely hoped for something more than the man she eventually married—who became Commander in Chief of Ireland, with mixed success—else she would not have turned him down in the first instance. That said, his close friendship with the Prince of Wales was worth a great deal. It took her to the heart of the Marlborough House set, where—thanks to her own force-ful determination to please—she remained. She entertained the prince, just as her father had done before her, although she was paying for the honor rather than being paid; it has been estimated that she spent some $6 million on throwing the kind of parties that he most enjoyed. Which, in turn, enabled her mother to go back to New York and buy the white marble house that had belonged to Edith Wharton's great-aunt, model for Mrs. Manson Mingott in *The Age of Innocence*, who had sworn never to allow Mrs. Paran Stevens through her door.

It may seem extraordinary to find fulfillment through spending an inheritance upon a succession of dinners for the heir to the throne. But what else to do, when the concept of female equality—although no longer unimaginable—still seemed so remote, like the notion that women might engage with life in a similar way to men? Minnie Paget was as clever in her sphere as any high-flying graduate today, not least because she understood that the social landscape was pretty much the only one in which feminine power then lay. So too did her mother, who had come to Europe—a gamble, like all emigration—and achieved from that journey exactly what she wanted.

The mothers, indeed, were the real drivers of these marriages. They wanted what was best for their daughters: that age-old desire, whose benevolence is not without egotism. A daughter's position reflects upon her mother, after all. And in some cases the egotism outweighed the benevolence, as for instance with the match decided upon for Consuelo Vanderbilt by her mother, Alva, which was brokered with a ruthlessness that would have been admired by Mary Tregonwell, mother to the London heiress Mary Davies.

This was the second time that Alva Vanderbilt would play the court card. She did so in a way that obliterated the scandal of her divorce, and returned her triumphantly to the heart of the quality.

By 1895, the year *The Strand Magazine* published "The Great Californian Heiress," the concept of the American girl in a coronet was a familiar one. These girls were celebrities: people would mass outside houses and venues where they were expected to appear, and newspapers on both sides of the

Atlantic were obsessed with them. Each country had a deep fascination for and with the other. In Britain, certainly, where homegrown aristocrats were also of undimmed interest, the remote glamor of America—its sheen, its newness, the sheer scale of what it represented—gave the heiresses a cinematic dimension before film stars were even dreamed of.

In the twenty-one years since Jennie Jerome set the ball rolling by marrying Lord Randolph Churchill, her two sisters had married into the Anglo-Irish aristocracy; Consuelo Yznaga had become the Duchess of Manchester and *her* sister, Maria, was now Lady Lister-Kaye. Tennessee Claflin, not an heiress but certainly a superb buccaneer—she had made money as a clairvoyant, a healer, and (with the help of her rumored lover, seventy-five-year-old Cornelius Vanderbilt) as a Wall Street broker—was now Lady Cook, with a husband thirty years her senior and a glorious mansion overlooking the Thames on Richmond Hill. The adopted Virginia Bonynge, whose real father was in San Quentin prison, and who was one of Consuelo's protégées, was married to Viscount Deerhurst, heir to the earldom of Coventry. New York–born Adele Beach Grant, who had also paid for Consuelo's services, was the 7th Countess of Essex.

In New York, meanwhile, the Astor-led society had become (as per *The Age of Innocence*) quite au fait with the figure of the traveling duke: his sidelong charm, his air of having been born on horseback, his self-effacing arrogance. Familiarity, however, had not bred contempt. When it was known that young Charles Spencer-Churchill, 9th Duke of Marlborough, would be attending a ball thrown by Alva in Newport at her "summer cottage"—the majestic Marble House, built (or "vanderbuilt," as the wags had it) in the style of the Grand Trianon at Versailles—people were simply unable to resist the lure. They were probably unable to resist Alva also: she was always such good value. And by August 1895, after just a few months in the wilderness, she was center stage once more. By November that year, Consuelo was the 9th Duchess and chatelaine of Blenheim Palace.

* * *

Ten years after her marriage, the Duchess of Marlborough was painted by John Singer Sargent, who surely captured better than anybody the women of the Gilded Age: their moneyed sexiness, their passive power. Consuelo was portrayed en famille, at Blenheim, with a husband, two sons, and a pair of spaniels, a companion piece to a Sir Joshua Reynolds painting of the 4th Duke. She is the very glass of elegance, not least because the artist— whose sardonic eye was a joke shared between him and his more perceptive observers—has placed her on some stairs, above her husband, thus accentuating the fact that at five feet eight she was six inches taller than he.

Aged twenty-eight she is beautiful—a stately young peeress— but as a girl she would have been the ultimate Sargent model with her mass of dark hair, vast sensuous eyes, and long, indolent body. Photographs of her aged eighteen, newly married, show her in coronet and cloak (with four rows of ermine and a two-yard train, as her rank decreed), a choker strapped weightily around her etiolated neck. Later she wrote that "my tiara invariably produced a violent headache, my dog collar a chafed neck"; such was the lot of the duchess.[3]

She brought $2.5 million to the marriage, given to her husband in trust, and an annual income of some $100,000 per annum, guaranteed to him by the New York Central Railroad Company, which no subsequent divorce could touch. Charles—or Sunny, as he was known—had no interest in Consuelo as a woman;

so she later affirmed. If her assertion was true then, in a way, it made things simpler, freed the ice-cool transaction from any pretense that the heiress was wanted for herself. This was old-school bartering, and no mistake.

The Marlboroughs had been in financial trouble for some time. They had already taken steps to address the issue, although what was actually required was a giant leap. Blenheim—stern, vast, and baroque, the only non-royal palace in England, set in two and a half thousand acres of parkland—was frankly a money pit, and the decline in land values had not helped. The 1st Duke, John Churchill, received his title and house in the early eighteenth century as a reward for his great victories on the battlefield; his wife Sarah's position as Queen Anne's "favorite" was also a factor, although her carelessness with the monarch's affections eventually led to a cessation of royal funding for Blenheim. It was always, in fact, a bit more than the family could afford. Although generally deemed Sir John Vanbrugh's masterpiece, some thought it almost too magnificent, a monolith rather than a house: Alexander Pope hit the nail on the head when, having duly admired the place, he asked: "But where d'ye sleep and where d'ye dine?" The remark was later echoed by Consuelo, who expressed wonderment at the fact that Blenheim had 170 rooms and not a comfortable one among them.

By 1875 the 7th Duke was petitioning Parliament for the right to break the entail on Blenheim and its contents. This meant that precious items could be sold: a Raphael, a Van Dyck, a famed Rubens now in the Metropolitan Museum of Art. Very nice to have such things to sell, but even the huge sums raised could not fill the gaps. American money, therefore, became the obvious solution.

Thirteen years after his brother Randolph married the delectable Miss Jerome, the 8th Duke of Marlborough had been spending a summer in Newport, as a guest of none other than Mrs. Paran Stevens. Also present was the woman whom the *New York Times* called "the widow Hamersley," formerly Lillian Price of Troy, thirty-three years old and heiress to some $150,000 per annum left by her husband Louis. It was not long before the Duke and Mrs. Hamersley were saying their vows at New York City Hall, then in front of a Baptist clergyman.

A full-blown church wedding was impossible, because George Marlborough was divorced. His first wife, Albertha, had gone down that seismic route in 1883 on the grounds of infidelity and cruelty (infidelity alone did not, of course, suffice). The couple separated in 1878, on account of George's adultery with one Lady Aylesford, and Albertha filed for divorce after Edith Aylesford gave birth to an illegitimate son in 1881. At which point things got *really* complicated.

The Aylesford affair, which ended the Marlborough marriage, also caused a serious rupture between the Randolph Churchills and the Prince of Wales. Bertie—who had himself dallied with Edith—became angrily uncomfortable with her very public new liaison; in this sexually interrelated circle discretion was not merely desirable, it was essential, if the social house of cards were not to collapse. When Lord Aylesford became determined to divorce his wife, citing George Marlborough, the scandal seemed to escalate to formidable heights. Accordingly Randolph Churchill—fearful for his brother's reputation—asked Bertie to talk Aylesford out of suing for divorce, and applied pressure by threatening the prince with exposure of his own love letters to Edith. Then Randolph and Edith tried similar tactics with the prince's wife, Alexandra.

Staunch brotherly behavior it may have been, but it was also blackmail, and very foolish. The prince challenged Randolph to a duel, which was really not his style (plus he knew that his antagonist would back down; I would fight a duel with anybody but my future sovereign, was Randolph's craven way out of it). Prime Minister Disraeli—taking urbane charge—arranged for George to be sent to Ireland as viceroy, with his brother as private secretary. On their return in 1884 the prince, who was not a vengeful man, allowed the Churchills back into favor (not that Jennie would ever have been out of it). Meanwhile Lady Aylesford, who had separated from her husband in 1877—they never divorced—made a truly bizarre claim for the Marlborough dukedom on her son's behalf, which was turned down by the House of Lords.

Given this extraordinary saga, plus the fact that she was related to half the ducal houses in England, Albertha Marlborough could be confident that she would suffer no disgrace from the annulment of her marriage. Indeed, the social stigma fell upon her ex-husband. He began to spend more time in the United States where, along with his contemporary Kim Mandeville, he became something of a fixture. The problem of Blenheim could not be ignored, however; not even at an ocean's distance.

George was a complicated man, highly intelligent but with a gift—shared by certain heiresses—for making trouble for himself. Albertha, who was a decent woman, had been willing to try again with him if he agreed to break with Edith Aylesford, but he left her photographs all around the house and willfully resumed the affair. After this imbroglio, which would have been more than enough for most people, he was cited in the notorious 1884 divorce suit of Lady Colin Campbell. His poor reward for his brother's loyalty was to try and thwart Randolph's attempts to stand as a Conservative in the Blenheim constituency of Woodstock (George was a staunch Liberal). Albertha could probably have helped him cope with the Marlborough money problems, but Albertha was out of the picture. The solution, therefore, was simple: a rich American. When Albertha told Consuelo Vanderbilt, who married her son and heir, to get pregnant immediately and prevent the "upstart" Winston Churchill from becoming the 10th Duke, it is possible that Lillian Hamersley rather than Jennie Jerome was the oblique target of her remark.

At first the Marlboroughs mooched about the Continent, the usual refuge of aristocrats who had blotted their copybook. Queen Victoria—who shared Mrs. Astor's views on divorce—refused for some years to receive the new duchess at court. Lillian, now known as Lily, whose income was being merrily lavished upon the resuscitation of Blenheim and the decoration of a London town house, must have surely wondered when she would receive her side of the bargain (Consuelo Manchester-style, she would later try to sue her stepson for the money that she had spent).

Eventually, the energetic charm of the American socialite won through, and the Marlboroughs did enjoy a spell in the sunlight. However George—never one not to wreck a good thing—remained profligate in his habits: what he received from his wife with one hand, he spent with the other. When he died suddenly in 1892, aged just forty-eight, his heir Charles found himself in a kind of Groundhog Day scenario in which he needed to marry another—preferably richer—American heiress. He was deeply attached to another woman, but recognized that Vanderbilt-level wealth was the only way to save his ancestral home: such was the lot of the duke. At the same time, Alva decided that an A-list title in the family was the only way to save her situation. A win-win, therefore; except for Consuelo.

Born in 1877, she was the exquisite embodiment of privilege. There was nothing that she did not have: looks, money, two resident governesses—and, as Alva would no doubt have expressed it, a mother who only wanted the very best for her. In fact marriage to an aristocrat, which was of course what was best for Alva, was also probably what she would have liked for herself. Arrangers often impose upon others what they crave and cannot have. At Newport she had created a house as splendid and refined as almost any in Europe (albeit with that mysterious American feel of enhanced scale, of space beyond as well as within): the pink marble dining room, the magnificent Gothic Room, her own Louis XIV–style bedroom. Yet Europe itself remained the prize.

The fact that Consuelo considered herself to be engaged to another man—Winthrop Rutherfurd—was a mere bagatelle. Alva stripped out Rutherfurd as if he were a layer of old wallpaper. The stories of how this was achieved are possibly exaggerated, although Alva herself later admitted to using "duress and fear." She was said to have intercepted letters between the young couple, like a spy; to have forbidden Rutherfurd entrance to the Paris hotel where mother and daughter stayed in the summer of 1895 (and where Alva ordered a wedding dress from Worth, even though Marlborough had then met the girl once); to have induced guilt in Consuelo by saying that the worry of it all was making her, Alva, dangerously ill. Back in Newport she confined her daughter to the great house, much in the manner of an eighteenth-century husband with an "errant" wife, until Consuelo finally agreed to marry the duke.

There was certainly some truth in this last story—told in Consuelo's 1952 memoir, *The Glitter and the Gold*—as people took delight in whispering to each other about it, saying that the Marble House was a fitting place for a woman with a marble heart. Alva was the big bad wolf, cast in that role both by society and by her daughter, whose life she undoubtedly controlled. "I don't ask you to think," Consuelo recalled her mother saying;

"I do the thinking." Some of Alva's pronouncements do sound pretty strong, especially today, when in some ways we are more easily shocked: "to leave a marriage to chance is a sin"; "not many men are in love with their wives after ten or twelve years." But Alva was a realist, as much as a cynic. She was the East Coast equivalent of Nancy Mitford's Lady Montdore in *Love in a Cold Climate*, who says things like "whoever invented love ought to be shot" and tries desperately to marry off her beautiful heiress daughter, Polly, to a suitable man. Meanwhile Polly marries for "love"—partly to spite her mother—and the whole thing is a complete disaster. In other words there were no easy answers, not even for girls who had everything.

What seems surprising is that, despite Alva's willingness to go through a deeply traumatic divorce, she should have placed such an absolute value upon marriage (indeed in 1896 she herself got married again, to Oliver Belmont, an attractive divorcé slightly her junior). Yet the blunt fact of the matter is that she was right to do so. Life for women was a great deal better than it had been a century earlier, but for the overwhelming majority there was little on offer without a husband: this was the paradox, that marriage was the end of freedom but also a liberation. It was, as the writer George Moore said to Maud Burke, later Cunard, "the springboard to wider horizons."

Alva had married a Vanderbilt with a cool head, to escape genteel poverty and enter the gilded paradise. Now she was determined to push on—to bestride the Atlantic—through Consuelo's marriage. She was a nightmare by modern standards, yet she must surely be given credit for her determination, her drive toward what she believed was the top: she was *Gypsy*'s Mama Rose transposed to Fifth Avenue, and in a perverse sense one may perceive a feminist quest in her ruthless playing of the social game.

There was collateral damage, of course. It was said, again perhaps truly, that a footman stood guard outside Consuelo's bedroom door on the morning of her wedding, lest she try a last bid for freedom. Her eyes, as immense and mournful as Anna Pavlova's when she danced the "Dying Swan," still bore signs of redness as she drifted into St. Thomas's Episcopal Church. But Caroline Astor was guest of honor at the wedding breakfast, and in England a palace awaited, along with a mansion on Curzon Street gifted by Willie K. Vanderbilt. In that world, it was a success to rate alongside the 1st Duke of Marlborough's victory at Blenheim.

Happy ever afters—as Alva would no doubt have said—were for fairy tales. At best they were a matter of chance for women. Notwithstanding Queen Victoria and the late Albert, the belief that marriage would bring love as well as advancement was a naive one. And, when an inheritance was involved, it was always better to go into a marriage with one's eyes clear: unclouded by too much emotion.

* * *

Yet some of these transatlantic alliances *were* happy. There was May Goelet's to the 8th Duke of Roxburghe in 1903, for instance, which was helped by the fact that he was very rich too; these were not the kind of men to *enjoy* being grateful for their wives' money. There was also Mary Leiter's marriage to George Curzon, in 1895. The Leiters were loaded—a younger sister, Marguerite, would marry the Earl of Suffolk in 1904— but Mary was a catch in every way, a highly educated beauty with a sweet, generous nature. She willingly spent a fortune on advancing her husband's political career, which was always supposed to end up at 10 Downing Street but never quite did (foreign secretary was as far as it went). Curzon, already thirty-six, had wanted Mary for her money—that was the name of the game—yet after their marriage he fell deeply in love with her. So much better that way around! He was by most accounts an arrogant man, who made too many enemies to achieve all that he should have done. Mary brought out his better qualities—surely the real value of marriage.

The couple had three daughters, including the future wife of Sir Oswald Mosley, but no son to inherit Curzon's titles.* It has been suggested that this family dynamic, of the rich American wife plus three girls, was the factual basis for the Granthams in *Downton Abbey*, although the Barony of Ravensdale was created with the specific condition that a woman could inherit (his daughter Irene took the title and became a life peer). Nevertheless, the lack of an heir always bothered Curzon, and his desire for a son in fact played its part in Mary's early death.

In 1899 the Curzons went to India, where they spent six years as viceroy and vicereine, "ruling" over some three hundred million people. There were concerns that Mary had been thrown in too deep—today, one would be thoroughly prepared for a comparable role—but in fact she was a great success, operating on sound and sympathetic instinct. A typical gesture was when she sourced from India the gold material for Alexandra's coronation dress (Edward VII acceded to the throne in 1901). This pleased both the country in which she was living, whose Delhi factory made the cloth, and the monarchs of the country to which she would return. Despite her happiness in India, however, the unaccustomed climate made her ill, as did the various

* He had several, all created for him: Earl and Marquess Curzon of Kedleston, and in Ireland Baron Curzon (extinct); Viscount and Baron Scarsdale (inherited by a nephew), and Baron Ravensdale.

operations she underwent to improve her fertility—the longed-for pregnancy (an heir, this time?) led to a miscarriage, which in turn led to infection. Her death in 1906, aged thirty-six, soon after the return to England, felled her husband completely. Possibly there was guilt attached to his grief. He ordered the construction of a chapel at the family church in Kedleston, with a sculpture of himself and Mary, hands half-clasped, overlooked by angels: a poignantly unembarrassed expression of love, all the more striking for being conceived by this tough, politicking man of the world. "There has gone from me," he wrote, "the truest, most devoted, most unselfish, most beautiful and brilliant wife a man has ever had."

Life went on, perforce. The greater part of Curzon's career was ahead of him. He had a long affair with the novelist Elinor Glyn, who in 1917 read of his engagement to another woman while she was staying at his house. This second wife was Grace Duggan (formerly Hinds) of Alabama, a vastly rich widow of thirty-eight, whose husband—Irish-born, an honorary attaché in Argentina—had left her fifteen large *estancias* in South America. Some years later, when Curzon was definitively passed over by the Conservative Party for the top job, Arthur Balfour joked rather nastily that he "has lost the hope of glory but he still possesses the means of Grace."

In 1918 the beautiful young Lady Diana Manners (later Cooper) went to a dinner party attended by the Curzons, at which George asked her repeatedly what she was going to do with her life—"stuck to it in the obstinate way powerful brains do, blunt to sensitiveness"—while Grace, whom Diana found charming, "told me an amazingly characteristic fact about George. On marriage he made her sign a pledge that, in case of his death, she would never remarry." Quite the prenup.

This second marriage was very different from the first:

Grace, who kept to the pledge after her husband died in 1925, was buried in the grounds of the church at Kedleston, leaving Mary and George inside together for eternity. Curzon too was a catch, albeit one twenty years older than his wife—he had served in the War Cabinet and was at that point fully expected to become prime minister—and Grace certainly had her eyes wide open when she married him. He, meanwhile, still hoped for a son, but the treatments that his wife endured were (as with Mary) unsuccessful. Again this seems to have harmed the relationship, albeit in a very different way: for instance Grace slept with her stepson-in-law, Mosley—or so Mosley confessed to his friend Bob Boothby—which does not exactly imply marital bliss.*

If she had married Lord Curzon for "position," however, she certainly achieved it. Her two sons from her first marriage, raised as Roman Catholics, became close friends of Evelyn Waugh, and she herself is occasionally referenced in Waugh's diaries and letters; the impression is that she fitted into English society very well. In a letter to Nancy Mitford, Waugh likens Grace directly to the stupendously grand Lady Montdore. For sure there is a very Montdore quality to the image of Grace on the campaign trail with her son Hubert in 1930, when he stood for Parliament in the deeply deprived constituency of East Ham; she canvassed energetically from her chauffeur-driven Rolls-Royce, sustaining herself with the contents of a Fortnum's hamper.

The following year, heavily in debt, she was obliged to sell the great Curzon mansion at Carlton House Terrace, where in 1921

---

* Mosley told his friend, the Conservative MP Bob Boothby, that he had confessed his extramarital liaisons to his wife Cimmie Curzon. "Well, all except her stepmother and her sister." The sister in question was Irene. Later Mosley had an affair with Cimmie's other sister, Baba Metcalfe.

she had entertained King George V and Queen Mary. In 1943 Hubert died; his acceptance of a priest at the last inspired Lord Marchmain's deathbed scene in Waugh's *Brideshead Revisited*. Yet the second Lady Curzon sailed on, grand and tough as some of these women were, until her own death in 1958.

Her other son, Alfred, was a rakish drunk who pulled himself together to become a respected historical novelist. In 1954 Evelyn Waugh attended a lunch thrown by Grace "to impress Alfred's American publisher and all she asked were old ladies who talked of nothing but what had Queen Mary done with the vase they gave her at Christmas 1915"[4]—which indicates just how deeply the widow from Alabama, via Buenos Aires, had integrated herself into the strange world of upper-class London, whose code is to most people as unfathomable as the Rosetta Stone. If one plays a part for long enough, it would seem, the mask will meld itself to one's face. The US-born Katharine McVickar, who became Lady Grantley, would have her son announced to her by a steward—"Mr. Norton"—when he left the nursery to have tea in her apartments.

Yet some years later, in his 1971 diary, the society photographer Cecil Beaton recalled being told of "Grace Curzon's difficulty in being received by London society. On her arrival as a rich widow from the Argentine, she said 'Mrs. Greville [an influential hostess] wrote, "I've invited that pretty Mrs. Duggan to lunch." It would have made all the difference if she had left out the word "that."'"

What this odd little snippet really shows is how important it was for a woman to be married (even now, if one is honest, it is a passport of sorts). Before Grace became Lady Curzon, she was a semiknown quantity: a widow with a lot of ranches whom society had still to assess. She was "that Mrs. Duggan." The phrase directly conjures the reported remark made by Prince William to his younger brother, when Harry began courting Meghan Markle—"take as much time as you need to get to know this girl." Ah, those demonstrative determiners! Apparently Harry perceived the phrase to be disrespectful, even snobbish; "this" not "that" did the damage, but it had the same effect of causing offense.

The irony is that the hostess Mrs. Greville had been in just the same position as a woman like Grace. She had been "that Miss McEwan" (and worse), the illegitimate heiress to a brewing magnate. Although she passed as William McEwan's stepdaughter, and her fortune was sought by impoverished young aristocrats—such as the Honourable Ronnie Greville, whom she married in 1891—most people were aware of her origins. One can almost hear the sneery gossip about how her mother had been McEwan's mistress, how an obliging employee at the brewery had pretended to be her father at the christening, how McEwan warned "never comment on a likeness" when people exclaimed over how much his "stepdaughter" resembled him. However Margaret Greville had the grit of an Alva Vanderbilt, and concentrated on playing the hand that she had been dealt. Once married, she "molded [Ronnie] affectionately into any shape she pleased,"[5] then got on with her own business: she was through the door that led into society, and used her inheritance to lubricate her progress. Royals, as so often, were the key. She developed the gift of making herself indispensable to them, to the point where she was not only invited to the coronation of Edward VII but—still more of a coup—allowed to use their entrance to the racecourse at Ascot.

"Some people need to be fed with royalty on a frequent basis, like sealions with fish," said the Countess of Strathmore, snootily, but her daughter, Elizabeth Bowes-Lyon—wife of the future King George VI—became close to Mrs. Greville, who promised to leave the young couple her gorgeous house, Polesden Lacey in Surrey (this she did not do, although she did bequeath the then Queen Elizabeth some sixty pieces of fabulous jewelry*). Mrs. Greville entertained like a professional, and Polesden Lacey was kitted out like a hotel, with central heating, en suite bathrooms, even a switchboard: a far cry from jugs of hot water and female arms alive with gooseflesh in arctic drawing rooms. Her town house in Mayfair's Charles Street, whose walls were adorned with what *Vogue* described as "beautiful Sir Joshuas," was found after Mrs. Greville's death to contain 142 bottles of Bollinger 1928. No wonder people wanted to stay with her. She was, recalled Diana Mosley (formerly Mitford), "an amazing old woman, very ugly and spiteful but excellent company; her standard of luxury was of the highest."[6] During the war, when George V had banned sugar and alcohol for the duration, his wife would nip over for tea in the knowledge that there would be cake ("Dear Queen Mary, always so welcome, but always so little notice!"). In fact, Mrs. Greville was such a good hostess that she was able to become a "hostess," one of the last of the breed, when such a role was a woman's surest route to power.

Nobody is grander than a successful social climber: a "social Napoleon," as she was brilliantly described.[7] Mrs. Greville was

---

* Among them was the "Greville Tiara," a fabulous wall of diamond and platinum honeycombs, made by Boucheron from the broken-down pieces of an old tiara, now loaned by Queen Elizabeth II to the Duchess of Cornwall (whose grandmother Sonia Keppel—daughter of Edward VII's mistress Alice—was also one of Mrs. Greville's goddaughters). Another of Mrs. Greville's tiaras, whose centerpiece is a socking great emerald (93.70 carats), was worn by Princess Eugenie at her wedding in 2018. There was speculation that this was the tiara that Meghan Markle had wanted earlier that year for her wedding to Prince Harry—provoking his alleged remark "Whatever Meghan wants, Meghan gets"—but had been offered a different headpiece by the Queen.

only human in her desire to enjoy the power for which she had fought so hard. Should she, or should she not, extend the ladder down from her Charles Street cloud? Not for the American Laura Corrigan, megarich widow and former waitress, who had every dinner invitation dismissed: "I am never hungry enough." Her snobbery was naked and vastly comical: "My dear, one couldn't be seen with Ramsay MacDonald!" she said of the prime minister, thus dissociating herself from a man who had also been born illegitimate (conversely, the hostess Lady Londonderry—whose social assurance was absolute—was good friends with MacDonald). Even the husband of Queen Ena of Spain was put on the probationary list: "although he was a Habsburg, one always felt that he had only just arrived."

What, therefore, would her reaction have been to a Grace Curzon? A hint of condescension, naturally, but also the recognition that here was a force to be reckoned with—all that glamor and wealth—and potentially worthy of her notice. Grace must have been aware that an invitation from Mrs. Greville meant something; was she really so hypersensitive to a careless use of the wrong word? Or was it, rather, that the unfortunate "that" touched a nerve, because she feared that she might *not* be accepted, and so was on the alert for any confirmatory signs? Oddly enough, somebody who would have understood this very well was the first Lady Curzon, the enchanting Mary. Despite the real love that she felt for her husband, and her absolute willingness to embrace the situation along with the man, she wrote to her father: "Just tell the dear girls [female relations, presumably] once a month or so they won't forget it never never never to marry away from home unless they find a George as it is always a sorrow to be an alien—and 50 years in a new country never alters your nationality and I shall never be an Englishwoman in feeling or character and oh! the unhappiness I see around me here in England among American women."

For it was not so simple, this transatlantic displacement (as the former Meghan Markle would assert). Money made it seem so, of course. One could travel across the ocean, back and forth; one was moving to a mansion in Hyde Park, not a rented room in Streatham; one was surrounded by other women in the same position, competitors but on the same side. Despite the snipes—and the initial shock of the new—Americans were accepted, often welcomed, into this society. Emerald Cunard, who had treated the move as an opportunity for self-reinvention, *was* London society. Nevertheless: we are "upstarts," she told her friend, the Chicago-born MP Henry "Chips" Channon, using the word that had been aimed so dismissively at the half-American Winston Churchill. "We are both from across the Atlantic." This was in 1948, more than fifty years after her arrival in London. Similarly, "Who is he, anyway? The son of an American oil magnate," wrote the diarist James Lees-Milne in 1945 of Baron Fairhaven, whose title had been taken from the name of a town in Massachusetts.

And in 1952 Consuelo Marlborough, whose husband (so she claimed) disliked everything non-British, wrote: "in time I learned that snobbishness was an enthroned fetish which spreads its tentacles into every stratum of British national life." Quite true, although this was not a trait confined only to Britain. The point, however, is that one feels things differently as an *émigré*: and the cultivated oddities of British society—so often wielded as weapons upon the unwary—would certainly have loomed like icebergs.

The circumstances of the heiresses were quite different from those of the GI brides who sailed to the United States after the Second World War, yet in a fundamental way they were just the same. Even if a woman married according to her inclinations, she was required to make a profound adjustment. However much Mrs. Astor's New York had resembled Europe, it was *not* Europe; nor, anyway, was the tight world of the Four Hundred a true representation of America. And however much a woman like Mary Curzon might adore her husband, a marriage that is also a financial deal is always chilled, to some degree, by that underlying reality.

MRS. MARLBOROUGH

IN AMERICA, MEANWHILE, these alliances were becoming regarded in some quarters as little more than high-end trafficking.
"Once we made it our boast that this nation was not founded on
any class distinction," said the campaigner Mary Elizabeth Lease.
"Now we are selling our children to titled débauchés." The 1893
marriage of Cornelia Bradley-Martin to the 4th Earl of Craven
proved her point better than most. Cornelia was just sixteen, and
had been snatched by Craven before her debutante season—and
the arrival of any competition—in a move straight out of the
eighteenth-century aristocratic playbook. Although the wedding received a great deal of detailed newspaper coverage, it was
also criticized as excessive, ill-judged, and the "palpable sale" of a
girl barely out of the schoolroom. In 1895, the year that Consuelo
Vanderbilt married her duke and Mary Leiter her viscount, the
Los Angeles Herald wrote that some $200 million had "gone away
from these shores" in the form of the heiresses' financial worth.
In 1908 a play entitled *The Stronger Sex*, staged at Weber's Theater on Broadway, took as its subject matter the pursuit of a rich
girl by fortune-hunting noblemen; a practice that, according to
one critic, "has become a public scandal."[8]

The practice was not really going anywhere—between
1933 and 1964 Barbara Hutton would marry five European

aristocrats—but as a fashion, an industry even, it was on the way out. "We have heard *that* story before—till we can barely hear it patiently again," wrote *The Times* in 1917 of a musical comedy at the Shaftesbury Theater, whose central character was an American heiress pursued by an impoverished European aristocrat, blah blah blah. Clearly that particular theatrical producer thought it worth one more shot. Perhaps there was already a nostalgia for the late Victorian era, when dollar princesses were the pre-cinema celebrities of a world that must, by then, have seemed almost prelapsarian.

In Britain, the scions of upper-class families were not chasing heiresses but being obliterated on the battlefields of France. And in the United States, even before the outbreak of war, the Gilded Age had given way to something more sober.

It had reached a symbolic high point (which, of course, implies a subsequent descent) on an evening in 1897 at the Waldorf Hotel, where the Bradley-Martins held a costume ball whose $369,000 cost would, it was estimated, have fed almost a thousand families for a year. "We are the rich," declared a wisely anonymous guest. "We own America. We got it God knows how, but we intend to keep it if we can." The scene within was, as so often, purest Versailles. Defying hubris, some fifty women came dressed as Marie Antoinette; in the case of Caroline Astor, with the addition of a tiara worth $200,000. The hostess, Cornelia Bradley-Martin—"so ablaze with diamonds from head to foot that she looked like a dumpy lighthouse"[9]—wore a costume referencing not one, but two doomed queens: she was dressed as Mary, Queen of Scots, and her ruby necklace, bought from the recent sale of the French crown jewels, had actually belonged to Marie Antoinette.

To call this event tone-deaf would be quite the understatement, given that it took place at a time of depression, the "Panic" as it was called, which had begun in 1893. It was not on the epic scale of 1929, and certainly it did not affect the 1,200 guests at the Waldorf. In fact, President Grover Cleveland had been obliged to borrow gold from the man who had come to the ball disguised as Molière: J. P. Morgan. In the New York beyond Fifth Avenue, however, the Panic led to the opening of soup kitchens and sent unemployment for a time as high as 35 percent. Again one thinks of Versailles, that apparently untouchable aristocracy. And Mrs. Bradley-Martin's belief that throwing a ball would help the economy, creating work for cooks, florists, and dressmakers (ordering from Worth in Paris was *mal vu*), has a definite air of "let them eat cake"; however sincere her motivation, at least some of that $369,000 would surely have done better handed over to a relief fund.

The Gilded Age did not come to an end after one night of ill-timed excess at the Waldorf. Change does not work that way. Its small, continual movements usually happen out of sight, and one event is seen—retrospectively—to mark the moment when all those hidden shifts suddenly coalesce; after which things start to be different, until everybody realizes that they have changed completely.

Another moment of change—superficial, but in its way not insignificant—came in 1902, when Grace Vanderbilt assumed the role of de facto New York society leader from Caroline Astor, whose reign seemed to have lasted as long as that of the recently dead Queen Victoria, although in fact it had "only" been about thirty years. During that time Mrs. Astor had lost two of her daughters—Emily died in 1881, Helen in 1893—yet she had remained steadfast in her position; until the apparently trivial moment when the young pretender outdid her in a key bid, to host a dinner for Prince Henry of Prussia, brother of Kaiser Wilhelm, who was visiting New York. By means of much strategic letter-writing, Mrs. Vanderbilt lured the prince to her home. Mrs. Astor left town before the fateful dinner could take place, thus silently handing over her crown and scepter: *La Reine est Morte, Vive la Reine!* It is reminiscent again of E. F. Benson, whose *Mapp and Lucia* books chronicle the sweet idiocy of social warfare between two women; one might also paraphrase Henry Kissinger (on the subject of academia) and say that the fighting in high society is so vicious because the stakes are so low. Yet the rise of Grace Vanderbilt was a sign of something more. It proclaimed that the old order had changed, as of course it had been doing for years. The world of *The Age of Innocence*—exclusive as a thoroughbred yearling sale and supremely careful: "it was not the custom in New York drawing-rooms for a lady to get up and walk away from one gentleman in order to seek the company of another"—was long, long gone.

The new century also brought the election of Theodore Roosevelt, for whom the New World aristos were "malefactors of great wealth" whose power should no longer be absolute. "There is not in the world," said Roosevelt, "a more ignoble character than the mere money-getting American, insensible to every duty, regardless of every principle, bent only on amassing a fortune, and putting his fortune only to the basest uses. These men are equally careless of the working men, whom they oppress, and of the State, whose existence they imperil." That was telling them; as was this, in 1907: "The life of mere pleasure, of mere effortless ease, is as ignoble for a nation as for an individual."

Consuelo Marlborough—who had recently separated from her husband—was starting to agree. Remarkably, so was her mother. Not that Alva Belmont, as she now was, had ever led a life of "effortless ease," the effort she had put in was quite extraordinary, but now these women were hearing a new clarion call: the one that reinvented that totemic word "social," by attaching it to hitherto alien terms such as "responsibility" and "conscience."

Thus it was that Alva's fierce energy, which had been directed toward pushing herself to the top of a money-encrusted elite—which in the first instance meant marrying the right man—was now turned full blast upon the suffragette cause. Incredible? Not really. Alva, with her instinctive brilliance, had always known where the metaphorical party was happening, where the action was: in the late nineteenth century what had mattered was getting Caroline Astor through one's front door, and in the early twentieth it was about aligning oneself with progressive politics.

Tennessee Claflin, later Lady Cook, had been battling on that front since the 1870s. She and her sister had left America mainly to escape sustained persecution for their feminist campaigning: they were banned from making speeches (not least because they supported "free love"), arrested, even imprisoned. Tennessee was an adventuress, and like Alva she sought advancement. But—again as with Alva—this went hand in hand with something more profound, the drive toward the elusive nirvana of female equality. Society as a whole denied power to women. The logical move, therefore, was to find power within "society." Tennessee, who in America had asserted that marrying for money was a form of prostitution, in England found herself a rich man and played hostess to the Prince and Princess of Wales; emerging from the marriage in 1901, a widow of fifty-six, with a decent income for life and a name sure to draw an audience when she resumed her oratorial activities. Her speeches had mellowed somewhat, but on her return to her home country in 1909, she was welcomed as a pioneering heroine by the female suffrage movement. That same year Alva founded the Political Equality League in support of a woman's right to vote, an aim that was fully achieved in the United States in 1920. Her close friend and fellow suffragist, Sara

Bard Field, found it hard to resolve the contradiction between Alva's political sincerity and her dismissive treatment of women whom she deemed socially "inferior," but perhaps that was what a lifetime of combat in Newport ballrooms did to you.

Consuelo, meanwhile, had become deeply engaged with charitable work, especially in relation to mothers and children. The down-to-earth help that she gave to the Blenheim tenants—turning up at their homes with coal, blankets, even a pig—earned her the name "the Angel of Woodstock." Easy to say, of course, that this was easy for her to do; nevertheless, she did it. She was not the first to play the Lady Bountiful role—it was an aspect of noblesse oblige—but the point was that philanthropy was now acquiring a political aspect. The delivery of sacks of coal was kindly and direct, welcomed for precisely that human touch. Better yet, however, would be if the coal could be afforded in the normal way of things, if charity and gratitude were no longer needed.

This, at any rate, was the attitude of Daisy Warwick, heiress turned campaigner: a sui generis figure who was also a sign of the changing times. Born Frances Maynard in 1861, she inherited the family estates (originally bestowed by Elizabeth I) by the usual means—her father died and there was nobody else left—and became, aged three, vastly rich. Her mother took a new husband, Lord Rosslyn, who brought the family into the orbit of Queen Victoria; to the point where Daisy was regarded as a possible wife for Victoria's son Leopold. What actually happened was that Daisy became a mistress of another son, the Prince of Wales. She also got married—to the future 5th Earl of Warwick—although her love affairs were on the Jennie Jerome scale, and only one of her five children (her oldest son, praise the lord) was legitimate.

Then she became a socialist. How is this possible, one might think? Daisy, with her millions and her two stately homes, her husband's Warwick Castle and her own Easton Lodge in Essex?

This was not just champagne socialism; it was akin to Queen Victoria becoming a republican. Throughout the high point of the Prince of Wales's leadership of London society, Daisy had been at the heart of the Marlborough House gang, a creature of privilege and sensuousness, whose affair with Lord Charles Beresford—brother of the prince's racing manager—caused one of the scandals that periodically galvanized the set. Lady Charles had opened a compromising letter sent to her husband, which attacked him furiously for having made his own wife pregnant; Daisy's attempts to reclaim this deeply embarrassing document generated a series of showdowns, much in the style of the Aylesford-Marlborough affair, and again dragging in the Prince of Wales. What lives they led!—sleeping with each other in turn, like suburban orgiasts chucking their car keys on to the table at the end of the evening, except in this case the table was a priceless piece of Louis Quinze. One might say that the women had little choice but to collude in it all, that they were in fact forced to do so, since this arena was the only one in which they could thrive, and they had to play by its rules. Yet one must also admit that the way in which some of them behaved—Daisy, Jennie, Edith Aylesford, the theatrical patron Gladys de Grey; adored by a procession of men, batting them off or welcoming them in, according to mood—has a cavalier nonchalance that can only be called liberated.

So what brought about Daisy's Damascene conversion? It seems to have been quite sudden, although in truth it can't have been: by the end of the nineteenth century a nerve in society had become exposed, and for Daisy it was touched—unignorably— by the left-wing journalist Robert Blatchford, who had written a damning article about her decadent lifestyle. If such a thing were to happen today, to the equivalent of a society woman—a star actor, or renowned athlete—then it would either be dismissed, or a PR team would be instructed to deal with it; what would emphatically not happen would be the celebrity seeking out their critic, in order to hear their opinions and why they held them. Yet that is what Daisy did. They *were* remarkable, some of these women, however dismissible they may appear with their abundance of unearned advantages. They were not all of a kind—no group of people is—but in order to survive in that arena they needed personality and vigor and guts; sometimes they had wit and intelligence, sometimes compassion; and, although they were aware of their position, sometimes to a fault, they were rarely pompous about it. And so Daisy sat with this journalist, she listened to his thoughts about what was wrong with a system that had given her two homes large enough to house hundreds of people, while hundreds of people had no home at all; and she became a socialist.

She was sincere about it. This was no act. Like Jessica Mitford, who left her family home in Knightsbridge in order to live with her communist husband among the dirt-poor Londoners of Rotherhithe, Daisy stood by what she espoused. This, logically, meant wealth redistribution. Accordingly, she gave large amounts of money to the Social Democratic Federation, Britain's first formal socialist party, then joined the newly formed Independent Labour Party. She backed the October Revolution in Russia, delighted in foisting left-wing clergymen upon the parishes within her gift, and was fiercely concerned with the issue of women's rights. Later she would effect practical solutions, for instance founding establishments that promoted improved skills for workers, such as the Studley Agricultural College for Women—unflashy schemes, and admirably to the purpose.

Yet for all her largesse she was deep in debt, having (before the raising of her political consciousness) spent much of her fortune in the most recklessly capitalist manner. In 1913 she took the typically bold step of trying to sell letters written by her ex-lover, the late Edward VII, to his son George V. Shades of Randolph Churchill—and once again the monarchy was deeply alarmed, fearful that the facts about Bertie's loose living still had the power to damage from beyond the grave. Strings were pulled to make sure that the High Court prevented Daisy from publishing. Raising the stakes, she threatened to go to America with her prize. Eventually a rich politician, Arthur Du Cros, stepped in to buy the letters—paying off Daisy with the then immense sum of £64,000—and was rewarded for his service with a title. But how strange to think of the Countess of Warwick making thousands from her old association with the heir to the throne, then handing much of it over to the socialist cause.

In 1923, standing as an Independent Labour candidate, she contested the seat of Warwickshire and Leamington against the future Conservative prime minister Anthony Eden, for whom all her family voted. "It was the last place in the world she should have stood for," said her son, who the following year became the 6th Earl. She also planned to gift Easton Lodge to the cause— there was excited talk of turning it into a socialist college—but this was less about principle than the desire to offload a scarcely affordable house, which the party was not inclined to take on either (a similar situation would arise when Jessica Mitford tried to gift a Scottish island to the Communist Party—there was nothing they wanted less).

So the Dowager Countess of Warwick remained at Easton, where she cohabited with the Labour membership: the main body of the house was used for conferences, meetings, and the like, while she herself retained the Jacobean wing, in which she lived with her animals. In the exquisite sunken gardens a white peacock strutted among the comrades, and sometimes Daisy would show trade union leaders the bed in which she had slept with the king.

* * *

During the First World War, other great houses, like Hatfield and Woburn Abbey, had been turned into hospitals. And the expat heiresses displayed loyalty to their adopted country through the American Women's War Relief Fund, whose president Louise Paget, daughter of the former Minnie Stevens of New York, had moved into action just three days after the outbreak of the conflict. Like Daisy Warwick she was hands-on in her cause; in 1915 she went to work for Serbian relief and established a hospital in Skopje, contracting typhoid fever in the course of doing so. Louise was a Florence Nightingale figure, although her name has not survived in the same totemic way. Yet in 1917 her work was recognized by both her countries: she became the first recipient of the Medal of Honor of the Federation of Women's Clubs of New York City—an accolade later given to Marie Curie—and was made a Dame of the British Empire. She had a title from her marriage, to a distant baronet cousin, but more to the point she had a title of her own.

Consuelo Marlborough, meanwhile, had taken her own leaf out of Daisy Warwick's little red book, and in 1917 was elected as a candidate for the Progressive Party in the London County Council elections, standing in the impoverished area of Southwark West. Her slogan was "Vote, Vote, Vote for Mrs. Marlborough." A brief piece of Pathé film shows her moving elegantly through the tight-packed streets, a head taller even than the men, incontrovertible physical evidence of wealth versus deprivation.

In 1920 she resigned from the council, and the following year the Marlboroughs were finally divorced. Five years later their marriage was annulled, most likely because the duke—whose new wife was another rich American, Gladys Deacon—wanted to convert to Roman Catholicism. One of the chief grounds for annulment was coercion. Thirty years after the event, Alva Belmont testified that undue pressure had been applied upon Consuelo: "I forced my daughter to marry the Duke." No doubt she wanted to say the right things but, genuine or not, the mea culpa eased mother-daughter relations. The Catholic Church, never one to hold back, denounced "the heathen practice of marriage by capture and marriage by purchase"—as if marriage had not been susceptible to this practice ever since the institution was invented.

But Consuelo had, indubitably, become the very image of the bartered bride, born as she was into a time when a woman's legal rights might have led her to expect better. And she has endured as the symbol of a practice—which might be called heathen, or perhaps simply amoral—that took possession of late-Victorian high society, in which marriage was turned into a kind of speculators' market, with money and titles traded as fervidly as commodities on the stock exchange. It was not always purely venal, as the Roxburghes and the Curzons would have attested. And the hunters were certainly not only male, which made things rather more equitable; to describe women like Jennie Jerome and Minnie Stevens as victims is plainly ludicrous.

So the marriage deemed to represent this socioeconomic trend—the Vanderbilt-Marlborough alliance—was not entirely typical of it. But it was the grandest, the most dramatic, perhaps the unhappiest (although Consuelo Manchester might have disputed that), and therefore it became the one that everybody knew about.

A quarter of a century after its annulment, by which time Sunny Marlborough was long gone—he died in 1934 at the age of sixty-two—Consuelo wrote in *The Glitter and the Gold* of how spectacularly unhappy she had been as the 9th Duchess of Marlborough, and how much she had disliked living at Blenheim (favorably though it compared with the terraces of Southwark West). She would not be the last highly privileged woman to write a misery memoir and look for pity. Nor was she the last heiress to exemplify the truism that money does not buy happiness. And she had a pretty fair point, of course, when she portrayed herself as the prey of both an ambitious mother and an avaricious husband; although her book—which has been described as "shockingly dishonest"[10]—did not tell the whole story. This was recognized from the first in a review by Lord Birkenhead, which noted Consuelo's "flashes of engaging malice" and concluded: "It cannot be but sad for any friend of the late Duke of Marlborough to see him laid so callously upon the operating table" (at least she waited until he was dead before taking out her scalpel). But Consuelo had the gift of gaining sympathy, as some women do.

Both she and Sunny Marlborough were attached to other people at the time of their marriage (the duke was in love with a young woman named Muriel Wilson, with whom he always remained friends). It is true that he made little attempt to hide the fact. No more, however, did Consuelo. Indeed, it has been suggested that Winthrop Rutherfurd—the man whom she had wanted to marry, whom in her memoir she calls "X"—was the father of the Marlboroughs' second son, Ivor.

In 1901 Sunny wrote a letter to a friend, the lawyer and Liberal MP Richard Haldane, in which he was astonishingly open about his marital situation.[11] Obviously he felt the need to confide in somebody; also to set out his side of the story, although the letter remained private. It states that Rutherfurd was back on the scene just three years after the Marlborough wedding, in 1898, and that Consuelo spent two weeks with him and his sister in Paris. The inference is that Ivor was conceived on this trip; certainly this is what Sunny's second wife believed.*

On her return Consuelo told her husband of the relationship with Rutherfurd, who had asked her to elope with him. "I need hardly tell you that I was placed in a most painful and trying position," wrote the Duke. One might say that he had no love for his wife—only for her money, which he had started spending on Blenheim while still on his honeymoon—so what right had he to be upset? Yet upset is what he seems to have been.

At the start of 1900 Rutherfurd was back in London. "She was anxious to go and see him, and finally I allowed her to do so . . . I stated to her that I would not ask her to stay in my house if she desired to elope with Mr. Rutherfurd but that in consideration of her youth, her inexperience and lack of knowledge of the world I would not force her away from her home and her children. I told her that the decision must be made by her alone and pointed out to her with great care exactly what her position would be whatever course she adopted." It is doubtful that Sunny expressed himself quite so reasonably at the time, but this was probably the gist of what he said. The next day Consuelo had a long meeting with Rutherfurd, whose feet had clearly grown ice-cold: "he declined to elope with her on the plea that he was too attached to her." She then told her husband that she had no choice but to stay. It would be a remarkable marriage that could repair itself after such a rupture, and the Marlborough marriage had only ever been remarkable for its exterior glitz.

"I have tried," wrote the duke, at the end of his letter, "during the last 18 months under circumstances and situations sometimes overwhelming in the sorrow and grief that they have brought me,

---

* Gladys Deacon confided to Hugo Vickers her belief that Ivor was the result of "two nights in Paris with an American."

forcing me to bear the deepest feelings of misery, to sink entirely my own personal feelings and inclinations for these higher considerations which I felt that I was called upon to recognize. That I should offer a young woman, the mother of my children, every equitable opportunity of repairing the error of the past and that I should strive, despite the shattered home, to save her from herself from these terrible issues which her manner of life would inevitably lead her."

It is hard to doubt the sincerity of this, but equally hard to discern the reason for Sunny's "sorrow and grief." Perhaps he had not expected so naked a desire in Consuelo to get out—his side of the bargain had been Blenheim and a coronet, by which his self-worth was measured, and here she was rejecting both. Perhaps he was already suspicious as to the parentage of his second son. Perhaps it was simply a belief that a marriage should be maintained—the façade at least—and that the failure to do so was shameful, a dismal repetition of his father's wayward history.

Sunny went off to the Boer War, with his cousin Winston Churchill. When he returned, after six months, Consuelo informed him that she was having an affair with another cousin—the Honourable Freddie Guest, who had been living at Blenheim while the owner was away—and would like it very much if he would never enter her bedroom again. Subsequently there were liaisons with two more Marlborough relations: the Honourable Reginald Fellowes, who later married the Singer heiress Daisy, and Charles, Viscount Castlereagh, heir to the earldom of Londonderry, whose wife Edith would become one of the great political hostesses. She had a lot to put up with from Charles, a truly shameless philanderer. When he wrote to her, he would generally include a letter for his current girlfriend in the envelope: "You might just send the enclosed [to whomever it might be] . . . That would be very sweet and dear of you."

The relationship with Consuelo was serious—the couple ran off to Paris together—although she cannot have thought that anything would come from this quasi-elopement. Rather she seems to have been on a mission, to make her husband realize how angry she was about having had to marry him.

By this time Sunny had met the woman who would become his second wife, gorgeous Gladys Deacon, with her brilliant brain, French accent, and pale turquoise gaze. Not yet the duke's mistress, she was enjoying the rivalrous attentions of numerous suitors. Proust and Rodin worshipped her, as did Anatole France, the art collector Bernard Berenson (and his wife), Daisy Warwick's son Lord Brooke, and the Italian poet Gabriele D'Annunzio. So, too, did Consuelo Marlborough, who wrote to Gladys in 1904: "I have never cared for any other woman like you."

This passion of Consuelo's, which was physical without quite being sexual, is best described as a slight obsession, of the kind that a straight woman will sometimes feel for another. Lady Diana Cooper was similarly mesmerized by her husband's lover Louise de Vilmorin, when Duff Cooper was British ambassador in Paris and the three formed a highly unusual ménage à trois. For Consuelo there must also have been the simple pleasure of a female presence, a confidante with whom she had much in common: Gladys was just four years her junior, born into a wealthy East Coast family that had known scandal, albeit of a kind that frankly dwarfed Alva Vanderbilt's divorce—her father had shot and killed her mother's lover. Equally compelling, however, was what separated them. Gladys had *lived*, had mixed with the kind of society represented by Madame Olenska in *The Age of Innocence*, while Consuelo had married in a state of absolute innocence and was now playing catch-up. And Gladys—unlike her friend—had a glorious natural self-confidence, as later described by her friend Diana Mosley: "She knew she was wonderful, and cared nothing for the world's opinion."[12]

Yet it was Consuelo, really, who exerted the more profound fascination, because Gladys was completely entranced with the fact that her friend was the Duchess of Marlborough. For all her cleverness and charm, she was—like so many people—in thrall to the image of a coronet. Back in 1895, she had written to her mother with a truly bizarre prescience: "I suppose you have read about the engagement of the Duke of Marlborough. Oh dear me, if I was only a little older I might 'catch' him yet! But *Hélas*! I am too young, though mature in the ways of women's witchcraft — and what is the use of the one without the other?" Of all the men who paid court to her, it was Sunny Marlborough that she wanted. "What did she see in him?" wrote Diana Mosley. "He was unprepossessing. The answer must be 'a duke.' "

So when the Marlboroughs separated in 1906, Gladys moved swiftly to claim the prize; although it was disingenuous of Consuelo to spread the rumor that Sunny had been stolen from her. No wife had ever been keener for a marriage to end. And Gladys very decently burned any of her friend's letters that made compromising reference to love affairs, before waiting fifteen years for Consuelo to divorce her husband.

"Life together had not brought us closer together," was the bland reasoning for the separation offered in *The Glitter and the Gold*, although in a letter to his wife the duke went straight to the point—as he saw it. "It is painful for me to dwell in detail on those immoral actions on your part which began in the early years of our married life. Your attachments to Mr. R. [Rutherfurd] and to Mr. G. [Guest]. The recollection of those terrible periods can never be effaced from my memory." Again, the hurt seems absolutely sincere, although whether to Sunny's self-regard—his sense of what was due to his ducal position—or in some obscure way to the heart, it is impossible to know. What does seem clear is that, through the collapse of his marriage to Consuelo, he became the cold, arrogant, psychologically damaged caricature of a man that she portrayed him as being from the first.

His resentment toward her smoldered on, perhaps because she was so good at controlling the narrative with her saintly air and tragic eyes. In 1912, by which time she had a reputation for charitable works, he forbade entrance to Blenheim to a group from the National Union of Women Nurses; he could not bear the prospect of them gazing at his wife's portrait in "mournful admiration." At the divorce hearing in 1920 Consuelo dressed in deepest black as if consumed with grief, ropes of pearls ringing her thin swan neck. She answered counsel's questions in a soft, sorrowing voice. As she left the High Court she took a black chiffon veil from her muff and tied it over her head, shrouding her face completely.

And she cast a long dark shadow over Sunny, no question. "Thank Heavens it is all over," he wrote, when the divorce was granted in 1921 "—the last blow that woman could strike over a period of some 20 years has now fallen— Dear me! What a wrecking existence she would have imposed on anyone with whom she was associated." He married Gladys, then aged forty, but the delights of that long courtship (in which they had exchanged letters calling Consuelo "O.T.": old tart) fell away almost immediately; they might have become a comfortable Prince Charles and Camilla, but instead they turned into Henry VIII and Anne Boleyn. The hanging about had gone on too long, and love turned sour in the interim. As for Gladys's dream of being a duchess—how foolish she must have felt, to have believed that therein lay a happy ever after. She should have taken heed of Consuelo, whose performative misery had also been very real.

A mere eighteen months after her wedding, Gladys wrote: "Most interesting to me is Sunny's rudeness to me. Not very marked in public yet—but that will come. I am glad, because I am so sick of life here." By 1925 she was writing: "I conclude that matrimony is a difficult and tricky business and that its success implies giving up all one's personal existence—that living in an anodyne atmosphere flat as a steppe is the best one can hope it to be." At a Blenheim dinner, after Sunny's conversion to Catholicism in 1927, Gladys placed a revolver on the table. "Why?" asked one of her guests. "Oh, I don't know," she replied, "I might just shoot Marlborough."

Given that her father had indeed shot somebody, and died insane after serving a short prison sentence, this was a particularly unhappy remark. Gladys's singularity had turned to eccentricity, and her beauty had been sabotaged by some horribly basic cosmetic surgery: "it left her with mouth awry and a chin which looked like a collapsed balloon."[13] It is easy to understand why the duke—whose capacity for trying to understand women had long been exhausted—decided to leave Gladys to her own devices at Blenheim. Nevertheless, his behavior had become increasingly unkind; and one has the sense that the real target of his rage was not his second wife, but his first. Consuelo had now remarried—the wedding took place a couple of weeks after Sunny's—to a French aviator named Jacques Balsan, who despite a roving eye had adored her for years. They lived mostly in France, where Consuelo received favored friends such as Winston Churchill, and seem to have been perfectly contented. How that middle-aged bliss must have taunted Sunny Marlborough! He, meanwhile, plunged headlong into a full-blown midlife crisis, which again gives the impression of being obscurely aimed at Consuelo: he took up residence in London, went dancing a great deal, and had a series of affairs (including, it was reported, a sexual tryst in a taxi). In 1933 he had Gladys evicted from Blenheim. When she moved into the town house instead, he sent in private detectives to disconnect the utilities. In retaliation she employed detectives of her own to obtain evidence for a divorce—of which there was ample—but her husband died before proceedings could begin; this was as well for his reputation, although history would not be kind to him anyway. He was the man who married for money, who captured an heiress and used her with one thought alone, to save his aristocrat's palace. That was the story, all one needed to know.

* * *

For Consuelo, the process of disentangling herself from the Marlborough marriage—which she began after just three years, with that brief flight to Paris in 1898—was also a series of steps toward autonomy. The fact that it affected her husband was not really the point, because the marriage had never been about the union of two people.

Its annulment, together with Alva's statement that it effectively should never have happened, made Consuelo free in a way that her divorce did not. It restored her to the self that had been forcibly buried when she was eighteen. She *had* been a victim, even if she also played the part rather well. Very Princess Diana; although in this case with a happy second act.

In 1957 she returned to Blenheim for the first time since the war (which she had spent in the United States, having fled France at speed in 1940). Her son was now the 10th Duke of Marlborough, and the palace presumably congenial to her at last. There was surely satisfaction in seeing what her inheritance had done for it—the replacement, and more, of what had been lost in the great sell-off of the late nineteenth century—the survival and triumph of something venerable and beautiful, thanks to her Vanderbilt millions.

Consuelo died in 1964, having outlived her first husband by thirty years. She was the last of her kind. Thereafter, if an heiress was unhappy in her marriage, it would be her own doing and nobody else's.

PART III

NEW WORLDS

"It's less sad to be rich."

Said by Emerald Cunard, recorded in the
1945 diary of James Lees-Milne

A CITY OF WOMEN

AND NOW, AT last, some agency.

During the First World War, Consuelo—who always held firm to the tenets of *noblesse* and *richesse oblige*—sat alongside her fellow heiresses on the committee for the American Women's War Relief Fund. The fund had its own military hospital, set up at Oldway, a 115-room mansion in Paignton on the South Devon coast, to which Consuelo donated a chapel for the patients' use.

Oldway was the centerpiece of a large estate, newly decorated in the style of Versailles (where else), including a reproduction of the Galerie des Glaces. By late 1914 the great mirrored and marbled rooms, which housed some 250 casualties at a time, were renamed the Astor Ward, the Churchill Ward, the Paget Ward, the Marlborough Ward, and so on; American wealth repurposing itself, as time shifted grimly forward.

The estate was owned by Paris Singer, lover of the dancer Isadora Duncan and son of Isaac, founder of the Singer Sewing Machine Company. Isaac Singer was a New Yorker, a onetime itinerant actor, who had sought social elevation to accompany his immense wealth and built himself a castle in Yonkers.* Eventually,

---

* Paris Singer, born in 1867 in the city for which he was named, later one of the creators of Florida's Palm Beach, had five children by his wife and a son, Patrick, from his affair with Isadora Duncan, whose dance career he supported. In 1913 Patrick drowned, aged three, along with Isadora's daughter by the theater designer Gordon Craig. Oldway was sold in 1929, became a country club, and is now a council-owned white elephant, standing bereft, beautiful and incongruous.

however, he gave up on the impossible dream—entry into the Four Hundred—and moved to Europe: Paris, then London, then Paignton. This unlikely little seaside town is where he died in 1875, leaving some $14 million to be fought over by his complexity of heirs. He had twenty-four children by five women, with Paris coming in as number twenty-two, and the ensuing imbroglio was much pored over in both the American and British press—a local English newspaper summed it up as "a pretty kettle of fish." One son received £500 from his father, another £3,000, while an illegitimate daughter received the rather more gratifying sum of £160,000. Others did better still, notably Paris and his full sister Winnaretta, who was born in 1865.

Years later, in the extremely different world of 1929, Winnaretta and Consuelo would found the Foch Hospital in a Paris suburb, a not-for-profit establishment still in existence. When it came to their heiress status, these women were two of a kind. They were products of the Victorian era with a twentieth-century take on their money. Before the First World War, Winnaretta had built a housing project in Paris that greatly influenced subsequent public policy, and in the 1920s she commissioned Le Corbusier, no less, to construct Salvation Army hostels (one of which contained a penthouse for her own use). During the war she worked with Marie Curie on an enterprising scheme to repurpose limousines as mobile radiology units.

But what brought her renown—and created a truly venerable legacy—was her patronage of the arts. Of music, in the main: Poulenc, Stravinsky, and Satie were among those who benefited from her discriminating largesse. She had taste, she knew her stuff, and she had the rare ability to anticipate trends, in culture as in philanthropy (she perceived that the age of the big orchestra was coming to an end, that the future lay in small-scale pieces; some works still in the repertoire were played for the first time in her Paris house). For her, an inheritance was an entirely positive thing, a means to enrich one's own life and that of other people, a responsibility worth having. It sounds so simple, put like that. What possibly made it simpler was that Winnaretta was a lesbian, and not at the mercy of a husband (even though she had two of them). Love still had its power, but it was not bound up with money.

In a photograph of Winnaretta, aged three, she gazes at the camera with a jaw as firm as her adult will. By the age of eleven, she was both a millionaire and a devoted lover of music. Her mother Isabella—model for the figure of the Statue of Liberty—had remarried to a violinist, and at the age of fourteen Winnaretta requested for her birthday a performance of a Beethoven string quartet. This stepfather, however, had designs upon her fortune (and, it was rumored, her person). The moment she turned twenty-one she scarpered, buying a mansion on Paris's Avenue Georges-Mandel (as it is now called) from which to plan her future.

Despite her highly developed artistic sensibility, Winnaretta saw herself becoming a member of le gratin, that is to say French high society—at the heart of the seizième, as was her new house—and for that she needed to be married. She also wanted to rid herself of her surname, with its taint of trade, even though she was quite capable of putting down idiotic snobbery when she encountered it (told that the aristocratic name of Fournès was worth more than that of Singer, she replied coolly: "Not at the bottom of a check"). Accordingly, she accepted a proposal from pretty much the first fortune-hunting aristocrat who came along, although Prince Louis de Scey-Montbéliard had not, as they say, got the memo as to the nature of their union. Winnaretta is said to have spent her wedding night on top of the wardrobe, threatening to kill her new husband if he came anywhere near her.

This was never going to last. The marriage was annulled after five years, on the grounds of non-consummation. Then, in 1893, Winnaretta entered into a *mariage blanc* with Prince Edmond de Polignac: thirty years her senior, penniless but of grand lineage, highly cultured, a very delightful person and, like herself, homosexual. "The Sewing Machine has married the Lyre," was the whisper—the prince was a gifted amateur composer—but it was, in fact, a tremendously successful alliance. The Polignacs lived in Paris and briefly in Venice where, in 1900, the year before her husband died, Winnaretta bought a Lombardi palazzo. Both these houses—desirable in the real sense, the ineffable one that cannot quite be bought—became artistic hubs. Instead of sex, the couple had *salons*; these evenings *chez* Polignac were not just a social occasion for those who fancied a bit of culture with their cognac, but an elegant incubator of turn-of-the-century genius.

The *salon* was not a new phenomenon, but it was about to acquire a renewed importance. It had been a part of Parisian culture since the seventeenth century (although it probably originated in Italy; as with ballet, it was a concept that the French took over with aplomb and made their own). Naturally enough it flourished in the age of Enlightenment, and was mirrored in the gatherings of the Blue Stockings in Georgian London. Being within the domestic sphere, it was a means whereby women might express themselves freely and wield a measure of power, including over the men whom they could choose to invite. Now, however, the *salon* entered a kind of *age d'or*, which would last well into the twentieth century and would, by degrees, allow women to flourish beyond the role of hostess.

In the late nineteenth century, Parisian *salons* had a definite *côté snob*. They were written about in the press with the avidity given, in Britain, to the activities of the upper classes, and in the United States to those of the Vanderbilts and co. A renowned *salonnière* would hold a gathering on the same day each week, and there would be intense public interest in who had made it on to the guest list; especially when the hostess was an A-list aristocrat like the Comtesse Greffulhe, Winnaretta's chief competitor in the *salon* stakes. At the same time, these were not mere socialite gatherings. They had a genuinely serious import. *Salons* had always been about "the art of conversation" but now they included art itself, proper stuff moreover: music programs, literary readings, *boutique* exhibitions. The hostess herself might also sing or play, but only if she could do it well. These were not arenas in which a Florence Foster Jenkins would disturb the peace. They were fashionable, they were *mondaine*, but they were underpinned by a class-transcending reverence for the cultural, even the intellectual, that would have made the average British aristocrat thank God that their social season was shaped around sport.

A *salon* had become a shop window, in fact, and like a latter-day Medici, Winnaretta was known as "*La Grande Mécène*": the Great Patron. Debussy, Fauré, Ravel . . . they all premiered work in the drawing room at Avenue Georges-Mandel, which could seat 200 people, and Ravel's "Pavane pour une infante défunte" is just one of several significant pieces dedicated to Winnaretta. The descriptions of private concerts in Proust's *A la Recherche du Temps Perdu* owe much to evenings spent in her house (it was Robert de Montesquiou, the model for Proust's character Baron de Charlus, who first introduced Winnaretta to Prince Edmond). According to Nancy Mitford, however, who knew "Winnie" quite well in later life, Proust's humble wish to dedicate his masterwork to the late prince went down rather badly: "she got her solicitor to warn him not to . . . I don't think he was generally accepted in society."[1] Winnie, it seems, had caught the disease of snobbery from some of the company she was keeping.

Yet she was also, paradoxically, inhabiting the iconoclastic milieu of the avant-garde. She herself was a fine pianist and talented painter; her 1885 self-portrait could be taken for an early Gertler, and another picture was bought in the astonishing belief that it was by Manet (she owned an example of the real thing, naturally). She was also entirely open about her love of women. One might perceive a slight irony in the fact that she was protected from any threat of social ostracism by her "princess" status, but in truth nobody cared anyway. This was the city of *La bohème*, where male homosexuality had been decriminalized since the French Revolution. It was not Mrs. Astor's New York nor Queen Victoria's London (the famous—probably apocryphal—story is that the queen did not believe that such a thing as lesbianism existed). Two other rich American lesbians, soon to be *salonnières* like Winnaretta, were living nearby at the turn of the century: Natalie Barney in the Parisian suburb of Neuilly, where she was conducting a relationship with the *philhellene* Eva Palmer, and Gertrude Stein in the Rue de Fleurus, across the Seine on the Left Bank. A different world from Winnaretta's, which was also in fact the same world, and which would coalesce into the society that was Paris between the wars: gloriously liberal, with regard to race as well as sexuality, and a veritable cornucopia of artistic riches.

Winnaretta never hid girlfriends from her husband, but after his death—notwithstanding that it was a great sadness—her love life positively bloomed. She had in her care a nephew and niece, the children of a sister who had killed herself in 1896, and she respected that responsibility; but it did not cramp her style. She had affairs with both gay and bisexual women. She was unabashed and fairly faithless, characteristics that convention likes to attribute to men. A betrayed husband once shouted up at a window of her palazzo: "If you are half the man I think you are, you will come out here and fight me." The married Olga de Meyer, rumored to be an illegitimate daughter of Edward VII, was her lover until 1905. Then came the profoundly gifted painter Romaine Brooks, another American, who adored Winnaretta yet feared what she called her "ruthlessness" (the affair with Brooks casually coincided with a fling with the composer Ethel Smyth, there was also a dalliance with Natalie Barney, later Brooks's long-term partner). Winnaretta did have a tough and dominant side, let loose when she grew into the freedom of widowhood. Montesquiou described her looking like Nero in middle age, but crueller: "one who dreamed of seeing his victims stitched up by sewing machines." Yet in the days before definable feminism, a woman hell-bent upon owning her life might well be perceived as ruthless, cruel or, indeed, "manly."

The contradictions within that life—which were many, but which with the help of money she boldly resolved—are hinted at in a couple of vignettes. First this, from a young woman who in 1913 visited Avenue Georges-Mandel: "I was shown into the largest room I had ever seen in a private house ... There were beautiful books everywhere. I picked one up and found it to be a translation of Sappho's poetry." The young woman was a suffragette, and was there to meet Winnaretta's house guest: Christabel Pankhurst. Then—in 1936—Winnaretta attended a party thrown by the hostess Sibyl Colefax in Chelsea, where chief among the other guests were the new king, Edward VIII, plus Mrs. Simpson. After dinner, Artur Rubinstein played. He had been one of Winnaretta's protégés; yet what interested her on this occasion was not the music but bagging the seat next to the king (who was openly bored until Noël Coward took possession of the piano). "I have never seen a woman sit so firmly," recalled the politician and writer Harold Nicolson: "there was determination in every line of her bum."

Back in Paris, back in time, the cultural reach of Winnaretta's *salons* extended to encompass Modernism. Into her carpark-sized drawing room came her brother's lover Isadora Duncan, Kurt Weill, Stravinsky and Satie, Colette and Cocteau, Diaghilev and the Ballets Russes—a truly extraordinary group, in possession of the special vitality that comes when one's gift collides with the times, and shunts them forward. No question about it: Paris was the place to be, and it would become still more so when the artists in its midst included Hemingway, Fitzgerald, Picasso, and Joyce. It was a place for creatives, a place for Americans; and, within and beyond all this, it was a home to an enclave of suddenly liberated lesbians. "Paris had become a city of women,"[2] as the novelist Jeanette Winterson put it, not strictly accurately but one knows what she meant. In his own way, Truman Capote made a similar point when describing a visit to Romaine Brooks's studio in the 1940s, where on display were portraits of the women she had known and/or loved: "The all-time ultimate gallery of dykes from 1880 to 1935 or thereabouts."

* * *

Most of these women were rich. They had to be, to live as they did. This was a counterculture created by the privileged (as perhaps they usually are). Romaine Goddard, born in 1874, was a bona fide heiress; her brother died in 1901, followed soon afterward by her mother, whereupon Romaine and her sister inherited the vast fortune left by their Philadelphia businessman grandfather.

In 1903 Romaine entered a *mariage blanc* with her friend John Ellingham Brooks (future companion of the novelist E. F. Benson). It is striking how many marriages there then were, within "society," in which either or both partners were gay or bisexual: the union of Vita Sackville-West and Harold Nicolson is merely the best-known example. Adherence to convention obviously led some people to marry but Romaine, who was not conventional at all, may have set up with Brooks out of simple loneliness. By her own account[3]—which there is no reason to doubt—her life up to that point had been a series of gothic horrors: her father was an absentee alcoholic, her brother afflicted with mental illness; while her mother, a demonic creature unhappily obsessed with her son, gave Romaine for a time to an impoverished foster family in New York, then stopped paying for her keep. "My dead mother gets between me and my life," said Romaine, at the age of eighty-five.

She had moved to Paris for the first time in 1893. There she fell pregnant and gave up the child. She then went to Rome, her birth city, where she began to study as a painter, but was subjected to sexual harassment. Given all this it is hardly surprising that she should have welcomed the chance of marrying a safe and familiar figure; fortunately for posterity, this did not work out either. Brooks objected to his wife's habit of wearing male clothes—her 1923 self-portrait, dressed in a man's coat and hat, is as superb an image as that of Dietrich in a tuxedo in the 1930 film *Morocco*—and, still worse, made the fatal mistake of referring to his wife's inheritance as "ours." Cue the heiress early warning system! Romaine left the marriage after just a year, taking with her the means whereby she could forge her own path, creating a life that was not always happy but that was, crucially, her own.

Without men, but with money. That was the formula for a new design for living.

These women—Romaine Brooks, Natalie Barney, Winnaretta de Polignac, Gertrude Stein—were near contemporaries of Consuelo Vanderbilt; like her they were American-born and moved to Europe at a formative age. Then their stories abruptly diverged. Their sexuality impelled them to seek a different path, and what a very good thing that was; one can even argue that it was *necessary*, at that time, in order to take full control. To become, as Romaine did in her self-portrait, their own men.

In the dusk-and-champagne-color streets of Paris, exquisitely formal yet alight with bohemianism, they found—and formed—a world that was briefly defined by the golden principle of freedom. What a time this must have been! The love affairs formed the same close circular patterns as they had among the Marlborough Set, although here the cast of characters was all female. The art was as jagged and alive as a crack of lightning; the air was charged with a sense of purposeful change (not just change for its own sake); it was an ambience in which a woman with sufficient means could be mistress, spectacularly so, of her own destiny. And the *salon* was at the heart of it all: the microcosm of the city, or at least the city as it was experienced by these eager, engaged people.

In 1905, after a short period in England, Romaine Brooks moved back to Paris, where she painted her new lover, Winnaretta de Polignac. The success of this work led to more commissions; indeed Winnaretta played *mécène* to Romaine, who was rich enough not to need a patron, but as an artist very glad to have one. In 1910 she staged her first solo show. It included the wonderful *White Azaleas*, which depicted a female nude relaxing in the shadow cast by a vase of flowers—the kind of subject reveled in by male artists—and showed how Romaine's characteristic tonal palette, with its variations on a theme of gray, could be voluptuous as well as melancholic.

She also (as observed by Capote) painted the lovers who succeeded Winnaretta: for instance Ida Rubinstein, with whom she had a three-year relationship from 1911. Ida, born in St. Petersburg in 1883, was bisexual, beautiful, and majestically unconventional. She inherited a large fortune at the age of nine, and at first was treated like the heiresses of old—when she sought to become an actress in Paris, her brother-in-law had her confined to an asylum to prevent her defiling the family honor. Released back to Russia, she married a cousin in order to get hold of her money. Then there was no stopping her. She was determined upon a stage career, and in 1908 was coached by the great choreographer Mikhail Fokine for a private performance in the role of Salome (which involved a dance of the seven veils that would have gone down rather badly with her brother-in-law). Although her gift was as a dance-actor, and her technique inevitably lacking, she was asked to join the Ballets Russes; Diaghilev, a showman as well as a cultural visionary, was given to these apparently wild casting ideas. Luisa Casati, a rich Italian goth and another of Romaine's lovers, had also been invited into the company. She declined. Ida, who must have had astonishing stage presence, seized the chance and was soon being partnered by Vaslav Nijinsky. In 1911 she left Diaghilev and struck out with her own dance company, which like the Ballets Russes was run as a collaboration between Modernists. She continued to dance well into her fifties. During the Second World War she was active in the Free French cause and became the mistress of Lord Moyne, former father-in-law of Diana Mosley.*

She was rendered, in Romaine's portraits, as a semimythic figure, the not untroubled spirit of freedom. The painting of Natalie Barney was homelier, comfortably feminine—"why

---

* Lord Moyne, whose son Bryan Guinness had been heartbroken at losing Diana to Sir Oswald Mosley in the early 1930s, played a leading role in ensuring that she would be imprisoned without trial (as was Mosley) throughout much of the Second World War. As well as reporting Diana to officialdom, he set one of his grandson's governesses to spy upon her and report back on her fascist sympathies. In 1944 Lord Moyne was assassinated by the Stern Gang, a Zionist terrorist group.

resemble our enemies?" was Natalie's take on Romaine's suits—although this woman was arguably the greatest radical of them all. Born in Ohio in 1876, the daughter of a talented painter (Alice Pike Barney), Natalie recognized her homosexuality at the age of twelve, and arranged her life accordingly. Liberated, as she saw it, from a world made by men, she rejected its conventions—such as monogamy—and she really did not care a jot when the neighbors in Neuilly objected to the young women in the garden, dressed in togas or nothing at all, celebrating ancient Greece and channeling the pagan spirit of Isadora Duncan. "What do I care," she said calmly, "if they vilify me or judge me according to their prejudices?"

"That her 'problem' might really be nothing more than another's 'prejudice' was a very modern view indeed," as Jeanette Winterson succinctly put it, observing that "while Radclyffe Hall [the British lesbian novelist] was begging for her right to existence, Natalie was throwing parties until dawn."[4]

Again, of course, she was protected by money. Like Romaine, she did not have to temper her art to make it marketable. In 1900 she published *Quelques Portraits-Sonnets de Femmes*, a collection of poetry that was explicitly homosexual in theme, although reviewers pretended not to notice. But her real gift was for living: "One must be idle in order to become oneself," she said, an interesting remark that could only have been made by a rich person, although the leisured days of the typical moneyed woman bore no relation whatever to Natalie's supremely energized existence.

Having created a proto-*salon* in Neuilly she became, like Gertrude Stein, a great *salonnière* of the Left Bank. In her eighteenth-century villa in the Rue Jacob—where she lived from 1909 until her death in 1972—she served chocolate cake to Ezra Pound, Paul Valéry, Sinclair Lewis, Ford Madox Ford, Rainer

Maria Rilke, and T. S. Eliot (who turned down the grant that she had arranged for him with Pound). There was a certain amount of crossover with Stein, but although F. Scott Fitzgerald attended *chez* Barney, Hemingway and Joyce did not. And what of the women? Well: there was Colette, there was the painter Tamara de Lempicka, there was Sylvia Beach—who opened the legendary bookshop Shakespeare and Company—plus her partner Adrienne Monnier, there was Edna St. Vincent Millay, there was Peggy Guggenheim, and there was Radclyffe Hall, reading from her hymn to love between women, *The Well of Loneliness*, which had been banned in Britain in 1928. The previous year Natalie had started an *Académie des Femmes*, a riposte to the French Academy established some 300 years earlier, which included no female writers. Her support for artistic endeavor was absolutely staunch and sincere, and so too her support for her own sex. In this world women became muses to each other, rather than for men. It was not a paradise (although Paris can sometimes seem so); there were rivalries and jealousies and destructive personalities; yet there was an integrity and a joy about this different way of living, which continues to intrigue and to inspire some hundred years on.

In the garden of the house at Rue Jacob stood a Doric temple dedicated to friendship. And friendship—so underrated, so much in love's towering shadow—was indeed at the heart of this colony-within-a-colony, this ring of rich women within the expat circle, whose lives compared so favorably with those of their more conventional heiress contemporaries, the ones who wanted husbands and boyfriends and children. The Paris "experiment," which broke so easily with the old mores by the simple expedient of removing men from the picture, showed a possible way forward. Just think of all the married women who began quite openly to have lesbian affairs—of how bisexuality became a kind of norm in society: in one way this was straightforwardly about sex, yet in another it was a symbol of independence, a recognition that men were neither the inevitable endgame, nor the only game in town. For instance Élisabeth de Gramont, the Duchesse de Clermont-Tonnerre, who had two children by her dreadful husband, at the age of forty-three entered into another marriage contract: with Natalie Barney. The two women had been lovers for nine years, since 1909. Natalie's relationship with Romaine Brooks ("my angel Romaine"), which lasted through-out most of their very long lives, had begun in 1915.

Natalie's refusal to be faithful—which she defended on philosophical grounds, although it was not merely a matter of principle—naturally caused distress and even some cheap jokes. (When Gertrude Stein asked where Natalie found all her girl-friends, Alice B. Toklas replied that she scouted for them in the ladies' room in the basement of the Galeries Lafayette depart-ment store.) Élisabeth and Romaine accepted each other, and the ménage à trois continued until Élisabeth's death in 1954. A less comfortable set-up had arisen in 1927, however, when Natalie brought Dolly Wilde into the mix and three became four.

Dolly was unusual in that she had little money and her con-nection with art was almost purely familial, through her famous uncle Oscar, who had of course died in Paris. Dolly looked like Oscar and dressed like Oscar; she had his conversational gift, but could not translate it into artistic creation; she had suicidal tendencies and became dependent on drugs and alcohol. Nata-lie, who was supremely well adjusted yet attracted to less sta-ble personalities, paid for several detoxes. These did not work. Dolly died in London in 1941, aged forty-six, probably from an overdose: "most Lesbians seem to live forever," wrote her friend Nancy Mitford—"oh why did she have to go?" Nancy, who lived in Paris after the Second World War, observed in 1962 that the city "still harbours many an old mistress of Miss Wilde."[5] Back in the 1920s, one of her partners was Marion Carstairs, known as Joe, a granddaughter of one of the founding partners of Standard Oil. The women had met in Dublin during the war, when Joe was driving an ambulance. She was emphatically not artistic—her great interest was powerboat racing, and her usual costume that of a sailor (plus tattoos)—and, perhaps because her life was thus rendered less complicated, she seems to have had one hell of a good time; subsequent affairs were with Garbo, Dietrich, and Tallulah Bankhead.

She could not have been more different from the woman who was born Pauline Tarn in London in 1877, who inherited a fortune from her father and whose mother—an American—tried to have her declared insane to gain control of her money. These old tricks were still being played, straight out of the Wilkie Collins playbook, even though by the late nineteenth century they really had no chance of succeeding. Instead of being locked away and rendered powerless, Pauline was protected as a ward of court. When she attained her majority and her inheritance, she went to Paris and transformed herself into an embodiment of artistic creation: a cross-dressing poet named Renée Vivien.

Renée looked like Chatterton, lived like a figment of the Baudelairean imagination, and treated love as a poetic concept (whereas women like Natalie and Winnaretta were able to keep it in proportion). She was rendered illogically guilt-ridden by the death of a childhood friend, a girl named Violet—Renée had broken off their romantic attachment on account of Natalie—and was devastated by the ending of her affair with a married member of the Rothschild family, Baroness Hélène van Zuylen. She acquired a kind of eroticized death wish—an obsession with sadomasochistic fantasies, with drugs, with starving herself down to around sixty pounds. In 1908 she made a failed suicide attempt, drinking quantities of laudanum and lying down with a bunch of violets held to her heart. The following year she died of natural causes, aged thirty-two.

She was a victim-heiress, one might therefore say, although unlike the heiresses of old, Renée had agency; she lived in a world rich with the promise of strength and fulfillment. Yet this cultured, well-traveled woman, with a flat on the Avenue Foch, with money (and, by the end, with debt), had deliberately denied the possibilities that came with freedom.

Or so it seemed. But can one say such a thing about a person who freely chose to live as she did? She had tried to make her life into a work of art, which for her meant art beset with Romantic agony. In this she succeeded; and her fascination is imperishable (which she surely also wanted). Not just for her extraordinary image, which predated even Romaine's in its gender fluidity, but for her many and beautiful Symbolist poems, whose motif—a reiterated signifier of love and pain—led her to be called "the muse of the violets."

* * *

Paris had become the center of the creative world, but it was not only about Paris. Venice, too, was irresistible to the cultured rich—how could it not be? Post–First World War it became fashionable, rather than merely exclusive, although not more accessible. Tourism had not yet blurred the city's peerless silhouette nor disturbed its lush, hushed atmosphere. These visitors did not have to queue for a vaporetto nor stumble through a St. Mark's Square like an open-air Boxing Day sale; their fears for Venice's survival were existential rather than real. "How long can it survive, its huge palaces supported on wooden piles?" asked the diarist James Lees-Milne in 1947, but for the time being it seemed that it would. The general attitude was that of Nancy Mitford, who as late as 1968 wrote this comfortable thought: "I always tell the Venetians that Lord Byron used to urge his friends to come, saying in another ten years it will be in the sea."

From the balcony of a palazzo, or the speedboat that took one to the Lido, Venice surely looked both more and less perishable than it does today. More dreamlike, with every turn of one's head revealing a clean new Carpaccio or Canaletto; less vulnerable to human foot and natural forces. Quite simply, it was unreachable to most people. There was no Marco Polo airport until 1960. Hotels like the Danieli (where Ruskin stayed in the mid-nineteenth century, researching his *Stones of Venice*) and the Hotels des Bains on the Lido (where Aschenbach takes his last holiday in Thomas Mann's *Death in Venice*) were outlandishly exclusive. Many of the houses that lined the Grand Canal were still privately owned, although very much up for rental by hugely rich Americans like Laura Corrigan—a great Venice hostess—or Cole Porter, who threw magnificent parties in the 1920s, hiring the entire Ballets Russes and tightrope walkers who crossed the canal. Diaghilev, who was buried on the cemetery island when he died in 1929, had preferred "old Venice": the more decorous, rarefied place that predated the First World War, before Elsa Maxwell turned the Lido—which she claimed to have "invented" in 1919—into an outpost of the Jazz Age ("There was nothing here until I made it. You can say I *am* the Lido"). But old or new, it remained the playground of the privileged.

To stay in a palazzo—which some hotels had once been—was to experience life as a series of tableaux, in which sun struck shadow with the force of love and an aqueous shimmer rippled across every surface. The Isabella Stewart Gardner Museum in Boston could not quite replicate those qualities, but the 1903 building was directly inspired by the Palazzo Barbaro, where the eponymous Mrs. Gardner—a significant art collector, heiress to $1.75 million in 1891—was a frequent guest of the Bostonian Curtis family, whose name is still on the back door bell. Their drawing-room *salons* attracted the likes of Henry James (who wrote the room into *The Wings of the Dove*) and John Singer Sargent (who painted it in *An Interior in Venice*), as well as Edith Wharton, Bernard Berenson, and pretty much any other American visiting the city.

Fifty years later, Peggy Guggenheim—a minor heiress within her superrich clan—would put her collection of twentieth-century art on display in Venice itself. Having exhibited in both London and New York, in 1948 she acquired the perfect mise-en-scène of the Palazzo Venier, a bungalow palace in the Dorsoduro: it could be the most beautiful home in the city, she was told by a grand old Venetian princess, if you threw away all that awful art. The Venier had previously been the home of the *grande horizontale* Doris Castlerosse, an interwar goddess with the legs of Cyd Charisse. She acquired the palazzo with the American heiress Margot Liddon Flick Hoffman, who had fallen beneath her lethal spell ("Doris got more out of [Margot] than from any of her rich men," said the Duchess of Westminster, "every jewel the size of a cherry"). Before that the house was owned by Luisa Casati, who rode in a gondola with her cheetah and kept wax figures of her own likeness. Her astonishing appearance—part Aubrey Beardsley, part Hammer House of Horror—made her a figure of renown in the city: crowds gathered as she strode through St. Mark's Square in Fortuny and a fur coat, and her parties were showier than Jay Gatsby's. Like Renée Vivien, she made her life into a work of art; or, in her case, into a one-woman *tableau vivant*. She was, thought Natalie Barney—who wrote her a poem—"ever trying by strange disguisements to escape from the inner strangeness." She had a long affair with Gabriele

D'Annunzio, and a short one with Augustus John; Romaine Brooks seduced her and painted her; she was photographed, brilliantly, by Adolph de Meyer, whose wife Olga had an affair with Winnaretta de Polignac.

In 1947, when James Lees-Milne visited Venice and wondered how long it would survive, he stayed at the palazzo (now the Contarini Polignac) that had been Winnaretta's home. "There can be few things more romantic," he wrote, "more transposing from this dismal modern age, than to find yourself, at dead of night, under the stars and dim spangled lamps, skimming down the small canals, the gondoliers shouting *Hoih! Hoih!* as you approach a corner. Rhythmically, swiftly, you glide, your wake gently lapping the palaces . . ." He described his bedroom, the Venetian view that confounds with its fantastical actuality: "a large bed with white and gold posts, raised on a dais, the windows looking up the Grand Canal through the high-arched Accademia bridge to the Palazzo Fornari, and down the Canal toward the Salute."

Winnaretta herself had then been dead for four years. Her last great love had been the woman whom Lees-Milne would marry in 1951, Alvilde Chaplin.

The pattern woven by this particular set of lovers was the most intricate of the lot, with a circularity worthy of Schnitzler's *La Ronde.* For ten years, from 1923, Winnaretta had been in a relationship with Violet Trefusis, the married daughter of Edward VII's last mistress, Alice Keppel (so many roads then led back to Bertie—rather as, from the late seventeenth century, they led to Charles II). Violet, a writer and Francophile, vastly amusing but deeply untrustworthy, was the woman of whom Harold Acton wrote that "she was the kind of friend that made one long for a foe." She was also the long-term lover of Vita Sackville-West, with whom Alvilde Chaplin would have an affair in the 1950s. James

Lees-Milne had previously had a liaison with Vita's husband, Harold Nicolson.

Both men were essentially gay, despite having real love for their wives. In his diary for 1943, Lees-Milne recounted a conversation in which Nicolson "extolled the advantages of homosexuality and relationships between men, who allowed individual independence." The same was true, of course, of some of the lesbian relationships that had similarly flowered: "individual independence," that blessed state, had certainly been achieved by Winnaretta and Natalie Barney. Yet Nicolson's generalization does not allow for the nature of love, which cannot always be controlled or compartmentalized—who would have thought, for instance, that the relationship between Natalie and Romaine Brooks would come to an end after fifty years? In the 1950s Natalie acquired a last love—an ambassador's wife—and Romaine, after several years of yet another ménage à trois, finally decided (in her nineties) that she had had enough. Meanwhile Winnaretta, who had been the dominant personality in most of her relationships, in her last seems to have become the supplicant; according to Nancy Mitford, "Princess Winnie" died of a broken heart and Alvilde was the one who did the breaking. "She [Alvilde] told me she suffers dreadful remorse over having been horrid to the Princess," wrote Nancy in a letter of 1947—"I never thought it was quite her fault, they were thoroughly on each other's nerves."[6] What surely most affected the dynamic of the relationship (although Nancy did not mention it) is that when it started, in 1938, Alvilde was twenty-nine and Winnaretta seventy-two. The hauteur that the Princesse de Polignac had displayed at the start of the century, with everybody from her first husband to Marcel Proust, had turned at last to vulnerability. Nevertheless she had lived on her own terms; more so, surely, than any heiress had ever done before.

Natalie Barney, eleven years her junior, did exactly the same thing. She lived as she chose—with the money to fund it—and she did not compromise. After the Second World War, which she and Romaine spent in Italy, she returned to a Paris that had been occupied and much changed, its artistic colony (and colony of women) dispersed. Yet she reinstituted her *salon*. Capote went, as did the bereaved Alice B. Toklas and, some years later, younger writers like Mary McCarthy, whose 1963 masterpiece *The Group* has a Europhile lesbian heiress at its enigmatic heart. By then, the villa on Rue Jacob was visited in a spirit of homage to a legendary past: to see the room in which Ezra read his latest impenetrable cantos and Colette ate *gâteau*, and in which Natalie continued to sit like a clever little goddess, a living symbol of a time long gone. But what a time it had been, and how it continues to beguile us!

CHAMPAGNE (AND A DASH
OF BENZEDRINE)

LONDON, MEANWHILE, HAD its equivalent of the *salonnière*: the hostess.

This figure, who had flourished in the society led by the future Edward VII, veritably bloomed in the interwar period. It was a role made for heiresses, who could afford warm houses and fine wines to lure the A-list; as times grew harder and money tighter, which in the 1930s was the case for most people, even the privileged classes were glad of the chance to dine properly at somebody else's expense.

Emerald Cunard (formerly Maud Burke of San Francisco) strongly disliked the term hostess: "a most objectionable word." She threw Cecil Beaton's first book on the fire because it committed the crime of thus describing her, although the pair made up their quarrel when, as Beaton recalled, "I rescued her from a carousel horse that revolved too merrily in the grounds of Gerald Berners' house."[7]

That does not sound like a situation in which Hemingway and Gertrude Stein might have found themselves. Lord Berners— the model for the fantastical Lord Merlin in Nancy Mitford's *The Pursuit of Love*—was an aesthete and amateur composer; Beaton was an inspired photographer and designer; both were supremely cultured men. Nevertheless their milieu was social—Berners was upper-class and Beaton wanted to be—and that, overwhelmingly, was the world of the hostess.

Sometimes it was social-cum-political, as in the case of the heiress Mrs. Ronnie Greville, who wielded considerable influence through the many parties thrown at her houses in Mayfair and Surrey. According to the Conservative MP Bob Boothby, whom she introduced to some of the right people, "as far as patronage was concerned, she was extremely powerful . . . a bit of an old bag, but very good to me."* Harold Nicolson, who served for a time in Churchill's wartime government, was distinctly unhappy about this power of Mrs. Greville's. Never one to veil his misogyny, he called her "a common, waspish woman who got where she did through persistence and money," and in 1939 wrote tetchily in his diary: "The harm which these silly, selfish hostesses do is immense. They convey to foreign envoys the impression that policy is decided in their drawing rooms. People . . . are impressed by the social efficiency of silly women such as Mrs. Greville."

It is doubtful whether Nicolson would have written in this way about Edith Londonderry, another megarich political hostess but irreproachably upper-class. He also seems to have been overrating Mrs. Greville's importance: politics and society bled into each other, as indeed they still do, and the idea that "foreign envoys" could not discern where the lines were drawn is absurd. That said, the relaxed ambience created by a hostess could lead a politician into indiscretion, and David Lloyd George

---

* Boothby, who became a life peer in 1958, was a successful and self-publicizing politician, but is now better known for his love life: in 1929 he began an affair with Lady Dorothy Macmillan, wife of the future prime minister, that lasted until her death in 1966; in 1963 a fling with an East End cat burglar led to forays for rough trade in the company of the gangster Ron Kray.

certainly feared that this was the case *chez* Lady Cunard, whom he accordingly described as "dangerous." Furthermore, a hostess could be manipulated, not least because vanity might easily conquer acuity. For instance when Von Ribbentrop was German ambassador in London, he used Emerald Cunard—who had cultivated Mrs. Simpson, and thereby gained favor with the Prince of Wales—as a means to make friends with the heir to the throne. But that, too, was the way of the world. Like it or not, it is how things worked and still work. In this particular instance, many upper-class people met Von Ribbentrop in the 1930s, quite a lot of them were pro-Nazi, and the future Edward VIII was chief among them; a fat lot of good it did them all in the end.

Whether by luck, judgment or sheer inability to insert herself into it, Mrs. Greville was not in the Prince's camp, and later espoused Noël Coward's view that a statue should be erected to Mrs. Simpson for her role in removing him from the throne.* Her firm friendship with the future George VI and Queen Elizabeth meant that, monarch-wise, she had made the right bet. She made the wrong call about Nazi Germany, however. So too, at first, did Emerald Cunard. In 1935, according to the socialite MP Chips Channon, London gossip reported her to be "*éprise*" with the ubiquitous Von Ribbentrop. Later she did much better, asking the ambassador sweetly: "Why, dearest Excellency, does Herr Hitler hate the Jews?" Meanwhile Mrs. Greville attended Nuremberg (these visits were announced in the court pages of

---

* In a diary entry for May 4, 1937, Chips Channon wrote: "There was a long Windsor argument at dinner, and Noël Coward was rather sickening and unoriginal putting forward the middle-class point of view, which was snubbed successfully by Winston who remains pro-Windsor to the end." From *The Diaries of Chips Channon*, Vol. 1, edited by Simon Heffer (Hutchinson, 2021).

The Times, like attendances at Royal Ascot), and voiced some pro-German stuff that would have been infinitely better left unsaid. Possibly this was why Nicolson—who, despite an early association with Oswald Mosley, was relatively quick to see the fascist threat—was so viciously opposed to her. By 1938 she had realized her error and was trying hastily to backtrack, then in 1940 donated money for an RAF Spitfire that was given her name: the Margaret Helen. "That damned Ribbentrop," she said to her friend Beverley Nichols, smoothly rewriting the events of a visit by the German ambassador to her sumptuous home, Polesden Lacey. "I told him that if ever there was a war he might beat the English, but he would never beat the Scots."

During the Second World War she lived at The Dorchester hotel, whose steel structure—resistant to wind and, it was devoutly hoped, bombs—made it a venue of choice for much of the middle-aged beau monde. Permanent suites were taken by Emerald Cunard, Somerset Maugham, Lord and Lady Halifax, and Duff and Lady Diana Cooper (housed cheaply close to the roof); those in frequent attendance included Evelyn Waugh and Ann O'Neill, who later married Ian Fleming. When the Blitz raged the hotel guests slept in the basement gymnasium, where Emerald read Balzac. Also at the hotel was another hostess, Sibyl Colefax, who by then had very little money, and charged half a guinea for attendance at her Dorchester dinners. Mrs. Greville, naturally, had splendid provisions sent from Polesden for her own parties, although when the King of Greece came to dinner in February 1942 he told Chips Channon "that he could hardly look at food since it made him think of his starving compatriots." Also at the party were Lord Mountbatten, who in 1947 would become the last viceroy of India, and his wife, Edwina. Twenty years earlier this marriage—at which the Prince of Wales was best man—had been encouraged by Mrs. Greville, who had chaperoned the motherless Edwina Ashley out in India, and at first had feared that Mountbatten was a money-grabber. Although a great-grandson of Queen Victoria, he was not rich, and he always had an eye to the main chance—in this case to Edwina, who had just become a notable heiress. Aged nineteen she inherited £2 million from her grandfather, Sir Ernest Cassel, plus Brook House on Park Lane, which had a dining room that could seat one hundred people and a vast marble hall known as "the giant's lavatory." Edwina, an intelligent woman with a reckless streak, was a *grande horizontale* on the Daisy Warwick scale ("But where shall I put the third gentleman?" a butler once asked, when she was in bed with one lover and a second was waiting his turn in the drawing room). Out in India, an affair with Pandit Nehru was strongly rumored. She was also a free spender; in 1922, the year of her marriage, she arrived at the Paris Ritz with no money, cashed an IOU with the hotel manager ("such a divine man"), and headed straight out again to the wildly expensive shops behind the Champs-Élysées. Brook House cost an estimated £16,000 a year to run. Twenty-nine servants were employed when Edwina and her husband were in residence, and seventeen when they were not. In 1931 the splendid Victorian mansion was put up for sale, contrary to Sir Ernest Cassel's wishes, and a block of flats built on the site. The Mountbattens lived at the top in what was described as "London's first penthouse," which had eighteen bedrooms and was reached by a private express lift (in which, on her first visit, Queen Mary got stuck).

However: "Edwina M. is now a complete Socialist," wrote Chips Channon after the dinner in 1942, "which for anybody in the position of a millionairess, a semi-royalty, and a famous fashionable figure, is too ridiculous." Mrs. Greville, meanwhile, "seemed aging and silent." At a party a couple of months later, she greeted Channon from her bath chair. Making a brave, bleak joke of it, she said that she had everything wrong with her "except leprosy." She refused to shelter in the Dorchester basement and, as the Blitz reached its height, wore her superb emeralds—the real ones, rather than the replicas she had always favored—as a *geste insolente* toward the threat of obliteration. At the age of seventy-nine (or, according to her, seventy-five) and with her health in tatters, she knew that death was imminent anyway, although her grip upon life remained clawlike. In August 1942 she stayed for the last time with her beloved royals at Balmoral, and Queen Elizabeth wrote in a letter that "it was too pathetic to see this little bundle of unquenchable courage and determination, quite helpless except for one bright eye . . . I felt full of admiration for such a wonderful exhibition of 'never give in.' "

What had partly kept her going was inter-hostess rivalry. Grace Vanderbilt was an enemy-friend, a little too close to the royal family for Mrs. Greville's liking, although generally at a consoling distance across the Atlantic.* Emerald Cunard was too close, full stop. "You mustn't think that I dislike little Lady Cunard," said Mrs. Greville, adding—in reference to the quantities of makeup that she wore—"I'm always telling Queen Mary that she isn't half as bad as she is painted" (in retaliation Emerald said that the quails at Mrs. Greville's dinner parties were inflated with a bicycle pump). However Cecil Beaton, who was very much in the Cunard camp, wrote that Mrs. Greville "was a galumphing, greedy, snobbish old toad who watered at her chops at the sight

---

* In 1919, the two women—by then comfortably advanced in years—were in France together, when their car met with an accident and they were obliged to flag a lift. Grace was afraid that passing motorists would take them for prostitutes touting for trade. "My dear," said Mrs. Greville, "we may take that risk."

of royalty . . . and did nothing for anybody except the rich [not quite true]. Emerald cultivated important people so she could play with them as if they were notes on a harpsichord . . . When Emerald took notice of me, I felt that I had not lived in vain."[8] Evelyn Waugh, conversely, stated bluntly: "Emerald has always given me the shivers."[9]

Such hyperbolic venom and praise! These women elicited feelings of inordinate strength, in both their detractors and their worshippers. The reasons are complex, like the nature of their dominance. They were self-mythologizers, but people bought into their myth; there was willing collusion in their hegemony, but with that went resentment and sometimes derision. Their power was at odds, too, with their apparently lightweight demeanor. Nor was it the "acceptable" kind of female power—that is to say, based upon sexual allure. It derived ultimately from money, and money that belonged to them alone. They could choose how to spend it, thus had a freedom that was still, overwhelmingly, traditionally male.

Other freedoms had been accorded to British women since the end of the First World War—the right to vote,* to join the professions and sit on a jury—and in 1919 the Virginia-born Nancy Astor (who called Emerald a "pushing American") became the first female MP to take her seat in the House of Commons. Yet for all that, a woman's natural milieu remained the drawing room, and the means to wield power came typically through her ability to curate (in the modern terminology) a guest list, bestowing and withholding patronage, just as Mrs. Astor had done when she ruled New York. This had been true even in Paris, despite that collective burst of intense female liberation; and this

---

* At this point, the suffrage extended only to women aged thirty and above.

was London, with its impenetrable hierarchies, its deep mistrust of the serious. If a woman of ambition and determination sought a position in that society, it had to be done according to the rules. The role of hostess was therefore perfect: a *salonnière* for the shooting classes. The woman played her female part—providing comfort, luxury, a five-star home from home—and thereby gained her entrée into a man's world; which did not mean that the guests who fought to accept her hospitality would not sometimes chafe against her ability to provide it.

Today Mrs. Greville might well be in politics herself (with a number of lucrative directorships), or a successful CEO. She had an extremely good business brain, even if her judgment was faulty in other respects. She did not merely derive an income from the brewery business established by her father, she knew exactly what was going on with it; even when she was dying, the directors of the company were summoned to report to her, and apparently she put them through the wringer. She was a clever, artful negotiator. There was something rather brilliant in the way that she leveraged her connection with the future George VI and his wife, dangling the hope that she would bequeath them Polesden (when there was no thought that the throne, plus several enormous houses, would ever be theirs). Of course she was a desperate snob, all the more so because her own antecedents were such a handicap; she was, as it were, getting her attack in first. Of course she was on a power kick. She loved being a confidante of Queen Elizabeth, who would sit on her bed and chat as if to a mother; she loved shaking her head sagely about Winston Churchill to the Canadian High Commissioner: "I have known him for fifty years and he has never been right yet."

So how much better—one might legitimately think—if she had put her brains and drive to a more worthwhile use than cozying up to royals and introducing politicians to one another over the Bollinger! Yet it is impossible to overemphasize—even to grasp—the limitations of a woman's life at this time, however great her freedoms when compared with those of her mother's generation. Therefore one has to say: here's to you, Mrs. Greville. What a woman she must have been, with her gusto and her grit. "She wasn't beautiful, she wasn't brilliant, she was a fabulous snob," wrote Beverley Nichols. "And yet, one had been genuinely fond of her."

* * *

After all: money alone was not enough to bring success in that highly competitive world, nor to cause Mrs. Greville to sigh (delightedly): "One uses up so many red carpets in a season." In those days a carpet was spread in front of the venue for a society party, and crowds would gather to watch the arrivals; in 1924, hours before a ball was held at Charles Street, the road was so jammed that Mrs. Greville was obliged to prove her identity to the police so that she could reach her own front door. This iconography—the red carpet and the spectators—is yet more proof that society people were "celebrities," as we now understand the word: objects of ongoing fascination, whose clothes were itemized and described in the press (albeit without the sidebar commentary) and whose activities were laboriously detailed. Lady A has taken a house on Green Street; the Duchess of B held a dinner party last night in Belgrave Square; the Earl and Countess of C attended the Epsom Derby . . . such was the stuff dutifully recorded each day in the court pages of *The Times*.

Inhabiting the same postcodes but a different world were the "bright young things," whose activities—an attention-craving, youth-flaunting round of costume balls, treasure hunts, and parties, at which they dressed as babies or in pajamas—were fairly devoured by newspaper readers in the 1920s. Minor celebrities they most certainly were, and with their iconoclastic attitudes (which were not entirely facile), they ever more tightly joined hands with the other kind of celebrity: artists, performers, film actors, the sort of people whom the upper classes had traditionally shunned and now, with their survivalist instinct, semi-embraced. When Ida Rubinstein first tried to become an actress she was put in an asylum, and when the director D. W. Griffith offered Lady Diana Cooper $75,000 for a film role in 1919, her parents forbade her to accept (Queen Mary told her that she would be banished from Court if she disobeyed). Yet the telling point is that Diana—famous for beauty, and almost as attractive to the press as that other Lady Diana would be in the 1980s—was perceived by Griffith as a potential bankable movie star. And three years later she *did* make a film, playing "Lady Beatrice Fair" opposite ex-boxer Victor McLaglen (what a double act) in *The Glorious Adventure*. She received a degree of opprobrium from the respectable classes, including an anonymous letter that asked: "How can you, born in a high Social position, so prostitute your Status for paltry monetary consideration? You THING!" Yet her mother, the Duchess of Rutland, had undergone a complete change of heart. She was enraptured by *The Glorious Adventure*, and merely wanted more more more: "Oh, why can't Diana be longer?" In 1935, after another film and a much-celebrated theater role in Max Reinhardt's *The Miracle*, Diana was offered the lead in MGM's *Anna Karenina* when Greta Garbo had a tantrum and left the production; before she could make her decision, however, Garbo was back on board.

Diana told an American journalist—with typical aristo honesty—that she acted "only for money and distantly imagined fun. Don't let my grimaces to order be called self-expression."

What she had done, however, marked a significant step on the way to a society in which Noël Coward would be Queen Elizabeth's favorite party guest, Winston Churchill's daughter Sarah would marry the American entertainer Vic Oliver, and Princess Margaret would yearn to be onstage with Danny Kaye. It also showed how quickly the mindset of 1919—when Britain had still hoped, rather poignantly, to re-establish the cap-doffing order knocked sideways by the First World War—had begun to shift. The spirit of Modernism was drifting out of the artist's studio, into everyday life, and its sharp, cool ironies were like ice picks driven through the heart of the old certainties.

In a sense, smart society *was* like a stage (or film) set. One showed up, dressed up, played one's part, and failure to perform meant exile in the wings. In another sense, social life was real and solid in a way that it no longer needs to be, now that people are literally screened from each other, and great tranches of time can be subsumed into Netflix and a smartphone. Then, there was no hiding place. One needed energy, zest, alertness, and smartness, a sense that downtime was wasted time, a willingness to push one's personality constantly outward—qualities that now are rare as red squirrels; and for that reason alone this period continues to fascinate. Of course its style was superlative, as revolutionary and highly defined as that of the 1960s, with its streamlined silhouettes and delicious snapping idiom. Its cast of characters was a bright and brilliant one: well-born starry girls like Diana Cooper, Nancy Mitford and her sister Diana, who dismissed the usual debs' delights, the Lord Many-Acres and Sir Aubrey Shooting-Sticks, and mixed instead with men like Evelyn Waugh and Cecil Beaton, both of whom had left their bourgeois origins somewhere on the road from Hampstead to Belgrave Square.

And the woman at the center of this genuinely glittering interwar society was Emerald Cunard, who ditched her given name of Maud—which she proclaimed to be dull—after the death of her husband in 1925. She was a greater hostess than Mrs. Greville, who dominated through dominance, as it were, and was immensely obvious in her methods. Emerald had charm, although there were those who resisted it (chiefly her daughter Nancy). She also had the kind of wit that London society treasured, charmingly vague but with a childlike directness: "Her nonsense can be funnier than any nonsense I have ever enjoyed," as James Lees-Milne put it. In reference to his key position within the National Trust, she once introduced him as the man who "looks after all the public houses." She was enormous fun, in fact—and she was, uncontestably, a true lover and supporter of the arts. Toward the end of her life, weak of heart and plagued with throat cancer (she died in 1948 aged seventy-five), she ranted at her doctors about the plays and concerts that she was missing, as well as the parties—all those things were important to her. "Do they really not care for the arts? How extraordinary of them!" she exclaimed, during a discussion about the lack of culture within the middle classes. "When Emerald gets talking about literature and music," wrote James Lees-Milne in 1945, "about which she knows so much and loves so passionately, I realize that, for all her faults, she is a woman out of the common run." He also wrote that he never thought of her as a society woman—"that hateful term"—although others took a different view, notably Evelyn Waugh. In 1932, when his novel *Vile Bodies* was dramatized and about to begin a run at the Vaudeville Theatre, Waugh wrote to a friend that "Lady Cunard (whom God preserve) has just been given seats in the 18th row and is gibbering down the telephone saying 'How can I take Prince George to the 18th row?' so I have confiscated all poor Maud Yorke's tickets and given them to the old trout."[10] Prince George was a prize, but it was his brother who really counted. "Little Mrs. Simpson knows her Balzac," Emerald cooed in sincere approval, when she first welcomed the Prince of Wales's new squeeze to her drawing room, where the couple were soon to become a regular fixture. Not long afterward, all thoughts of French literature were out the window: "How could he do this to me?" she wailed plaintively, when Edward VIII's abdication scuppered her chances of becoming a lady-in-waiting at court (and her support of his love affair made her persona non grata with the royals).

No doubt about it, Emerald was easy to mock. For all her sense of fun, the joke was usually on her. Nancy Mitford described attending the theater with her in 1945, a roaring farce at which "E. sat very seriously as tho' at Shakespeare or Ibsen, looking at the actors through opera glasses."[11] There was also the story that her last word—delivered to her doctor and maid—was a plaintive cry of: "Champagne!" It is easy, too, to dismiss the priorities of somebody who cared so much about society, and used her inheritance to achieve advancement—then power—within it.

Yet she could command the admiration of an exigent man like James Lees-Milne, as well as making fickle London dance to her insistent tune; as with Mrs. Greville, money alone did not account for what she became. And then there is this more general defense, again from Nancy Mitford, as offered by the Duc de Sauveterre in her novel *The Pursuit of Love*: "You should never despise social life—*de la haute société*—I mean, it can be a very satisfying one, entirely artificial of course, but absorbing. Apart from the life of the intellect and the contemplative religious life, which few people are qualified to enjoy, what is there to distinguish man from the animals but his social life? And who understand it so well and who can make it so smooth and amusing as *les gens du monde*?"

That was Emerald.

* * *

Her origins were somewhat mysterious. She may have been illegitimate, and her $2 million dowry a legacy from her real father,
although there is another possible source for the money. Again
like Mrs. Greville, she lied about her age; no doubt out of vanity,
but also (one senses) from a deeper instinctive secrecy. The 1939
Register has a date of birth of 1880, which is pretty much impossible, and the register of deaths states that she was seventy-one
when she died, which means that she was born in 1876–7. The
more likely year, however, is 1872.

She was "adopted" as a teenager by a Horace Carpentier, a
former Civil War general who had made a great deal of money
through dubious land speculation. Probably it was he, rather
than a mystery-man father, who gave Maud her dowry. It was
said that he collected books and young girls, and preferred
both in the same condition: with their leaves uncut. In other
words his creep factor was galactically high, but the young
Maud Burke made use of him. Some girls can do this. They
are born with an ability to handle male attention and turn it to
their advantage. Oddly enough, this concept would have been
less shocking in the late nineteenth century than it is today,
when we are so alert to the dire implications of inappropriate behavior. There is no evidence that Mr. Carpentier actually
slept with Maud, whom he described as his favorite "niece";
and, if he had hoped to marry her, she managed to hold him off
without wrecking their association. Instead she allowed him to
impart to her a sophisticated education in opera and literature—
about which she cared so passionately, but which she also knew
would help her in society—and, in her early twenties, she
accompanied him to New York, where she began to husband-
hunt among the cruising gangs of European blue bloods (who

in some instances were not much better, morally speaking, than Mr. Carpentier).

Before this, in 1894, she had visited London. There she met the distinguished Irish novelist George Moore, who was twenty years her senior and fell madly, loudly, and demonstratively in love with her. "Dearest Maud, dearest Primavera!" he wrote in 1904. "I do not know what primavera means . . . It means Spring, doesn't it? It means joy . . . And you, dearest, mean all these things to me, for you are not, I am convinced, a mere passing woman but the incarnation of an idea." She recognized his quality and admired his work; but she knew that what she needed, in order to make her way in the world, was a husband who would plant her firmly within British society. She set about finding one with the profound determination that characterized this mistress of reinvention, this adventuress with a core of sincerity.

Sir Bache Cunard, whom she married in 1895, was not attracted to Maud's money, having plenty of his own from the family shipping line. Instead he fell for the flirtatious, eager vitality that overrode any lack of conventional prettiness, and which seems to have had an immense (perhaps deliberately contrived) attraction for older men—Sir Bache was forty-four. His mansion, Nevill Holt, was pinned deep in the midst of Leicestershire hunting land, long hours from the salvation of Covent Garden. In his settled rural passivity, however, she saw possibilities.

He adored the kind of country pursuits that bored his wife to death, and was also a man of hobbies: for instance he enjoyed carving coconuts, which he then mounted in cups, and he spent long weeks assembling a collection of horseshoes and fixing them on a gate, where they spelled out the words "Come into the garden, Maud." That touching gesture failed to touch Lady Cunard's heart. She was hell-bent upon London; where she was presented at Court after her marriage and where, felicitously, Sir Bache owned no property. When she "needed" to be in town, she could be there alone. By 1911—fourteen years before her husband died—the marriage was effectively over.

A daughter, Nancy, was born in 1896; their relationship was fraught (of which more later). Sometimes Nancy claimed to be the product of an affair with George Moore, which is a possibility. The man who truly engaged Lady Cunard's affections, however, was the renowned self-taught conductor Thomas Beecham, seven years her junior, with whom she began an affair in 1909. According to Cecil Beaton, she spent "most of her fortune" on promoting his artistic projects (and, according to Diana Cooper, helped Beecham's businessman father acquire a title in 1914: he paid £10,000 for it, of which £4,000 went to Maud, as she was then still called). By the end of her life she was debt-ridden—the jewels that she bequeathed to Diana were found to be fake, the real things long sold—and the willingness to squander one's money for love is, of course, a hallmark of the hapless heiress.

Yet it does not seem to have been quite that way. For a start, the effort that she put in for Beecham was justifiable on artistic grounds: the man was mounting opera seasons and conducting for Diaghilev, not bulk-buying Charvet ties and crashing Lagondas. Also he had family money. Her help was a contribution, rather than the purchase of a career in exchange for love. Furthermore, somewhat ironically, some of the money that she spent had been George Moore's: he left Emerald £80,000 when he died in 1933. Possibly Beecham played her for a fool, and certainly he was not faithful during their affair (like her, he was married and estranged), although Emerald was unprepared for the brutal cymbal crash that extinguished the relationship. At the start of the Second World War, she had followed Beecham to New York—for which she was accused by Margot Asquith of having "done a bunk"—and taken the suite next to his at the Ritz-Carlton. As from nowhere she heard that he intended to divorce his wife, in order to marry a woman whom he had previously dismissed as being "descended from a long line of dentists": thirty years of devotion were obliterated by a snippet of gossip. In the uncompromising analysis of Bob Boothby, Beecham "took most of her [Emerald's] money for his operas, and then married Betty Humby without telling her. She never recovered from the shock." Emerald by then was nearly seventy, and Nancy Mitford wrote in 1945 that she "continually talks of suicide"—although the fact that she talked about it, as it were socially, was a sign that she didn't really mean it. Cecil Beaton, with his more romantic but not unperceptive viewpoint, wrote that "she rallied bravely, and never spoke ill of the man who had treated her so ruthlessly." In fact her spirit had a natural upward curve, which external circumstances could never entirely suppress. Returning to London after that great blow, establishing her base in room 701 at the Dorchester and disdaining the V2 bombs as a propaganda invention; teetering in high heels to Diana Cooper's wartime farm in Sussex, where she wore pearls and leopard skin and was butted to the ground by a cow; describing a heart attack as "extremely pleasant—one was floating among the clouds!" . . . like her counterpart, Mrs. Greville, she had guts.

Beecham had been at the center of her life, where he had not deserved to be, but there had been much more to that life. From her home at 7 Grosvenor Square—sold at the start of the war—Emerald had thrown dinners and parties that seem to have had a quality of enchantment: an innocence, even. For all her worldliness, she had nothing of the cynic. She retained an inquisitive brightness, like the beady-eyed birds to which many people likened her. "I thought I had never seen a more amusing-looking little parakeet," wrote Beaton; "her hair as pale yellow and fluffy as the feathers of a day-old chick; her feet and legs were more like a wagtail's, so staccato and expressive." Naturally there were those who yearned to be bitchy rather than entranced; such is the nature of social life. Emerald's power in that sphere laid her open to attack and—as is so often the way with women—her appearance was a handy Achilles' heel. She aged, and tried not to do so, and this made her vulnerable. She was likened to a "canary of prey" and, by the ghastly Harold Nicolson, to a "third dynasty mummy painted by an amateur." In her midforties, which then was far from young, she was described by a half-sneering Margot Asquith as a "rococo, spontaneous, frivolous foreigner of excellent heart and digestion and no occupation, dressed like a girl of 20 in white muslin at night, and décolletée by day."[12]

But Beaton was right to celebrate this quality of agelessness, which turned ingénue Maud into interwar Emerald with barely a trip upon the red carpet. "Emerald's clothes were witty confections and retained, with her perfumed Edwardian aura, the romantic aspects of the turn of the century—yet Emerald's mind could never be bound by Edwardian conventions." Like Winnaretta de Polignac, her near contemporary, she embraced Modernism with fervor; although less rich than Winnaretta, she was immensely generous with her money (not just to Beecham) and with her fundraising activities, including for the Ballets Russes. In an era before subsidies and grants, rich enthusiasts like Emerald were a necessity—indeed, patrons are still highly desirable—and according to Beaton she did "more to help the masses appreciate and enjoy theater, ballet and opera than all the reforms made since the war." One must allow here for his worship of the woman, but he was not alone in thinking that, given the extent of her social connections, her impassioned advocacy for the arts was of significant value.

It has been said that she "collected celebrities with the eagerness of a greedy child in a sweet-shop."[13] No doubt there is truth in that. Her real passion for culture comingled with an urgent desire to be at the heart of fashionable society. "There are people about that are of no interest to me," wrote George Moore, after an irritable visit to Grosvenor Square, "as little intelligent they seem as squeaking dolls" (did he mean the Prince of Wales, whose love of Balzac was almost certainly nonexistent?). Undeniably, Emerald was frivolous. Sometimes she was absurd. Yet did that really matter? To the struggling creative there is nothing more welcome than simple appreciation, particularly in a country that tends to give it grudgingly, and her way of promoting the arts was arguably the right way, in a country that tends toward philistinism; a Natalie Barney or Gertrude Stein could never have thrived in London as they did in Paris. And with what Diana Mosley described as her "astonishing personality," Emerald would gather together her disparate guests and orchestrate an evening, much as her lover did his musicians: she had, wrote Beaton, "a deft way of pulling in the reins."

Unlike the Paris *salonnières* she had no artistic gifts of her own, nor did she seem to crave them. As Moore wrote in a book inscription: "Her genius is manifest in her conversation, and like Jesus and Socrates, she has refrained from the other arts." What can this conversation have been like? It is almost impossible to imagine, not least because its blend of intelligence and instinct, sophistication and silliness, effort and ease is simply no longer required; but in it, surely, was the sound of that lost and eternally seductive era. To Cecil Beaton she was the very symbol of a magical world that as a young man he had longed to enter, and that did not let him down. "To me," he wrote in 1948, "Emerald was the quintessence of the civilization that is now in eclipse."

James Lees-Milne was a sterner judge, not always in sympathy with the society in which Emerald was revered, and at first resistant to her inconsequentiality. Yet when she died, he too was compelled to mark her passing in his diary.

"I admired her more than I admire most women, for her lightning perception, her wide reading, her brilliant repartee, her sense of fun, and sparkling, delicious, wonderful nonsense. If only I could have attended her dinner parties as a dumb servitor, the awkwardness of trying and failing to contribute to the conversation would not have arisen. I would have been content to listen to her and watch her deft manipulation of the conversation until eternity . . . I knew I could never entertain her, and so I avoided her too often. Yet I am glad I knew her for no one will ever take her place."

In fact Lees-Milne was oddly felled by Emerald's death, which, in the years after the Second World War, seemed like a last light going out from a livelier past. "My day quite overclouded by it," he wrote abruptly. During his daily walk to Brooks's club "I kept saying to myself, 'Why do all these ugly and stupid people that I pass live, and yet Emerald dies?'"

* * *

At a small dinner party at the Dorchester, the last thrown by Emerald at which Cecil Beaton was present to record events, she said the world had become so dreary, "and life unlike everything she believed it should represent, she was not sorry to go." Raising a glass of champagne, she said: "I drink to my death."

Beaton—whose major triumphs, such as his Academy Award for the design of *My Fair Lady*, were still ahead of him—was in fundamental agreement. The era that Emerald had represented, in her thistledown yet oddly substantial way, was over; her death merely emphasized the fact. In 1947 Lees-Milne had written: "A whole social system has broken down. What will replace it beyond government by the masses, uncultivated, rancorous, savage, philistine, the enemies of all things beautiful?" Two years later, Cecil Beaton recorded Duff Cooper saying that "the life of taste, culture and refinement, as we knew it, has gone for good." These were the words of fearful people, who were at odds with the society being formed by the postwar consensus. By modern standards their views are problematic—yet one has sympathy with this much: that they regretted the passing of a world in which money had moved in step with style, taste, a reverence for artistic endeavor, a life elegantly lived: money for its own sake was not what these people worshipped.

That change was what Emerald had seen at the end of her life, and as usual her sentiments are both susceptible to ridicule and astute. Just a couple of years earlier, however, she had been out and about in the ugly new world, undaunted by age, facing down bombed-out London as if its grimness were merely a mirage—as indeed, on a night in February 1946, it was. "Oh the BALL last night was such heavenly fun," wrote Nancy Mitford to Evelyn Waugh, describing a grand occasion attended by war-wearied society in all its unearthed finery. "Chips [Channon] said to Emerald 'This is what we have been fighting for' (we?) as he surveyed the scene to which clever old Emerald replied 'Why dear, are they all Poles?'"

A few weeks previously, the joke had been on her. In mid-January, a cocktail party was held at the Tower of London, which doesn't exactly sound like the most desirable outing for a lady in her seventies, nor indeed for anybody in their right mind in the depths of winter; but, in their dogged and rather impressive way, everybody turned up and, as Nancy relayed to Waugh: "Violet T[refusis] said to me 'When I got to the Traitor's Gate I heard 2 well-known voices & it was Emerald & Daisy.' " This was rich, coming from a woman far more outlandishly treacherous than Emerald. With regard to Daisy, however, it was hard to argue: Daisy Fellowes was a tough nut. Born Marguerite Séverine Philippine Decazes de Glucksberg in 1890, she was the niece of Winnaretta de Polignac, and aged six had inherited her mother's sizable portion of the Singer fortune. She was also the heiress who, more than perhaps any other, lived as a pure and unrepentant hedonist. She frankly loved having money—was said to cross herself in gratitude if she passed a sewing machine in a shop window—and she did exactly as she pleased. No guilt, no regrets, just lots of sex and Schiaparelli.

There were others, of course, of this straightforward kind: for instance, the Paget sisters, the Honourable Dorothy and Olive, nieces of Arthur Paget, who had married the American heiress Minnie Stevens. Their father, Almeric, had also married an American, Pauline Payne Whitney. So there was a lot of money sloshing around, together with impeccable social connections; and in 1916 the sisters inherited $4 million from their mother, topping up the large chunk of money left by their great-uncle, an original investor in Standard Oil who had never married (one's favorite kind of great-uncle). From a very young age, they were beautifully set up to live just as they pleased. The paths that they took were completely different, which in itself implies that they followed their own inclinations.

Olive, born in New York City in 1899, worked as a nurse in the First World War and married three times. In 1926, she and her second husband acquired Leeds Castle in Kent, a spectacular and beautiful building, medieval in origin—former residents included Edward I and Eleanor of Castile—but largely rebuilt in the nineteenth century, with a lake, two bridges, and gardens landscaped by Capability Brown. It was also in a state of extremely poor repair. When her marriage ended in 1930, Olive kept the castle, became its chatelaine, and spent much of her inheritance on restoring it. A huge undertaking—a life's work indeed—but what work! Much praise has rightly been given to Deborah Mitford, who in 1950 became the 11th Duchess of Devonshire, and did wonders for the family's ancestral home of Chatsworth; yet Olive was there before her, sourcing designers, architects, and craftspeople, re-creating a home that was also a storybook fantasy, and even having enough money to heat it.

From the 1930s she became a "hostess," albeit not one whose own personality—as with Mrs. Greville and Lady Cunard—became the focus of events. Invitations to her weekend parties at Leeds were, naturally enough, much sought after. Guests included the political associates of her third husband, Sir Adrian Baillie, as well as the unholy alliance of the Prince of Wales, Mrs. Simpson, and Herr Von Ribbentrop; although such were Olive's fence-sitting skills that she could also command the attendance of the Yorks, the future George VI and Queen Elizabeth. Perhaps the most interesting sign of the times, and of the special brew being stirred of old and new celebrity, was the number of "stars" who visited the castle: Charlie Chaplin, Errol Flynn, Robert Taylor, Gertrude Lawrence, Douglas Fairbanks *père et fils*. (In 1936 Fairbanks senior had married an English aristocrat—Sylvia, Lady Ashley—with whom he partied at Leeds. Sylvia's rise was even more amazing than that of the illegitimate Mrs. Greville or the mysterious Maud Burke, not least because she lacked even the meanest inheritance. Born Edith Hawkes, the pretty daughter of a Luton publican, she became a chorus girl and married Lord Ashley, son of the 9th Earl of Shaftesbury. After Fairbanks she went on to acquire

three more husbands, including Clark Gable. Shape-shifting—
especially for what Jane Austen called a "woman of decision"—
was very much the order of the day; just as it had been a century
earlier, but now the loosening of society meant that a skilled
operator like Sylvia could penetrate its very heart.)

In the Second World War, Leeds Castle was used as a hospital, like many of its kind, and thereafter its social life resumed
in more decorous, mature style. Queen Elizabeth—from 1952
the Queen Mother—continued to visit, as did Jock Whitney, US
ambassador to Great Britain in the late 1950s and one of Olive's
cousins. She died in 1974; through a charitable trust her home
was left to the nation.

Her younger sister Dorothy, born in 1905, predeceased Olive
by fourteen years—worn out, perhaps, by the singular thrills of
her sui generis life. Dorothy never married. She had a female
companion, Olga, but by some measure her greatest love—upon
which she lavished her most tumultuous passions—was horse
racing. Known as the "sport of kings," it is in fact the sport of
anybody who has so much money that they can afford to chuck
most of it away; a definition that used to apply almost solely
to monarchs and aristocrats, who throughout the eighteenth
century ran racing as their private open-air playground-cum-
gentleman's club. Then, by degrees, the door opened—slightly—
to encompass the plutocrat, the banker, the sheikh, the
occasional actor and footballer. Far less frequently were horses
owned by rich women—indeed, it was only in 1918 that the
name of Lady Jane Douglas, owner of the Epsom Derby winner
Gainsborough, was permitted to appear in the racing annals.
Lillie Langtry, mistress of the future Edward VII, had used the
racing name of "Mr. Jersey." The Duchess of Montrose—a major owner in the late nineteenth century—was "Mr. Manton."
It was, indubitably, a man's world: women attended, especially

the social events of Royal Ascot and Goodwood, but only rarely were they directly involved in their own right. What changed this, more than anything, was the accession to the throne of Queen Elizabeth II, who in the year of her coronation—1953— owned the Derby second, and whose profound engagement with racing normalized the concept of female participation. Before the Queen, however, there was the Honourable Dorothy.

Both women had grown up with racing as an intrinsic part of life. The Queen's parents were enthusiasts, although not to the same devoted extent as she herself, and so too were the Whitney family. Jock owned a winner of the Cheltenham Gold Cup, as Dorothy would later do. She also won the Epsom Derby, which the Queen has never done.

In fact Dorothy Paget, by the time of her death in 1960, had owned more horses than any other woman in the history of racing, and in doing so spent some £3 million (which would now buy a single A-list yearling, but was then an astronomical sum). She was hugely successful, winning more than 1,500 races. These included four Champion Hurdles at Cheltenham and a truly astounding seven Gold Cups, five of which were won in 1932–6 by a legendary steeplechaser: Golden Miller, still the only horse to win the Gold Cup and the Grand National. Her Derby winner, Straight Deal, was a home-bred from her Irish stud farm, Ballymacoll (a highly prestigious establishment and still extant). The horse's victory came in 1943, so technically he was the winner of the Newmarket Derby—the race had been moved from Epsom for the duration. Dorothy turned up to collect her trophy in the same outfit that she wore to Aintree, Ascot, and everywhere in between, a blue tweed coat of outsize proportions. Despite having ridden and hunted in her youth, she adored confectionery and became immensely fat; fripperies such as vanity were not on her radar.

Bolstered by money and protected by social position, indifferent to convention or to changing times, Dorothy was in every sense a monumental figure, redolent of an earlier and bolder sporting age. Racing had always been a repository of eccentricity, a place where people heedless of public opinion could live without care, grappling with the only thing that eluded their command: the thoroughbred. It was to this world that she naturally belonged. She behaved very much like the Duchess of Montrose, in fact, who was born in 1818 and an owner in the demanding, capricious mode; for instance, she temporarily dismissed the vicar at her local Newmarket church because he had prayed aloud for a good harvest. He should have known, she ranted, that her St. Leger horse would only go on soft ground (that is to say, after a great deal of rain). This was very much the sort of thing that Dorothy Paget might have said and done. She fairly terrorized her trainers (she had at least seventeen) by moving her horses around on a whim; although on one occasion the biter was bit, when a Newmarket yard gave Dorothy a day's notice to remove her entire string, failing which it would be turned out on to the High Street. No doubt this particular trainer was heartily sick of being telephoned in the middle of the night, when she tended to do most of her planning and wanted to talk things through. Bookmakers kept an employee on call at all times, fearful of missing out on her latest 4 a.m. plunge: she was an epic gambler, quite ready to put £10,000 on one of her own horses. In order to keep her sweet she was allowed to place bets on races that had, in fact, taken place some hours earlier, on the previous day. The fact that she was doing so in good faith was proved by the fact that most of her selections had already lost.

But this was not about money. For people like Dorothy, the love of racing is about an emotional connection unlike any other, an intensity of feeling for the thoroughbred—that creature of supernal beauty, who is in one's possession yet can never quite be controlled—and when her horses competed she would tremble with nervous excitement inside the tweed coat. Superstitiously fearful of not reaching a racecourse on time when she had a runner, she always took two Rolls-Royces for safety's sake. When—unbelievably—both cars broke down en route to a meeting, she handed over £300 for a Baby Austin parked outside a butcher's, then went on her way with the car's owner as her passenger.

There was another, unexpected side to Dorothy Paget: she had a great care for the fate of Russian refugees. Her finishing school in Paris had been founded by two such, one of whom—a princess straight out of Tolstoy—was the aunt of Dorothy's partner, Olga. With the help of the princess, Dorothy financed a large old people's home for *émigrés* within a chateau south of Paris, as well as a plot within the graveyard of Sainte-Geneviève-des-Bois, now known as the Russian Cemetery. Among those buried in its grounds is Rudolf Nureyev.

* * *

Daisy Fellowes did not go in even for minor acts of philanthropy, although like most of her class she sat on a few charity committees. In a profound sense, however, she was an heiress of the Dorothy kind: blessed with an uncomplicated desire to enjoy her money.

The blue tweed coat, though . . . Daisy would have died before ever contemplating such a garment. Her *chic* was a thing to behold. Having favored Chanel, in the 1930s she became a muse to Elsa Schiaparelli: "shocking pink" was conceived for Daisy—she wore, for instance, a black suit with a motif of pink lips—and with extreme panache she carried off the famous Surrealist "shoe hat" shaped like a stiletto. In general, her style was sleek and bitingly simple, with a razor edge of subversion: black to a wedding, red to a funeral. She could afford to keep things plain. Her jewelry collection was said to be the finest outside the Crown Jewels, and photographs do indeed show items that were utterly dazzling, for instance a diamond parure consisting of heavy neck collar, two exquisite winged clips for each lapel, and—very twenty-first century—a delicate little ear cuff. An immense necklace from Cartier in Christmas tree colors—emerald, ruby, and sapphire— was sold for more than one and a half million pounds in 1991, then a world record for art deco jewelry. In 1939 a cache worth £30,000 was stolen from her house at Neuilly, but this was almost an irrelevance—there was plenty more where that came from.

Daisy could also keep it simple because she had a body worth revealing. She received friends while having her bath, wearing a specially made cellophane cape. Almost a century before such *régimes* became the rage, she was following a diet that comprised elements of keto and intermittent fasting (also a dash of Keith Richards c. 1971): grouse, cocktails with a slug of Benzedrine, and morphine. Later she took to cocaine, which is renowned for its slimming properties, and to which—according to Evelyn Waugh— she introduced Lord Berners. Of course she was not alone in taking drugs. Before her marriage Diana Cooper, then Manners, took chloroform ("jolly old chlorers") and lay "in ecstatic stillness" after injecting herself with morphine. Coke, or "naughty salt," was frequently taken at dinner parties. However, Daisy was unusually dedicated in her usage, which continued into her fifties at least.

Aged about twenty she had a reasonably successful nose job, without anesthetic, and in later life had four facelifts, or so it was alleged by Truman Capote: "the Doctors say no more." None of this made her conventionally beautiful. But my goodness she had style, together with a kind of fierce energy that blazed away at life as if it were there to be conquered and laid waste. She had, said US *Vogue* editor Diana Vreeland, "the elegance of the damned."

She also, according to Nancy Mitford, had a "terrible cleverness." In fact her intelligence was probably the unexpected key to her character, which always had an element of the self-aware. "You are sitting next to the siren," she said to James Lees-Milne, at a dinner in 1946: both true and a knowing little joke. She was not clever in the manner of Nancy, whose lightly worn learning was surprisingly thorough. Daisy's lover, the literary Duff Cooper, was dismayed when she asserted that Flaubert had written *The Charterhouse of Parma* (imagine Emerald's horror). But she had the shallow flashing brilliance of one of her jewels. Although she could have spent every day of her life in the bath or in bed, idling about until it was time to display the couture, her agile mind would not permit this. She was Paris editor of *Harper's Bazaar* and wrote poetry, plus a couple of witty little novels, notably *Les Dimanches de la Comtesse de Narbonne*, which in 1960 was published in Britain as *Sundays, a Fantasy*. "That old Daisy has written a nouvelle which isn't bad at all in a sort of Firbank way," was Nancy's judgment.

Nancy, who had none of Daisy's rapacity—she was immensely clean-living, and preferred the serenity of Dior to the snap of Schiap—nevertheless got on with her. She appreciated the wicked humor: Daisy's nickname for the eager-to-please British ambassadress in Paris, Lady Harvey,* was "Tout

---

* In 1947 the Harveys, Maud and Sir Oliver, succeeded the glittering Coopers—Lady Diana and Duff—at the British Embassy in Paris, which had been a home from home for the beau monde after the war. Theirs was not an easy gig, and Nancy Mitford's initial reaction was to write to Evelyn Waugh that "the Harveys are utter ghastly drear personified," although later she changed this opinion. Her last novel, *Don't Tell Alfred* (1960), was a fictionalized version of the *régime* change: Diana became the beautiful Lady Leone, who camped out at the Embassy and set up an alternative social court (in reality the Coopers moved to nearby Chantilly, less intrusive but still a little too close for the Harveys' comfort).

Simplement Délicieuse," which is very Mitford. In 1954, however, Nancy relayed to Evelyn Waugh what sounds like a typical series of events. "Just to say I'm off on a yacht," she wrote cheerily in August, having been invited by Daisy on a short cruise. (Daisy had two yachts—"the big and the dinky," as Harpo Marx described them—and, in a touch still more revealing of her wealth, their itinerary was embroidered upon seat cushions). A month later Nancy was back, her tone a little less joyful, having been "chucked . . . off the boat at a moment's notice" in order to make way for Daisy's boyfriend, Lord Sherwood.

This was the man known as "H. L.": hated lover. Another Mitfordian nickname, although Daisy would have meant it. By the time of the cruise she was sixty-four, so H. L. may have had less competition than hitherto, but one of the glories of Daisy is that she was untrammeled by that kind of convention. Again like Nancy, who talked frequently about the bliss of being middle-aged, she was free in a way that we struggle now to be, such is the obsession with youth; had a woman like Daisy been asked about "aging" (as a journalist surely would today) she would have jangled her jewelry and laughed the question to scorn. She was *herself*. How was that not enough? Unlike Emerald she did not ape the image of her youth but simply strode on, armored with confidence. At the age of sixty, as a guest at the "party of the century"—held in Venice at the Palazzo Labia, owned by Charlie Beistegui—she was dressed as the "Reine d'Afrique" with swathes of leopard skin across a stark ballgown (Diana Cooper went as Cleopatra, and used Cecil Beaton's photograph of herself thus costumed for her passport). In 1957, again from Venice, Nancy Mitford wrote that Daisy had become engaged in a truly ludicrous squabble with Lady Marriott, known as Momo, an heiress of similar vintage. "A dinner given by Momo and sabotaged by Daisy . . . Momo riposted by stealing Daisy's hair appointment and trying to steal her evening coat. As they are all too old for love now it's the best they can do I suppose."[14] Nancy, whose long-term affair with Gaston Palewski had just come to a semi-ending, may have been speaking for herself here. There is no reason to believe that Daisy thought herself too old for anything, let alone love.

Her sex life, eventful in the extreme, was also a defiance of convention for which a woman would—in some quarters—be judged even today. Jennie Jerome and Daisy Warwick had been similarly active, but *this* Daisy was so performative about it; one would say that she was attention-seeking, as when she commanded a man to prove his love for her by jumping into a swimming pool drained of water, except that again such behavior—including its ironic nod to her own reputation—seems to have been entirely natural. She would assuredly not have cared that Harold Acton described her as "a female dictator of untouchable severity."

From the age of six she and her brother Louis had been in the care of their aunt, Winnaretta de Polignac. Their mother, Isabelle-Blanche Singer, who had married the 3rd Duc Decazes de Glücksberg, had killed herself in 1896; a grim circumstance echoed in the life of Barbara Hutton, whose mother, Edna, was found dead, apparently from suicide, when Barbara was aged four. So Daisy was raised in that supremely artistic, worldly, luxurious Paris household, and before too long she would have seen that Winnaretta, whose own upbringing had been a somewhat remote business, had a ruthless streak in her love affairs. Daisy may also have inferred that this did her aunt no harm, and that playing the victim was for losers.

She married her first husband Jean, Prince de Broglie, in 1910. There were three daughters, although (what a surprise) she later casually admitted that the youngest was not Jean's. In fact, the actual quotation went thus: "The eldest, Emmeline [born 1911] is like my first husband only a great deal more masculine; the second, Isabelle [born 1912], is like me without guts; the third, Jacqueline [born 1918], was the result of a horrible man called Lischmann."[15] Although she was playing to the gallery, her non-maternal aspect is confirmed by the story of how, walking one day in Hyde Park, Daisy saw three exquisitely dressed little girls and exclaimed to their nanny: "Oh what heavenly children, whose are they?" to which the reply came: "Yours." This may be a bit too good to be true, although those who heard the story found it perfectly credible.

Also implied within the above quotation is the fact of the Prince de Broglie's homosexuality. He died in 1918 while serving with the French Army in Algeria, officially of influenza, although it has been suggested that he committed suicide after his proclivities had been revealed; there was another story (with Daisy there are hundreds) that she had found him in flagrante with the chauffeur. So widespread, and so accepted, was homosexuality within high society, it is easy to forget that it could carry a stigma outside that charmed circle. In France, where it was not illegal, it might still be viewed as immoral. In Britain it was not decriminalized until 1967, which goes a long way to explaining why a number of homosexuals sought to form relationships with women, although there were other factors. In the case of a complex man like James Lees-Milne—who, as well as being in love with Nancy Mitford's brother Tom, was crazy about her sister Diana—there was a profound connection with his wife, Alvilde. With other men there would have been a straightforward desire for children, perhaps specifically an heir (or even an heiress); presumably this was the case with de Broglie, although Daisy's money would have been a still greater consideration. Why Daisy married him is more mysterious. She was already the daughter of a French duke, although the de Broglie name was more prestigious, and gave her children the title of Princess. Perhaps, too, she thought that he would be no trouble.

Her lofty position in the *haute bohème* gave her an entry into British society, but now she sought to establish herself at its heart. She was said to have set her cap at the 15th Earl of Pembroke, with whom she had a brief fling; he got cold feet and was challenged to a duel—on the grounds of breach of promise—by Daisy's brother, now the 5th Duc Decazes and apparently still living in the eighteenth century. So in 1919 she married instead a former squeeze of Consuelo Vanderbilt, the Honourable Reginald Fellowes, with whom she had a fourth daughter, Rosamond, in 1921. Reggie seems to have been an amiable sort, but he was another unlikely match for this turbocharged woman (and again may have been chosen on that very account). In the parlance of the time, he was a bit of a dud. He was interned throughout the First World War, trapped by accident in Germany, where he had been accompanying his father on a health cure; then came the collapse of the venerable old stockbroking firm in which he was a partner, leading to huge liabilities and a declaration of bankruptcy. Reggie had behaved like a dimwit rather than a crook, although the Official Receiver ruled that he was "not wholly without responsibility." How fortunate, therefore, that despite her extramarital liaisons he was not wholly without Daisy. The social pages of *The Times* recorded in 1924 that the newly bankrupt Reggie was in the South of France, then Monte Carlo, with his millionaire wife; what Daisy must have thought about it all, who knows, but essentially she had gotten what she wanted. The couple stayed together until Reggie's death in 1953. Daisy attended Court at Buckingham Palace, and presented her debutante daughter, Rosamond. She was on hand for receptions at the French Embassy, in honor of figures such as Paul Valéry and, later, Nabokov. She was one of the select band of women costumed and photographed at the highly publicized·"Olympian Ball" in 1935, where Diana Mosley—then Guinness—appeared as the figure of Venus and Daisy as Justice, plus chariot.

She was, in sum, an integral member of society in both Britain and France. A leader, one might say. She knew all the usual suspects: Beaton, Waugh, Maugham, Barbara Hutton, the Aga Khan and his Begum and, of course, the Prince of Wales and Mrs. Simpson, who cruised with her on the "big" yacht in 1935. She had a chateau at Neuilly, with a garden full of statues by Cocteau, where she threw splendid parties such as the costume ball for Elsa Maxwell's birthday, at which everybody had to come as "somebody else" (Daisy dressed as a cloakroom attendant). She also owned a villa at Cap Martin on the Côte d'Azur, so lavish that the walls of the boathouse were covered in Tiepolos, and in London she favored hotels: Claridge's and the Dorchester. She was said to move around a lot in order to avoid taxes on the vast Singer income. Aunt Winnaretta had done much the same thing.

After the Second World War she acquired a flat in Belgravia, an apartment in Tangier—which became very fashionable—and a fabulous country estate, Donnington Grove near Newbury, formerly the home of Beau Brummell. She bought it on the advice of that man of wealth and taste, Lord Berners, the first night of whose droll ballet composition, *A Wedding Bouquet*, she had attended with Winnaretta in 1937. As Diana Mosley recounted, Berners adored Daisy—her highly constructed appearance, her "malicious remarks made in silky tones"—and, although entirely gay, he "became so devoted to her that I sometimes thought he almost resented the presence of her lover, Hugh Sherwood." Daisy and Berners were two of a kind. When she told him that

Evelyn Waugh prayed for her every day, he replied: "God doesn't pay any attention to Evelyn."

Waugh, who had scolded Nancy Mitford over her adulterous affair with Gaston Palewski, must have had his hands full with Daisy (although one is reminded just a little of William Gladstone, consorting with prostitutes in order to save them). On the front of the house at Donnington she placed a statue of St. Joseph, whom with her saving self-mockery she called "the patron saint of cuckolds."

Unlike the similarly libidinous Peggy Guggenheim, who out of straightforward desire slept with most of the artists whose work she promoted, Daisy did not necessarily go for sexy men. Power over the powerful seems to have been more her thing. For instance she made a play for Winston Churchill (a cousin of Reggie's), recalled by his private secretary Jock Colville: "She was a wicked but attractive woman who, according to Mrs. Churchill, tried to seduce her husband shortly after their marriage. It was unsuccessful and she was forgiven, even by Clementine." There was a decadence in Daisy, for sure; as with the story of how she and a lover followed poor old Reggie to a brothel in Monte Carlo and watched him at play through a window. Again, is it true? But again, if not, it was the kind of thing that people felt able to invent about her, knowing full well that they would be believed.

In late 1919 she began a long-term affair with Duff Cooper— another plain-looking politician, although very much an *homme aux femmes*. One senses that his wife, Diana, was not terribly interested in sex. Her great gift was for friendship, which she often extended to Duff's mistresses; like the Churchills, however, she and Duff had only just married when this particular liaison began. Equally recent was the wedding of Daisy and Reggie. Small wonder Diana described Daisy as "the very picture of fashionable depravity." Duff recalled how opium lowered her inhibitions to absolute zero. At Deauville in the summer of 1921, the intoxicated man would spend every afternoon with his mistress, and one evening abandoned Diana at the casino and went back for more; Diana, who surely knew exactly what was going on, nevertheless affected to believe that Duff had been murdered and called the police. It was a good, but pointless, revenge—the affair continued and so did the marriage. Diana was simply too grand and large-spirited to bear grudges, although her forgiving nature was poorly rewarded. During the Second World War, when she was running her farm in Sussex, Duff installed Daisy at a house in Chapel Street left to Diana by her mother. After the war Daisy returned to Paris and devastated Duff's "official" mistress with her presence; the beautiful, incandescent Diana found herself in the bonkers position of consoling one of her husband's girlfriends about whether he might prefer the other.

But that was Daisy: able to create trouble, and more than happy to do so.

She was, in her own words, always "on the scent." The language in which she described conquest was that of violence, transgression. "It's a thrilling feeling, like tasting absinthe for the first time. Soon the man asks: 'When may I come to tea?' — that's when I sharpen the knife." One senses her excitement, her desire to exercise the power of sex backed by that of money; she was a force of nature, glamorized by every artifice that a twentieth-century fortune could buy. "I felt mesmerized like a rabbit by a stoat," wrote James Lees-Milne in 1947, when face to face with her over dinner. The young Claus von Bulow, no less, years later acquitted of murdering his American heiress wife,*

* Claus von Bulow married Martha "Sunny" Crawford—who inherited a reported $100 million at the age of three—in 1966. In December 1979 (by which time the marriage was generally perceived to have run its

had the same reaction. He had been invited to a "party" and wrote that he felt like "a rabbit with a rattlesnake" when he turned up and discovered that he was the solitary guest. What transpired is unknown. What is certain is that with regard to men, as was said of Peggy Guggenheim, "they came to grief, not she."[16] She had no interest, none at all, in vulnerability.

How very fascinating it would have been to put this woman in the path of one of those earlier, predatory heiress-catchers—a William Pole or an Andrew Stoney—and see how they all fared. One feels that she would have chucked their cruelty and their sex-weaponry back in their faces; that she would have stuck a knife into them if they had tried their tricks and dazzled a judge into directing her acquittal; in her own era she would have done those things, for sure. But in theirs? Who knows how much would have been different, in an age when passivity was the default female position, and an inheritance the paradoxical means to render a woman still more powerless. The law decreed it so; the law that was made by and for men; only when the law changed were women able to keep their money and shape their fate.

We know all this. We know that not until the early twentieth century—when the slim ghost of feminism began to hover and

---

course) Sunny was found unresponsive at the family home in Newport. She recovered and was diagnosed as hypoglycemic. In April 1980 she was admitted to hospital again, confused and disorientated. On December 21 that year, she was found unconscious, with a brain injury so severe as to lead her to fall into a persistent vegetative state. In 1982 von Bulow, who was accused of causing this injury by injecting his wife with insulin, was convicted of attempted murder. At a second trial he was cleared. He had a crack legal team led by Alan Dershowitz; Truman Capote, among others, testified as to Sunny's excessive drug use; nevertheless, her two children by her first husband remained convinced of von Bulow's guilt. Sunny died in 2008, aged seventy-six, having never regained consciousness., persist, when the First World War performed its brutal purgative changes, when the interwar years danced before they darkened— were heiresses able to live with the freedom of Natalie Barney, Dorothy Paget, and Daisy Fellowes; able to enjoy their equal and unequal rights.

So was it just about the times, and those giant social and political shifts? Or would these people always have been, essentially, who they were? Was the folly of a Catherine Tylney— marrying a gorgeous monster when she could have had a safe, fat husband and become Queen of England—of its time, or for all time? Would the determination of a Winnaretta Singer have managed, in any era, to create a life of her choosing? It is a big question. It would have interested Natalie, bored Dorothy to death, and given Daisy the opportunity for a bon mot, delivered crisply, before moving on. She had things to do, drawing rooms to conquer, money to spend.

* * *

Yet one could, as in a fiction, shift the viewpoint on Daisy Fellowes's story, and tell it thus.

Marguerite Séverine Philippine Decazes de Glücksberg, who was born beneath the weight of a surfeit of names, from the age of six acquired a new burden: the millions inherited from a mother who had killed herself. The father, a cold aristocrat, gave Marguerite away to an aunt who was entirely absorbed in her own life, spending money for her greater glory and conducting as many love affairs as possible. The huge Paris mansion formed a strange, loveless environment for Marguerite—known as Daisy—and her brother. Her innate sense of insecurity was compounded when her father told her that she was ugly. As soon as she could, she embarked upon a series of cosmetic procedures;

these became a lifelong obsession, as was the pursuit of extreme thinness that led her to become a habitual drug user.

Her first husband was a homosexual, rumored to have committed suicide. Thereupon Daisy sought sanctuary, or perhaps oblivion, in sexual encounters: she became addicted to that particular buzz, just as she was to morphine and cocaine, and was heedless of the havoc that she created and the marriages that she damaged. All that mattered was the shot of pleasure that alleviated her pain. In the same way she acquired clothes, jewels, properties, yachts, dodging the tax man as much as she could by living constantly on the move, a woman haunted by the past and seeking escape.

Her second husband was a feckless fool, who embarrassed her by being made a bankrupt, although she had long since betrayed him with the politician Duff Cooper (and others). But he had given her a position in London society, where she mingled with the privileged, dressed to shock and impress, filled her days in an attempt to alleviate the void in her heart. She was amusing but her jokes had a vein of ice, and she could be cruel. When company was gathered together on her yacht—effectively trapped at sea—she would pick one of its members to bully and tyrannize. It was as though she were afraid of kindness, the smothered emotions that it might uncover, whose force would shatter the brittle unreality of her life.

She spent much of the Second World War holed up in London, waiting for visits from Cooper, who was then minister of information in the War Cabinet. Did she enjoy this situation? How did she feel about it afterward, when she learned of what had been happening in France? Two of her four daughters were accused of collaboration. Emmeline, wife of the Comte de Castéja, spent five months in Fresnes prison, sharing a cell with four prostitutes. The reason for her incarceration was not entirely clear. One account states, straightforwardly, that she had had an affair with a German officer; yet in 1946, James Lees-Milne wrote in his diary that she had "just left a French prison for having betrayed her girlfriend to the Gestapo during the war."

The fate of Jacqueline, the other daughter, was to have her head publicly shaved. Her story, too, is slightly mysterious. It would seem that she had been working for the French Resistance, as had her husband—the Austro-Hungarian Alfred Kraus, whom she married in 1941. Apparently unbeknown to her, Kraus was engaged upon counterespionage and giving information to the Abwehr. To save his wife, who was in the sights of the Germans, he betrayed some of her fellow Resistance members.

Therefore Jacqueline—unlike Emmeline—was a victim of grave injustice, whose "Princess" title may have triggered the spirit of vengefulness that infected the newly liberated Paris. If, that is, she was genuinely unaware of what her husband was doing; although an odd fact is that she remained married to Kraus until 1958.

For Daisy, meanwhile, there must have been an intensity of shame. Ever in denial, she trampled it down. She returned to Paris, where in her magnificent *hôtel particulier* on the Rue de Lille she achieved such a perfection of décor, it was as though the war had never happened. There was "not a frill out of place," a guest recalled, "gleaming, rich—no bibelots missing, carpets, cushions on the chairs and all the candles lighted on the stairs." Duff Cooper was now British ambassador in France, and his wife Diana invited the charmless Emmeline to the Embassy ("I hope I never go to prison with her," she wrote). That magnanimous gesture surely only increased Daisy's sense of guilt: about the war, the Coopers, her failures as a mother.

Yet how could she ever have made a good parent, given her own upbringing, which had left those great holes inside her heart? And what, as she approached the age of sixty, could she now do about any of it? The only course was to press on with more parties, more lovers, more dress fittings, to become an aging Agatha Runcible—the desperate, thrill-chasing socialite in Evelyn Waugh's *Vile Bodies*—who did not know how to stop the merry-go-round.

Daisy had cared little for her husband Reggie, but after his death in 1953 she was cut adrift. Her sole child from their marriage, Rosamond, led a thankfully normal life. However, her other daughter—Princess Isabelle, a historian and essayist—died in 1960 at the age of just forty-eight. For the seventy-year-old Daisy, this must have been the worst blow of all. What had it all been for: the delirious highs, the delights of conquest, the thrill of the wisecrack, the gleaming soirées at which she had disdained the competition in her jaw-dropping outfits? How much happier might she have been, with less of what she had had—and more of what mattered? What had her life been, except an expense of spirit in a waste of shame?

And an expense, full stop. She died in 1962 in Paris, her heart weakened by grief and hedonism, and from the Singer millions just £77,712 remained.

* * *

Gruesome, yes. But revealing, because that florid little passage is both true and not true. Daisy's life *can* be interpreted in that light, as if her every action had a hidden meaning. The point is whether she herself saw it that way, to which the answer is: No. That was simply not her attitude, and in the end that is what counts. She was superficial but she was strong, and sadness or shame—which she must have experienced—were allowed no power over her. She called off those hellhounds and sent them slinking away.

"Her gaiety is infectious," wrote James Lees-Milne in 1946, when she thumbed her nose at the aftermath of war in a style that only money could buy, by taking a party of people to the Savoy in her Rolls-Royce: "It has a glass roof." Her inheritance enabled her to gratify huge appetites, but fundamentally she was always their mistress. Like Diana Mosley, she would have said at the end: I've had a fantastic life.[17]

Yet one can, as has been shown, reinvent her story in such a way as to render that life a sad and empty business. Certainly it would be easy to do so today, when we tend to see every quirk of character as pathological—requiring to be pressed into shape by the steam iron of therapy—and redefine the old mantra of "keeping up appearances" as "being in denial" (*The Crown*—the Netflix extravaganza about the lives of the British royal family—gains much of its force from applying modern behavioral standards to people who, through choice, showed emotion only to their dogs and horses). The people themselves saw it differently. Diana Cooper, for instance, probably did not like the fact that her husband was unfaithful—pathologically so, indeed—but her splendid shrugging acceptance was both an act and a reality; the two were not divisible. Do you want to go home, she was asked by Emerald Cunard, when Duff was preparing to move in on some new woman at a party. "Why?" said Diana. "He's not bored yet, is he?" That was the style, when one's life was also one's social life.

There is, of course, a logical corollary to this. Given that the wicked and wonderful Daisy Fellowes can, with a shift of perspective, be viewed as a tragedy queen, might one not do the reverse with a woman like Barbara Hutton, that textbook poor little rich girl? Have we—the prurient onlookers, with heads full of tropes about the victim-heiresses of fiction—in fact written her story as a slow decline into misery, in order to gratify ourselves that money really does not bring happiness? By the time Barbara had reached adulthood, rich women had been liberated to become painters, poets, Derby winners, and sexual conquistadors. Why, then, would they retreat into the helplessness of their earlier incarnation?

Because—in answer to that earlier question—it was not just about the times. It was also, and always, about people. The twentieth-century heiress was freer than any class of woman in history; but freedom is not always such an easy thing to handle.

PART IV

UNPROTECTED, REVISITED

"Somehow there was nothing to surprise or delight."

From the 1961 diary of Cecil Beaton, describing a ball
at Barbara Hutton's palace in Tangier

ALICE

TAKE, FOR INSTANCE, the story of Alice Silverthorne, born in 1899 in Buffalo, New York, to a timber millionaire and a Chicago socialite. Her life, like Barbara Hutton's, had many parallels with that of Daisy Fellowes, which makes the differences all the more striking and interesting.

Alice was a beautiful heiress. It is a retrograde description, but a century ago there was—like it or not—no better thing for a woman to be, and Alice was perhaps the most beautiful of them all. With heiresses, beauty is easily confused with the lush gleam of money. Alice's physical allure—which can be judged not just by photographs, but by the effect that she created—was of a special order: lit by personality, shadowed with complexity. With her soft, widely spaced features, smooth dark hair, and slight body, she had an air of demureness, like an off-duty member of the Ballets Russes; yet the look in her eyes was that of a wild girl, and wild was what she was. A photograph shows her seated with a hand casually cradling a Masai lion cub, too large for his position on her lap, his tail falling to the ground like a thick rope. This was Samson. Alice loved him with the peculiar passion—both troubling and comfortable—that one feels for a soulmate.

Her intensely feminine *chic* was very much of its time, but she has an entirely contemporary aspect. A woman of today would want to look like her. And, although her appearance was conventional, it was clear that the person inside it was not: her fabulous eyes slanted away from the world into which she was born. She craved freedom, just as Samson had surely done, but this went extremely badly for her. She harbored an equally fervent life force and death wish—a kind of despairing vitality. Today, one would surely explain it in terms of mental illness, but that was not the language of the time.

Her upbringing—like that of both Daisy and Barbara—was problematic. The Silverthorne marriage exemplified that familiar American tug between old and new money: Alice's father, although descended from early settlers, was regarded as *nouveau* by his mother-in-law, who was a member of the Armour family and thus, effectively, Chicago aristocracy. William Silverthorne was also a ladies' man, much like Barbara's father, Franklin Hutton, whose relentless infidelities may have led his wife to kill herself. Juliabelle Silverthorne, fragile in health, was similarly unhappy in her marriage. It has been said[1]—although there must be an element of speculation—that in 1906, after an almighty showdown with her husband, he locked her out of the house all night in the middle of winter. Juliabelle contracted vascular laryngitis, died six months later at the age of thirty-five, and was instantly embalmed and buried. The sequence of events is highly suggestive of neglect, but inconclusive; Alice, meanwhile, became the heiress to a large fortune placed in trust.

Her father remarried almost immediately, back into the Armour clan: Juliabelle's belief that he had been having an affair with her cousin was completely justified. He did not, however, shunt his daughter to one side, as the Duc Decazes had so readily done. Instead, he and his new wife took Alice on their honeymoon and a couple of years later, when Alice was twelve, she and William sailed to Europe on their own. Imperfect as he undoubtedly was, William was the center of his daughter's life. In 1913, however, a New York court ruled that Alice should be removed from his custody and given into the guardianship of the Armours.

One's thoughts fly naturally to the possibility of inappropriate behavior, although the Armours' motivation was at least as likely to have been financial—*their* suspicion was that William had been nibbling at Alice's trust fund. The journey to Europe, taken while William's second wife was pregnant, was perhaps ill-advised, and working back from the evidence of Alice's troubled maturity it is easy to locate the problem in childhood. Of sexual abuse, however, there is no evidence at all. The fact is that these things were almost always, and only, about money.

In its less newsworthy way, the Silverthorne hearing was a precursor to the lurid 1934 court case in which the Vanderbilt family fought for custody of ten-year-old "little Gloria,"* whose mother had married into their, by then, quasi-regal clan. She too was called Gloria, and was one of the "magnificent Morgans," twins born in 1904, who as young women went on the gorgeous prowl for rich husbands. Thelma married Viscount Furness,

---

* Gloria Vanderbilt, whose childhood was steeped in the sad tropes of the poor little rich girl, and whose later life was by no means free of them—she had grave financial problems; she married four times; one of her four sons died in a possible act of suicide—nevertheless made herself into a modern phenomenon: the worker-heiress. She was a model, actor, and artist who, in the 1970s, licensed her name and developed a fashion brand, whose most renowned and pioneering product was an early example of designer jeans. The Vanderbilt name was embroidered on a back pocket. Her great-great-grandfather Cornelius would have been proud of her, although she lacked his fearsome business instincts. The mother of CNN's Anderson Cooper and, it is sometimes claimed, the model for Holly Golightly in Truman Capote's *Breakfast at Tiffany's*, she died in 2019, leaving a mere fraction of what had been in that coveted trust fund.

lived in Britain, and became a long-term mistress of the Prince of Wales; indeed it was Thelma who took a six-week trip to America in 1934, leaving "the little man" (as she described him) in what she believed to be the harmless hands of Wallis Simpson. Gloria married Reggie Vanderbilt, twenty-four years her senior, divorced with a child and cast in the oh-so familiar dashing but louche mold. His sister Gertrude, who had married a Whitney, was aunt-by-marriage to the Paget heiresses: what a world this was! And it was Gertrude who played the assassin's role against Gloria senior at the custody trial, saying—as the Armours had done about William Silverthorne—that she was an unfit parent to her ten-year-old daughter.

An additional factor, and of huge significance for all such families, was the 1932 kidnap and murder of the son of aviator Charles Lindbergh. Indeed Barbara Hutton's son Lance, born in 1936, was targeted—luckily by an idiotic amateur—when he was two weeks old. It was entirely reasonable to say that "little Gloria" needed protection, not least as she was tormented by nightmares about the Lindbergh baby (possibly encouraged in this by a deranged nurse). And, for sure, Gloria senior was not going to win prizes for hands-on motherhood—she was a beautiful woman who liked visiting Europe and enjoying herself— although the truth is that it was quite normal in that world to have a child, arguably far too young, and foist it onto somebody else. Daisy Fellowes had done exactly that. So too would Alice. Both had grown up without mothers, as did Barbara Hutton, while Gloria senior's mother would testify against her in the custody case. Thus the lovelessness, the lack of that maternal anchor, perpetuated itself, and for some the fallout was lifelong.

What was particularly unkind, perhaps, was to be placed at the center of a familial civil war, with oneself cast in the role of spoils; as happened to Alice, but far more so to the young

Gloria, whose early years were described as "Snow White sur-rounded by some quite sinister beauty queens and a platoon of dwarf-like lawyers."[2] In familiar heiress fashion, little Gloria was wanted, primarily, not for herself but for her money. At the heart of the Vanderbilt case was a trust fund. Reggie had died insolvent in 1925, when his wife was just twenty, but millions remained locked away for his two daughters; Gloria senior had to ask for living expenses to be paid out of this fund. Given the might of what was assembled against her in court, she never stood a chance.

No more did William Silverthorne. Yet Alice had adored her father, who would not even be invited to her wedding, and the abrupt severance of the relationship was deeply damaging; as, more insidiously, was the Armour insistence upon her prepara-tion for entrée into the world of the social elite. Alice was sent to Mount Vernon seminary in Washington, DC, and given a wartime debutante ball. It was like taking Samson the lion cub to Henley Regatta. Instead of falling into the seemly embrace of a blue blood straight out of early F. Scott Fitzgerald, she be-gan going about with a mobster—a type in which Chicago then abounded—who escorted her to nightclubs, where he knew all about how to circumvent those pesky Prohibition laws, and took her closer to life's gleaming razor edge. It is by no means un-known, this posh-girl fascination with low life, and often it is just a phase. With Alice, it was more like a sign.

* * *

In 1921 she went to Paris and, before she could tumble headlong into the Jazz Age, she did the "right thing." She got married. Like all those rich American girls had done before her (and like Bar-bara Hutton would later do, repeatedly), she married a European aristocrat, Comte Frédéric de Janzé: courteous, Cambridge-educated, excellent on paper. Although his family was keen on the Silverthorne money, Frédéric fell madly in love with Alice herself. "The dark red lips nearly maroon," he wrote in 1928, in a fictionalized recollection of his wife, "the wavy shingled hair—a marvellous work of nature, a more marvellous work of art." His passion for poetry may have led him to see her through a literary haze; if it is dangerous for susceptible young girls to read too much Byron, then the same applies to romantic young men and Baudelaire. He described Alice with a besotted bafflement reminiscent of another man—a contemporary named Jean Lenglet—who wrote a novel about life in Paris with his wife, the novelist Jean Rhys. Alice resembled Jean Rhys, both physically and in her urge to self-destruction. What blighted Jean's life was the lack of money. What saved it was her superb writer's gift. Alice, who had an imagination but no creative outlet, could do nothing but spend money, and try to follow the rules of a society that she did not value.

Almost certainly, she had no particular interest in Frédéric de Janzé. She fell almost immediately pregnant, with the first of two daughters, and grappled with her new relations, with whom she shared the ancestral chateau in Normandy. Even Nancy Mitford, the love of whose life was France, found the *gratin*—as opposed to the *haute bohème*—sticky: the opening scene in *Love in a Cold Climate*, when the guests at a dinner party gamely bowl conversational balls toward a fabulously unreceptive old duchess, was surely written from the heart. Moreover Alice—who was *bohème* through and through, and should really have been living as the honorary heterosexual alongside Natalie, Romaine and co.; not least because she still had a strong American accent—also had to contend with a representative from the British aristocracy. Her new sister-in-law Phyllis was an earl's granddaughter, extremely well connected within British society, a friend of Nancy Mitford, Evelyn Waugh, Diana Cooper—the usual. In fact Phyllis was quite capable of going to a nightclub with a mobster, and had been one of the women followed by the detectives employed by Gladys Marlborough when she sought evidence of the duke's adultery. Like all her class, however, Phyllis carried off such behavior with a confidence so impregnable that scandal simply bounced off it: no shame penetrated.

These were the kind of people with whom an heiress inevitably found herself associating. Her money decreed it. Barbara Hutton was a fixture of high society—as if there were no alternative worth considering—and Daisy would not have dreamed of considering an alternative. Alice, however, was part of a world into which she did not actually belong, and by which she was bored to the point of rage. Therein lies a paradox: the heiress always has the means to buy escape, but for that very reason she never quite escapes.

Yet the illusion that she might do so came in 1925, when she traveled to Kenya for the first time with Frédéric. She was disorientated and transfixed by the place—the deep shadows cut by the blinding sun, the absolute darkness of the night sky, the proximity of the majestic animals—and above all, perhaps, by the belief that here was freedom.

Of course Kenya at that time was full of European settlers, what Evelyn Waugh described as "English squires on the Equator"; on the one hand was the alien glory of a giraffe, on the other a club serving Brown Windsor soup and vast amounts of alcohol. "Everyone drank about ten pink gins before lunch," Waugh recorded in his diary during a visit to Kenya in 1931. There was also—as in artistic Paris—a colony within a colony, what was known as the Happy Valley set, about whose delinquency so much has been written. The set was led by the lethally attractive Josslyn Hay, who in 1928 would become the 22nd Earl of Erroll, and his wife Lady Idina, who like Daisy Fellowes had the habit of receiving guests in her bath. Daisy would have fitted in just fine, in fact, although her lust for life (rather than mere lust) was not quite Happy Valley. These people were decadent in a bone-deep way. They were the same kind of socialites as would be found in London; yet somehow they were not quite the same, because the world in which they operated was different. It was their creation, it was all that there was, and within those giant open spaces it had a strange, unhealthy exclusivity. The usual rules were observed—people dressed for dinner, went horse racing, had parties at the Muthaiga Country Club in Nairobi—yet there was an underlying sense of what-the-hell, anything goes. In Europe there was a constant sexual merry-go-round but in Kenya, where the focus of attention was so narrow, the incestuous nature of these liaisons was intensified. It was not that the settlers were necessarily idle. Like their leader Lord Delamere, who had been in the country since 1901, they farmed thousands of acres, had an exhilarating outdoors existence (which all too often included the ghastly practice of big game hunting), and held administrative posts. But they had none of the usual things to think about, the distractions of "real" life whose banality can be a salvation. What they had was pleasure, and—to prevent it from becoming pleasureless—a hunger for novelty.

Into this cruel, beautiful, and beguiling world came Alice, and very soon she began an affair with Joss Erroll that would continue, on and off, until his murder in 1941.

In the fifteen intervening years, her life became a succession of dramatic, appalling and, on the face of it, completely unnecessary events. Her marriage, which like so many had been contracted for no good reason, was ending from the moment that the de Janzés arrived in Kenya, although the couple's shared love of animals kept them together for a while: Frédéric also adored Samson, whom he had rescued when the cub's mother was shot by a visiting maharajah. They fed and nurtured the young lion—at this point there were also a monkey, two dogs, and a baboon—while their children, Nolwen and Paola, remained in France in the care of their de Janzé relations. Alice was determined to stay in Kenya, which she now identified with happiness, and she had the means to do as she pleased. She bought Wanjohi farm in the highlands, plus its 600 acres, with Frédéric helping to broker the deal.

He was a *mari complaisant*, powerless in the face of Alice's complex attraction. Childlike for all her sophistication, she had almost no maternal instinct (it has been suggested that she suffered from postnatal depression, although she may simply have been overwhelmed by having two children in such quick succession) and this, too, Frédéric seems to have accepted. Perhaps he thought he could "save" her. In 1928 he wrote some short stories based on his time in Kenya, and has another character pronounce upon his fictionalized marriage: "she cares too much for her pets and he cares too much for her." True enough, but there had been another factor, as he knew perfectly well. In 1926 Alice had begun a relationship with the man who took the picture of her seated with Samson, a young Englishman called Raymund de Trafford. This may have started as an attempt to provoke Joss Erroll into jealousy (his marriage to Idina was coming to an end), although in their arrogant self-assurance the two men were not unalike. In any event, just a few months after meeting Raymund, Alice told her husband that their marriage was at an end, and gave the children over to his care.

The problem was that Raymund did not especially wish to become her second husband. At first he said that he did, but in the cold light of day he began to share the misgivings of the de Traffords, grand old Catholics who disapproved of divorce, and who would cut him off if he were to marry her. Alice could have easily funded his preferred lifestyle, but Raymund was not prepared to sever ties with his family. Had they been penniless, he might have done so. Instead, abruptly, he broke off the relationship with Alice, despite the fact that she had just left her husband on his account. In other words, Raymund was not a good man; although he was clever, literate, and "diabolically handsome."[3] He had been forced to leave both his school, Downside, and the Coldstream Guards, and ended up in Kenya, where he met Evelyn Waugh, who of course adored upper-class Catholics (and was enchanted by the country). In 1932 Waugh wrote indulgently that Raymund was "something of a handful v nice but SO BAD and he fights & fucks and gambles and gets D.D. [disgustingly drunk] all the time."[4] The previous year, during a stay at Raymund's house in Njoro, Waugh recounted in his diary that his host "got very drunk and brought a sluttish girl back to the house. He woke me up later in the night to tell me he had just rogered her and her mama too."

During the Second World War, he would spend three years in Parkhurst jail on the Isle of Wight, having killed a woman cyclist while driving—drunk—back from Cheltenham races (on his release he joined up). Yet this very ruthlessness seems to have made him irresistible to Alice, or perhaps to have presented a challenge that roused her, while Raymund recognized in her a similar nature to his own: Waugh called him a "fine desperado," and there is no better way of describing Alice. He must have known that she would react badly when he ended the relationship but, at the same time, as an experienced leaver of women, he would have felt perfectly able to handle her—until, that is, the day in March 1927 when they were kissing for the "last time" at the Paris Gare du Nord, and Alice shot a bullet into his chest. Then she turned the gun on herself, and fired into her stomach. "Take care of my dog," she said, before passing out. She had brought a friend's Alsatian with her on this extraordinary afternoon, which consisted of a farewell lunch with Raymund to mark the end of their affair, followed by a visit together to a gun shop near the Louvre, where Alice bought the elegant little revolver that she would use on them both half an hour later.

They survived their gunshot wounds. Was this the intention? Surely not. Alice had missed Raymund's heart by millimeters (the line in the film *White Mischief*,* saying that she shot him "in the balls," is droll but incorrect). If she had felt psychologically unable to fire into her own chest, she had still done herself plenty of harm. She suffered abdominal pain for the rest of her life.

She was imprisoned for a time in the Saint-Lazare women's jail—according to rumor, in the cell once occupied by Mata Hari—and, in December, tried for "wounding and causing bodily harm." The sensation of the court case prefigured the one that followed the shooting of Joss Erroll in Kenya, fourteen years later. How could people not be fascinated by this exquisite girl, this heiress, whose slight figure contained the passions of a Medea? It was reported that, when asked by the police to explain her actions, she had replied: "It is my secret." At the trial her sphinx air would be penetrated, perforce, although to nothing like the extent that it would have been in a British courtroom (this was France, after all, with its defense of the *crime passionnel*). She was asked by one of the judges to confirm that she had abandoned

---

* Released in 1987, the film—based on a book by James Fox—was a depiction of the Happy Valley set and an account of the murder of Lord Erroll. Alice was played by Sarah Miles (brilliant but not quite right—too obviously mad) and portrayed, inaccurately, as a drug addict.

her husband and children for Raymund de Trafford. Yes, she said. The judge repeated:

"Your children?"

The reply has an air of honesty. "It's so hard to explain, but I thought only of myself."

These questions were put in order to establish how much Alice had given up for her victim; not, as they would have been in Britain, to show what a frightful selfish woman she was.

Asked then about her intention when she bought the gun, Alice stated simply that she had wanted to kill herself. "But," said the judge, "you shot Monsieur de Trafford while you were kissing him."

"Not quite. I was holding my gun when he kissed me. I don't know what went on in my head. I saw, like a drowning woman, all the memories of my life. I wanted to kill myself, but at the last moment in a sort of trance, I fired on him."

Whether this was the weird and actual truth of the matter, or whether it had been carefully contrived by a lawyer, it succeeded in conveying that there had not been malice aforethought. Much emphasis was placed upon the fact that Raymund had promised to marry Alice, and had broken his word. "I am responsible," he told the court, in the voice of the gentleman that he occasionally managed to be.

Alice de Janzé was fined the equivalent of sixteen shillings and sixpence, and given a prison sentence of six months, suspended under the 1887 First Offenders Act. She left almost immediately for Africa. Just over four years later, at Neuilly town hall, with her bulldog at her side, she married Raymund de Trafford.

* * *

There may be a simple explanation, on Alice's part at least, for this marriage. In early 1928 she had been ordered to leave Kenya because she was a "prohibited immigrant"; not just a convicted criminal but—almost as bad—a divorcée, in a country where single women were generally not permitted entry. The lurch toward gender equality had clearly not reached the colonies (although, once married, a woman could live as she pleased). And Alice, with her spectacularly wayward past, her pet lion, her disturbing allure, her penchant for topping up cocktails with a slug of absinthe, was an undesirable; the Happy Valley set was one thing, but this woman did not even really fit into that well-bred gang of debauchees. So getting married—again—was a means of getting back to what she thought of as home.

That said, there were more complicated reasons as to why she chose Raymund rather than another man (she could very easily have found somebody else). He did not want to marry her—he never had wanted to—although his own perversity may have led him to do so. Alice's behavior would have flattered and intrigued him. He was not the sort of upper-class man to be embarrassed by an unconventional girl (good lord, Marigold isn't wearing any stockings!); had he been, he would have stayed away from Alice in the first place. He knew how he ought to behave, even if he rarely did so, and he may have liked the idea that he was righting the wrong that he had done to her. There was another factor, however, which unsurprisingly was money. Alice had lots of it, as did the de Traffords, and marrying her would no longer alienate the family, because her union with Frédéric had now been annulled. Like the heiress-hunters of old, Raymund may have seen potential value in being tied to a woman who would, if nothing else, pay him to go away.

For Alice, meanwhile, there was a blood tie—literally—with this man. With him, she had enacted something like the events in the hunting lodge at Mayerling, the eroticized death game in which the Habsburg prince Rudolf shot his mistress and then himself; except that this time the woman held the gun, and nobody died. Perhaps she could not quite bear to leave such a story unfinished. Perhaps she just wanted to win her battle. "I always get my own way," as the fictional Alice says in one of Frédéric's short stories. "I take what I want and I throw it away." Raymund was not the only thing in her life: since 1928 she had spent time in France with her children—although tenuous, a relationship did exist—and in London, where she was a regular at the uber-smart Embassy Club favored by the worldlier royals. Yet she longed to return to Kenya. The melancholia that always threatened was held at bay there, or so she felt, and she chose to use Raymund as the way to achieve this.

She got what she wanted, then both of them threw it away— just three months after the wedding she was holidaying alone in Slovakia while Raymund was in Venice with Evelyn Waugh, celebrating Diana Cooper's fortieth birthday at one of Laura Corrigan's rented palazzos. In late 1932, Alice gave her husband a first-class fare to Australia and a living allowance for several months, and he was off. The baroque drama of their liaison had come to its sudden end. Alice was left at her beloved Wanjohi farm, with a British passport and the entrée that came with being Mrs. de Trafford. She was sleeping again with Joss Erroll (although he too had remarried), so she got what she wanted in that respect also. Her feelings for him are a still deeper enigma.

In 1933 Frédéric died, aged just thirty-seven; Alice did not attend his funeral. In 1936 she visited her father, who was living in South Carolina and whose medical bills she was paying, but their bond had long since been broken. In 1937 she was divorced from Raymund, who had turned up occasionally and made an aggressive nuisance of himself, although she wrote to him regularly when he was in Parkhurst. She saw her children, but not often. Her de Janzé relations kept in constant touch, although they must have surely regretted the day that this lunatic of an American walked into their lives. In 1939, she was hospitalized with the abdominal pains that had plagued her for the past twelve years. Afterward she visited Paris and spent some time with her children which, as it happened, was a good thing. Then she took the decision to spend four months alone, traveling and exploring in the Congo. As ever, it was wayward—she knew that war was imminent—yet at the same time it makes one feel, more than anything, the waste of Alice's life. She had the money to undertake this splendid adventure, she had the profound independence of spirit to want to do it; why, then, was she doing imbecilic things like marrying the wrong men and shooting herself in the stomach?

Love and freedom are near-impossible things to reconcile. Alice was a lone wolf, who loved other wild things (although she had now acquired a tiny dachshund to go with her African lion dog and eland), but at the same time she wanted men in her life, where they had always been. When potent new blood entered the Muthaiga Club in 1940, her competitive female instincts were aroused. Diana Broughton, aged twenty-seven, thirty years younger than her husband Sir Jock Delves Broughton, was a middle-class girl on the make, a shape-shifter like Sylvia Ashley, and with all the vitality that came with it. Next to her, Alice de Janzé looked like a *neurasthénique*, which by then is what she was—beautiful still but pale, wan, drinking too heavily and taking too many sleeping pills. Diana was blond, tough-looking, nakedly vampish, with a touch of the gangster's moll despite her rigorous *chic*. She had an instant affair with a Coldstream Guards officer, Dickie Pembroke, whom Alice had marked down for herself (and who would in fact be her last lover). Then Joss Erroll, whose second wife had died in 1939, moved in for the kill. This was Happy Valley, where sex was a game whose rules required one to be a good loser, and Jock Broughton appeared to accept what had indeed been inevitable; that it was only a matter of time before his wife looked elsewhere, not least when what was on offer was a sexy earl. And Joss seems to have been promising more than just a fling. His intentions may not have been honorable, but they were sincere. Accordingly, in January 1941 Jock instructed his lawyer to begin divorce proceedings, and at the Muthaiga Club raised a gentlemanly toast: "To Diana and Joss . . . may their union be blessed with an heir." A few hours later, early the following morning, Joss's car came off the road as he was driving home from a nightclub. He had swerved to avoid a person, identity still unknown, who then leaned through the window and put a bullet into his neck. Jock Broughton was tried for the murder and acquitted, although he remains chief suspect.

It has been suggested, however, that the guilty party was in fact Alice, the woman who had previously shot an errant lover, and whose passion for Joss had been ignited into warped obsession by his relationship with Diana Broughton. It is possible. There were rumors that she owned a gun. A mysterious hairpin was found inside Joss's car, not belonging to Diana, although knowing him it could have been pretty much anybody else's. Dickie Pembroke had supplied Alice with an alibi, but given the behavioral code of that society it meant little. A more convincing argument in her defense, however, is that the manner of Raymund's shooting was so different from that of Joss Erroll: that galvanic moment at the Gare du Nord was as flagrant as a scene from romantic opera, not an undercover act on a deserted road, from which the culprit scuttled into the night. Alice's behavior at the mortuary, where she kissed Joss's dead lips and said to him: "Now you are mine forever," might be construed as a confession in the gothic style, and her regular visits to Jock in prison as bad conscience; she also attended the trial every day—all twenty-seven of them. She was not alone in that, however. It was the hottest ticket in Nairobi. And perhaps the strongest evidence for her innocence is that she did not shoot herself, there and then, beside Joss's body, but instead waited eight months to do it alone.

The death of Joss Erroll seems to have taken away what remained of her capacity for happiness, which had been running low for a long time. Six days after the murder, Alice's father died. In July, after Jock Broughton's acquittal, Dickie Pembroke—who had been on leave from the Guards for misconduct, but was madly keen to get back (and away?)—rejoined his regiment in North Africa. Alice had come to rely upon Dickie, and soon after his departure wrote that "the fact of you going away in these uncertain times, even for only a short time, as we hope, is pure and absolute pain." In September she underwent a hysterectomy; before leaving home for the operation, she gave her dachshund a lethal dose of Nembutal. This, more than anything, for a woman with a profound and passionate love of animals, was a sign that she had lost her grip. Life need not go on, she wrote to Dickie. "In Joss's case someone decided that, in Minnie's case I did, and the length of our own lives lies entirely within our own hands (unless someone else gets at us first!)." A couple of weeks later she filled her bedroom at Wanjohi with flowers, wrote five letters, including to her children, put on her best nightdress, and took a large dose of the drug that she had used on her dog. Then she shot herself. This time she aimed at her chest, and the bullet found her heart.

* * *

A pointless life? A wasted life? Alice de Janzé had had such grace, and she had found delight in many things: Africa, animals, her farm, even love sometimes. Yet this had been the end of the story. Dickie Pembroke received a postmortem letter that concluded: "I simply can't write again, and there is nothing more to say," and her children—who were living in Chicago for the duration of the war—read about her death in the newspapers before her letters could arrive. It was typical Alice that she should have left them Wanjohi farm, while stipulating in her will that they must spend eight months of the year looking after it: a clear impossibility. Eventually, the house became a school. "My mother's wishes to the wind," said her older daughter, Nolwen, with admirable magnanimity.*

She could stick to nothing except Africa, and in the end even that failed to give her pleasure: "Oh God, not another fucking beautiful day," as her famous cry had it. It is hard, very hard indeed, not to think that she would have done better with less money—she had thrived on her only job, working for a fashion house in Paris in the early 1920s—but, as it was, the twin hellhounds of melancholy and accidie had time and space to breed, and indolence permitted obsession to grow unchecked. Like the Happy Valley set to which she semibelonged, she needed more "real life"—something that an heiress always struggles to find. Nor can it be bought. It is the possession of the non-moneyed, and for all its vagaries and anxieties it is more of a gift than we realize.

---

* The lives of Alice's daughters were happier than one would have dared to expect. Nolwen became a fashion designer and died in 1989. She married three times, lastly to the renowned art historian and broadcaster Kenneth Clark. Her sister, Paola, died in 2006. She married John Ciechanowski, the son of a Polish diplomat, a racehorse trainer and renowned amateur jockey.

That said, might not Alice have found real life by staying with her first husband and her two daughters? She had fought to leave Paris, as though family life were a trap that must be sprung, and the attendant guilt surely haunted her. With Dickie Pembroke she had found—too late—a tremulous stability. Might she have been happier if she had accepted this need twenty years earlier? Was not Dickie, in fact, very much like Frédéric, the husband whom she had never wanted?

Again one confronts the unfortunate mystery that people rarely fall in love with those who are kind to them, but instead seek out those who are cavalier, challenging, and sometimes downright nasty. Heiresses, for whom obeisance was on tap, were particularly drawn to men who refused to bow and scrape; one understands the paradox, although a woman like Daisy Fellowes—who bowed to nobody—did not succumb to this temptation. Alice de Janzé could not resist it. In the end, what she really liked about Raymund and Joss was that they were never going to impinge upon her freedom. At the same time freedom was a truly terrifying thing. Such are the existential problems of those who live with too much money, which by then equated with too much choice.

Alice did not *want* a normal family life. Plenty of women feel that way, and in her social world it was extremely easy to be a hands-off wife and mother (Daisy again); but even that was not enough for her. She lacked the requisite light touch when it came to arranging her life. With her it was all or nothing, and—as is so often the case—it ended up by being nothing. As for Frédéric, the man who had offered her his love . . . yes, his kindness was apparently that of a living saint. He had remonstrated with Raymund de Trafford on Alice's behalf, when Raymund broke off the relationship in 1927; he had offered his ancestral castle for Alice's convalescence, when she shot herself in the stomach and was released from prison to await trial; he had taken on the children after the divorce, and agreed to an annulment so that Alice could marry her godless Catholic.

Did he, however, achieve a peculiarly appropriate act of revenge upon his wife? If so—or at least if she believed so—it may explain her decision not to attend his funeral, which on the face of it is wholly indefensible.

Perhaps more than anything—any person, place, thing—Alice had loved the lion cub, Samson. After the breakdown of the de Janzé marriage, the animals became the focus of much of their attention; where they should go, how they could be transported back and forth, from Kenya to France, so that somebody was always available to care for them. At the time of the shooting incident in 1927, Samson (plus the monkey and a baby Nile crocodile) were living in a Paris flat with Frédéric and the children, whose nanny not unreasonably objected. While Alice was recovering from her gunshot wound at the de Janzé chateau in Normandy, Frédéric arranged for Samson to be taken to the Jardin d'Acclimatation, a children's zoo in the Bois du Boulogne.

After the trial Alice traveled to Kenya, accompanied by her monkey. Frédéric, uncharacteristically, had forbidden the transportation of the lion, saying that Samson could not now be removed from the zoo (to which he had been given without Alice's knowledge or permission). It is highly unlikely that she accepted this as a final decision, although a full-grown lion undeniably presented difficulties. When she returned to Paris a few months later, in her new position of "prohibited immigrant," she had the intention of visiting Samson in the Bois du Boulogne and, if possible, reclaiming him. Too late: the lion was dead.

This was Frédéric's story, as told in his 1929 quasi-autobiography. After Alice's departure for Kenya he had visited the Jardin d'Acclimatation, where he learned that its big cats had been transferred to a circus. Arriving at this circus he saw a Masai lion, now full grown, with a Z-shaped scar that he recognized. "It couldn't be Samson," he wrote, "but no two lions could have that same scar!" Determined to buy the lion back, he returned to the circus every day for a week until, during his final visit, the animal sprang in weary rage at his female trainer and was instantly shot. "I felt him shudder and he collapsed on my feet, knocking me over. I got up from under him and took his great head on my lap; a trickle of blood flowed from the side of his jaw onto me, then down to the floor; he tried one or two manful licks and snuggled his great shaggy head into my lap; he died in my arms—content, I hope, on the heart of a friend."

It is possible, of course, to take this account at face value (even though the book in which it appears begins with a disclaimer: "go your way, untrue stories of mine"). As presented, the facts were these: Frédéric had given a huge Masai lion to a children's zoo and, although he loved Samson deeply, he was happy to hand him over without checking whether the zoo would be able to home such an animal indefinitely—according to Frédéric, Samson was kept for just a few months. He was amazed to recognize the lion at a circus, although he had been told that he would find him there. He visited the lion for a week before arranging to buy him back, despite the fact that Alice would have given the money in an instant. And he had refused to let his wife take the lion back to Africa, because it might upset the zoo.

Another possibility is that the account, with its novelettish coincidences and melodrama, was not in fact true, but was invented with a bland intent to distress.

Or perhaps, more poetically, one can see something else in this story: the deadly revenge of the kindest of men, destroying the thing that his miscreant wife loved so much, acting always—as he insisted—with the best of intentions; and the pointless insertion of a bullet into something impossibly beautiful that did not wish to be caged.

REBELS

ALICE DE JANZÉ was a rebel against nothing in particular, but Nancy Cunard was a rebel with a cause. She may have started her career as an anti-heiress out of a straightforward desire to upset her mother. It was said of her that if no cause for battle existed, she would set out to invent one. Yet she developed into the real deal, a civil rights activist, in an age when Margot Asquith could make this casual wisecrack about her behavior: "So what is it now, Maud, drink, drugs or n***ers?"

Born in 1896, and thus a precursor of the Mitford sisters by a generation, she had something in common with their more politicized representatives. Like Jessica Mitford—that definitive Hon and Rebel—Nancy Cunard turned vociferously upon her own upbringing and, to an extent, the system that created it. Like Unity Mitford, who was a close friend of Hitler and attempted suicide when Britain declared war on Germany, she had fanatical tendencies that led to self-destruction. And, as with the Mitfords, the political was also the personal. Unity had been influenced by the example of her sister Diana, who married the Fascist leader Sir Oswald Mosley; Jessica acted in reaction against both Diana and Unity. A competitive family dynamic played its part in forging their convictions, just as Nancy Cunard's antipathy to her mother forged hers. The nature of her feelings is made plain by this story from Nancy's debutante year of 1914; when asked, during a parlor game, whom she would most like to see enter the room, she replied "Lady Cunard, dead."

Several of these heiresses were motherless. Nancy lived as if she were, or wanted to be, and through her cool eye one sees Maud/Emerald in a wholly contemporary light. A century ago, this self-created woman was an arbiter of high society, a force to be reckoned with; she was subject to mockery, but her power never really waned. Today she can be portrayed quite differently: as an airhead whose love of the arts was tainted by folly (John Galsworthy, in her assessment, "looked like a gentleman and may have been one"), for whom those outside her charmed circle simply did not exist. This, a century ago, is how her daughter saw her—and, by extension, the society that she commanded. She disliked Emerald's fluffy, fluttery appearance, so at odds with her own stark, shorn-headed sleekness. She disliked her ditzy way of speaking and her frou-frou manner, especially when it was aimed at her friends. She was fond of Sir Bache Cunard, and considered that Emerald had treated him badly (which of course she had; in revenge he cut her out of his will).

At the same time, her disapproval did not prevent her from living off her mother's fortune (strictly speaking, she was an heiress once removed). And Nancy had this much in common with Emerald: she loved the arts. She believed in what she called the "sacred mission of art to change history." She became a dedicated patron, spending wads of money on the promotion of experimental writers through her Hours Press, a private publishing and printing house that she established in 1928 at her farm in Normandy. In 1930, a poem entitled "Whoroscope" became the first separately published work by Samuel Beckett, with whom she had a short affair and who admired her "spunk and verve." Other Hours Press writers included Ezra Pound—also a lover—and George Moore, about whom Nancy later wrote a fond memoir.

Was she Moore's daughter? Illegitimacy was so common among the upper classes as to be a near-irrelevance, except when it affected the inheritance of a title; Lady Diana Cooper professed delight at being the product of a love affair rather than the daughter of the Duke of Rutland* (it was different for a woman like Mrs. Greville, although she rode out that particular example of snobbery by being the biggest snob of the lot). Nancy did actually ask Moore whether he was her father, although the general opinion is that he was not. Moore enjoyed proclaiming his love for Emerald—"I never cease to think of you"—but that sort of talk does not always go with action. Indeed it was said of him that he told, but did not kiss.

Against that is a vignette recalled by Chips Channon,[5] probably dating from when Nancy was in her late teens and—as he put it—"involved in the first of her many public scrapes." Chips was discussing this with her mother, when Moore was announced: "Emerald leaped up, saying: 'There's little George Moore' as she always called him." The conversation about Nancy continued, and Moore "made some tactless remark . . . whereupon Emerald lost all control and in a frenzy of rage struck him with a paper cutter that lay on a Buhl table [the detail of the Buhl is very Chips]. She shook him, chased him and rained a volley of abuse on his

---

* Her real father was a man named Harry Cust, an MP, unusually good-looking (as was Diana's mother—her beauty was no matter of chance) and a rather romantic character who beguiled men as well as women. William Waldorf Astor invited him to edit the *Pall Mall Gazette*, although he had absolutely no experience of journalism. He was the father of a number of illegitimate children, including, according to rumor, the mother of Margaret Thatcher, whom Diana would blithely describe as her niece.

bald, shining head . . . it was odd to be present at this little scene between the greatest writer in Europe and the most sophisticated woman in London, and one wonders what their relations were that they could have been so intimate as to exchange blows."

Her behavior does seem like that of a woman incensed by a lover—one, moreover, who might have been Nancy's father—although, having presented this possibility to himself, Chips went on to say that he did *not* think the couple were "intimate" in a sexual sense. "I think he was really an old monk," he wrote firmly of Moore, adding that Emerald was perhaps his only real friend; "his manner with her was always that of the courting suitor." Which was astutely observed. And which therefore implies that Emerald's behavior—quite extraordinary, even allowing for exaggeration—derived from her raging frustration with Nancy: Moore had, as they say, touched a nerve.

Certainly Nancy was difficult. Jessica Mitford was capable of throwing great wobblies over, say, her mother's refusal to send her to school, but she always had a funniness and pouting charm. Nancy, conversely, was in an eye-rolling sulk all the time, driven by her mother's reverence for social success to behave in as oppositional a way as possible. Again, she feels very contemporary. She is perhaps the first woman in this book to defy conventions that governed the lives of even the Paris iconoclasts. Small, silly things; like the fact that she was still in her nightdress, in the sordid throes of a terrible hangover, when Emerald came skipping into the drawing room one late morning in 1916, accompanied by Diana Manners and her future husband Duff Cooper. "Diana was disgusted," wrote Duff. Perhaps she reacted so fiercely because Nancy had not bothered with the façade behind which they all lived, and which made transgression acceptable: the "don't frighten the horses" philosophy. Metaphorically speaking, Nancy was ready to scare the horses to death. A half-century before those aristocratic girls who left their pearls in Wiltshire and started having fun with rock stars in Chelsea, Nancy ditched London's spacious squares and moved to a studio in Fitzroy Street where she lived, not without privilege, but certainly in defiance of its trappings. Whoever believed that sex began in 1963? "Come to Fitz, Diana," Nancy would say, but for all her broadmindedness Diana could not cope with Bloomsbury living (which, in this incarnation, meant beds that there was little point in making and champagne bottles broken at the neck). Nancy lived at the studio with her friend Iris Tree, of whom Diana wrote: "Iris quenches a dozen blue-flies' thirst, and God knows her face betrays her. Nancy too is in the same boat of so-called iniquity . . . God help them both! They have more courage than me." Also at Fitz was Phyllis Boyd, later Vicomtesse de Janzé, who had more in common with Alice than she had cared to let on.

The similarities between Alice and Nancy were more obvious. In 1916 Nancy married in that same wrongheaded way, as a means of aimless escape, from a society that she disliked into what was simply a different kind of trap. She wore gold for her wedding to Sydney Fairbairn, attended by Sir Bache Cunard, George Moore, and Thomas Beecham; her mother gave the couple a house in Montague Square, which was presumably the point of the exercise, although escape from Sydney—who had been wounded at Gallipoli, and later was awarded the Military Cross—soon became uppermost in Nancy's mind. She fell in love with a man named Peter Broughton-Adderley, who was killed a month before the end of the war, thus making him impossible to get over; it was suggested by some of her friends that she never really did. But the affair ensured that her marriage came to an end—insofar as it had ever started—and in 1919, when Sydney was demobbed, she told him that she could no longer bear to be with him. Alice again: that desperate and despairing selfishness.

The difference was that Nancy had intellectual gifts and interests, which Alice did not possess. She had already contributed to an anthology of poems, *Wheels*, edited by the Sitwells, and her writing was greatly encouraged by George Moore, although she had decided that she would be unable to produce anything as long as she was married to Sydney. However, the marriage had done its strange illogical job of allowing a woman to be more liberated, and in 1920 Nancy left London and went to France.

In Paris, where she was not part of the heiress enclave, she became instantly absorbed instead into the creative colony that had taken possession of the Left Bank. She played tennis with Hemingway and was friends with Joyce. Modernism she already knew about, of course, but now she encountered Surrealism, Dadaism, thrilling stuff that fed Nancy's hungry soul (food itself she disdained) and led her to produce quantities of poetry, five volumes in the next decade. With her uncompromising stare, her angularity, her streamlined elegance—an Ibizan hound body and a Wyndham Lewis head—she looked the living spirit of the new age, and artists could not resist her. Brâncuşi sculpted her, Man Ray photographed her, Kokoschka painted her. Her very brain was Cubist, skewed but honest. Her friend Michael Arlen, the Armenian-born novelist whose work *The Green Hat* became a lurid, shallow, rather delectable record of the postwar ennui that bred the Lost Generation, modeled the central character upon Nancy: she was Iris Storm, melancholic and magical, promiscuous and obsessed with purity, driving to her death in a yellow Hispano-Suiza. She was also said to be Myra Viveash in Aldous Huxley's *Antic Hay* and Lucy Tantamount in his *Point Counter Point*. Novelists of Huxley's caliber do not transpose people directly into books; that is not quite how it works; but his affair with Nancy—and the penetrative piquancy of her personality, her style—assuredly had its influence.

The vitality of this period was all the more remarkable because, not long after her arrival in France, Nancy had had a hysterectomy that led to peritonitis. She was lucky to survive. The near-death experience led her to attack life with increased ferocity and, perversely, to become more careless with her health. She had always been a party girl, but she became by degrees a functioning anorexic, a serious drinker, and possibly a drug user; unlike Daisy Fellowes, who was all these things but on her own terms, Nancy gave the impression of somebody who at any moment might spin out of control. The effect of the hysterectomy, meanwhile, is incalculable. Had she had children, Nancy would probably have become yet another of the rather terrible mothers who plague this book. Nevertheless to lose one's reproductive organs before the age of twenty-five is a serious physical and psychological assault. No woman really wants to know that she *cannot* have children—to choose not to do so is entirely different—and, with the death of Broughton-Adderley, she had also lost the man with whom she had hoped to spend her future. From that point she was able to do as she pleased, live as she chose, and sleep with whomever she wished, without fear of consequences or emotional attachment. It may have been a freedom too immense, even for Nancy Cunard.

* * *

Emerald would almost certainly have been happier as a childless woman, although she was not anything like as bad a mother as Daisy or Alice. She was self-absorbed, for sure, but in her way she made an effort. After the hysterectomy, Nancy published a well-received book of her own poetry, entitled *Outlaws*; Emerald went into full-blown agent mode and promoted it as hard as only she could. She took Nancy on holiday to Monte Carlo, which sounds more than acceptable. She also asked Duff Cooper, so often a diplomatic intermediary, if he would persuade Sydney Fairbairn to give Nancy a divorce, which finally happened in 1925. A few years later, in the summer of 1930, Evelyn Waugh described a large dinner party thrown by Emerald—with whom he was never at his best; she was "obviously dissatisfied with me as a lion"—attended by sundry Sitwells, Oswald Mosley, Harold Nicolson, and others. "The party," he wrote, "seemed to be half for George Moore and half for Nancy Cunard." In other words, Emerald was trying to be involved in her daughter's life, or try-ing to make Nancy involved in her life; and Nancy did attend the party. Why, one has no idea. Because by 1930 her rebelliousness had found a new and serious direction, making her contempora-neity never so shiningly clear, and her break from the world her mother inhabited near-complete.

A month before this summer dinner, Waugh had described in his diary a very different sort of occasion: cocktails at the home of his old friend Harold Acton, who lived on Lancaster Gate. Among the guests were "Nancy Cunard and her negress and an astonishing, fat Mrs. Henderson." Wyn Henderson was the manager of Nancy's publishing firm, Hours Press. The iden-tity of the black woman is unknown, but her presence at the party signifies the fact that Nancy had, by this time, become as intensely engaged with the anti-racist cause as she had been with the Modernist movement. In 1928, after an affair with the poet Louis Aragon, she went to Venice with her cousin Victor Cunard, a rich homosexual who would later become Nancy Mitford's companion of choice when she visited the city every summer. There Nancy met Henry Crowder, a black jazz pianist. She does not seem to have been especially interested in the world of Crowder's music—unlike Baroness Nica de Rothschild, whose own rebellion took the form of total absorption into the

American jazz scene. Nancy was attracted to the man (although she was not faithful to him), but still more so to the cause that his skin color represented. *That* was what absorbed her, particularly when she subsequently went to Harlem and learned about race issues in the US. She was, by nature, a rebel—against her background, her money, her mother—but she was entirely genuine in her devotion to that cause. Like Jessica Mitford, who moved from Knightsbridge to Rotherhithe with her first husband in deference to the communist creed, Nancy did not merely pronounce her beliefs: she lived them. "I've always had the feeling," as she put it, "that everyone alive can [do] something that is worthwhile."

Today, she might well be open to "white savior" accusations; in fact her lover seems to have seen her—rather humorously—in that light. Be more African, she told him. I'm American, he replied. She would certainly be accused of cultural appropriation in her wearing of African-inspired jewelry: bangles made of bone stacked in rows up to her elbows, necklaces of fat wooden cubes, as in the truly fabulous Man Ray image that shows her delicate, intelligent, dead-white mannequin's face resting on her hand, above forearms ringed as if with pieces of armor. At first the interwar fashionistas found this bizarre—wood and bones, when one could afford diamonds?—but then, as they do, they perceived in it a new expression of *chic* and called it the "barbaric look." Nancy, who wanted to shock, doubtless preferred it when everybody was gazing on in amazement. Her punk sensibility did not want the approval of Boucheron, which eventually created its own African-style gold cuff. That had not been the point of the exercise; although it was, one might say, a mark of her success.

She lived with Henry Crowder in Paris, a more liberal city than most in matters of race. For that reason, Thomas Beecham wrote to warn her to stay there. Which, of course, was a sure way to make her leave and come to London. At this point, relations with her mother took a very unpleasant turn. She and Crowder were harassed by visits from the police, for which Nancy blamed Emerald, saying that her mother had employed detectives to follow them. She also accused Emerald of threatening to have Crowder deported. All this may well be true—Nancy had not taken up the cause of anti-racism for no reason. A slight complicating factor is that she had been told, when still in Paris, that her mother was reducing her allowance by a quarter. The reason given was that Emerald had lost money post-1929 on her American investments, but Nancy believed that it was an act of revenge because of the relationship with Crowder. That, too, is possible. It is also possible that Nancy came to London with the intention of blaming her mother for any difficulties created by racist authorities (she could be fairly sure that there would be some). What is odd, in the circumstances, is that she attended a dinner party at Grosvenor Square in the summer of 1930, in the midst of all these tumultuous happenings.

But her rage against Emerald smoldered on: part political, part personal. For Jessica Mitford, her sister Diana Mosley became the very embodiment of fascism and of the suffering caused by the Second World War. For Nancy Cunard, her mother became symbolic of all the blind smugness within Western high society. She herself, meanwhile, had become the Anti-Heiress, despite the fact that she used her inherited income to print a pamphlet entitled "Black Man and White Ladyship." This was an account of the manifold injustices suffered by black people, but also an attack on her mother, who (in her rather brilliant phrase) was "as hard and buoyant as a dreadnought." In 1931 she sent copies of the pamphlet to Emerald's friends as a Christmas card. Among the recipients was the Prince of Wales. Henry Crowder, who held more nuanced views than those of the woman who was trying to save him, thought the whole thing "idiotic"; Emerald claimed to fear for her daughter's mental stability.

Yet if one set aside this obsession with her mother, what Nancy was doing was admirable, impressive, and years ahead of its time. Her sensibility, again, was very now. She would have been an absolute dynamo on social media. As it was she edited a huge volume, *Negro*, published in 1934 and funded not by her inheritance but by the proceeds of multiple suits won against newspapers, after their libelous coverage of her time in London with Crowder. The 800-page book, which sold (or rather, sadly, did not) at the then immense price of two guineas, was a highly significant artifact. It celebrated black achievement, being a collection of work by writers including Zora Neale Hurston and Langston Hughes; and it was a denunciation of racism, of what Nancy called the oppression of "14 million Negroes in America," which she underlined by including some of the anonymous insults and death threats that she herself had received when news of her project became public. *Negro* was, in effect, a declaration of the twenty-first-century creed: Black Lives Matter. It was a pity that Nancy still could not stop herself making vicious digs at her mother, "an American-born frantically prejudiced society woman," and so on, but the magnitude of the achievement remains.

In her compelled and combative way, and despite her venom toward all that Emerald represented, she continued to socialize within that accursed world. The fact was that mother and daughter had many friends in common. "Nancy and her black lover were often to be seen at Lancaster Gate [Harold Acton's house] when visiting London," wrote Diana Mosley; Acton, perhaps the most amusing and sought-after of all these people, was also a regular guest at Emerald's house, as were Cecil Beaton, who photographed Nancy, and Evelyn Waugh, who, in

Brideshead Revisited, reimagined her as "Nancy Tallboys," hostess of a party much like the one that the real Nancy held in 1933 in the basement of a hotel: a fund-raiser on behalf of the Scottsboro Boys, nine African American teenagers accused in Alabama of the rape of two white women.* It was attended by the more bohemian London socialites—including Augustus John—who danced and mingled with Nancy's black friends, a scene in which her two worlds felicitously collided. At the same time, rather less happily but unsurprisingly, she was under surveillance by Special Branch. An internal report commented upon her preference for black men and added that she was "reputed to be a drug addict." Mrs. Simpson was also being watched in this manner, although a few years later Nancy was in more exalted company—including Duff Cooper, Noël Coward, and Winston Churchill—when her name was placed by the Gestapo on the list of those who would be arrested in the event that Britain were invaded.

This, too, was to be expected. Nancy had widened her political stance and become a vociferous voice against fascism. She had written extensively about the danger presented by Mussolini and, particularly, by Franco. In 1936 she traveled to Spain and reported on the civil war, which she described as "a prelude to another world war." The following year she joined forces with

---

* The case was also referenced in Nancy Mitford's novel *The Pursuit of Love* as an example of a gross miscarriage of justice (with, of course, a powerful racial bias); further evidence that it became a cause célèbre within London society. In 1932, all but one of the nine teenagers—aged twelve to nineteen—were sentenced to death for the rapes (for which there was no evidence except the testimony of the two women). After a succession of appeals and retrials, and the admission of African American jurors, charges were dropped against four of the defendants. Nevertheless, the others received sentences ranging from seventy-five years to—in one case—death, although this was commuted.

Stephen Spender and W. H. Auden (whose poetry she had published), and compiled a questionnaire that was sent to 200 writers, the results to be published in the *Left Review*, charging them to state whether they were "for, or against, Franco and Fascism? For it is impossible any longer to take no side." How contemporary this feels, yet again; reminiscent of the "silence is complicity" charge leveled by twenty-first-century anti-racism campaigners. Naturally most of the replies were pro-republican, although Nancy's old friend James Joyce was one of those who chose not to answer, and five writers—including devilish Evelyn Waugh—voted in favor of Franco. George Orwell, meanwhile, wrote: "Will you stop sending me this bloody rubbish . . . I was six months in Spain, most of the time fighting, I have a bullet hole in me at present and I am not going to write blah about defending democracy."

One takes his point. It was not unreasonable to see Nancy—as perhaps Henry Crowder had done—as a willful agitator, in modern parlance a virtue signaler, ranting at those who did not actually disagree with her but who were more realistic, or perhaps cynical, about the limits of what protest can achieve. She was not wise; the quality sits uneasily with her kind of passion. Yet it could never be said that she did not follow through on her principles. She volunteered in the refugee camps—as did Nancy Mitford, who fictionalized her experience in *The Pursuit of Love*—and established a shelter that prepared meals for as many as four thousand people every day. The crisis was truly appalling, even if the behavior on the republican side was not always exemplary, nor the situation as binary as that questionnaire had made it seem; but that was Nancy through and through, one was with her or (like her mother) against her. Eventually her health, never robust, gave way and she returned to Paris to convalesce. When the greater, still more evil war that she had predicted broke out, she came to London and worked as a translator for the French Resistance, again pushing herself with a frenzied masochism, working six night shifts in a row, refusing the comforts of sleep and food. "Somewhere, someone is suffering," she would say, as if for her not to do so also would show an intolerable deficiency in empathy.

It was a long, long way from the world of The Dorchester hotel, which had by no means been safe or anxiety-free, but had done that old-style thing of keeping up a front and (in the case of Mrs. Greville) putting on one's priceless jewels when the bombs threatened annihilation. Nancy, with her fierce unfiltered sincerity, had always refused that kind of façade; for her it was a grave dishonesty, and as a matter of principle she had become as one with the destruction wrought by a near decade of European war. The intensity of her engagement was noble, but it had been a kind of madness from which she was unable to retreat. Now her brain began to follow her body into a state of permanent fragility.

Toward the end of Emerald's life—so much happier than her daughter's, but afflicted by the rupture between them—she was driving through London when her chauffeur swerved to avoid a woman who had stepped, seemingly obliviously, into the road in front of her car. It was Nancy. This strange, wordless encounter was their last meeting. When Emerald knew herself to be dying she asked a friend to intercede for her with her daughter, but there was no response. Nancy was traveling. A month before her mother's death, in June 1948, she sailed from Trinidad on the *Empire Windrush*, alongside the first large group of West Indian immigrants to arrive in the United Kingdom.

She was left a third of what remained of her mother's estate, and with it bought a house in the Dordogne to replace her Normandy home, which had been in the eye of the wartime storm. By the

1950s, most of the money had gone. She had wanted it that way, yet without the protective barrier that it formed against the world she began to disintegrate. There was a series of incidents, such as the one in which Nancy emerged from an Italian café, raging drunk with a cigarette up each nostril, throwing tomatoes at stray dogs. Another, the cause of her being certified in 1960, was recounted by Nancy Mitford in a letter lamenting the poor health of her close friend, Victor Cunard. "I think it was partly brought on by the madness of N. Cunard [his cousin]—I mean by her going mad. She went to an hotel at 3 A.M. & when the night porter aged 90 showed her her room she ordered him to sleep with her. She then set fire to a policeman. She is now in a bin whence she writes heartrending letters to poor Vic." In a highly characteristic remark, she concluded: "Women should never take up causes, that's what it is." She meant it, beneath the flippancy. She had seen the repercussions for three of her sisters: Diana, who had gone to Holloway jail on account of her fascist sympathies; Jessica, whose baby daughter had died in a measles epidemic in Rotherhithe; Unity, who had lived brain-damaged until her death in 1948, having shot herself in the head on the day that Britain declared war on Germany.

Nancy Cunard, who had fought so hard on the other side from Unity—the right side—was in a comparable condition. During her confinement she ranted continually against Spain, the CIA, and the British Foreign Office, whom she blamed in turn for certifying her. On her release she resumed her old habits, no food and as much drink as possible, but her rage was as new and strong as a summer sunrise: "How I should like to machine-gun the evil whites," she said, apparently meaning just that. In 1965, in Paris, she went on a prolonged alcohol binge that left her catatonic. When police eventually found her, she could not remember her name. Two days later she died, weighing less than seventy pounds. "Her body had wasted away," said her former lover, the Nobel laureate Pablo Neruda, "in a long battle against injustice in the world. Her reward was a life that had become progressively lonelier, and a godforsaken death." There was anger in that eulogy, aptly and justifiably so. There was also, whether or not it had been intended, an implicit religious dimension; as if Nancy had done whatever had been necessary, whatever it had taken, to get her through the eye of the needle.

* * *

Brâncuşi's sculpture of Nancy, *La Jeune Fille Sophistiquée*, sold at Christie's in 2018 for $71 million. Such was the value of her image in bronze. Of herself she had written: "I should own absolutely nothing." The anti-heiress indeed. Few human beings are true radicals, but Nancy had become exactly that. She had moved from teenage malcontent to committed activist to self-identifying anarchist to self-destroying nihilist; in the middle of that journey had been a long stopping point, a wonderful moment of achievement, which a century on is still worthy of acknowledgment. Then the story went the wrong way. She might have mellowed, as Jessica Mitford did, and become a productive member of the civil rights movement, a truth-teller who did not alienate, but that was not Nancy's style. As with Alice de Janzé, it was all or nothing.

The differences between the two women are as clear as the similarities: one led a life of passionate engagement, the other let life fall through her hands—but both had psychological issues that are impossible to diagnose at a remove, together with a capacity for happiness that they refused to fulfill. In that last sense, therefore, they resemble the heiress who has come to symbolize the word, in all its intimations of fairy tales and doom: Barbara Hutton.

Barbara was not a rebel, however. She was sixteen years younger than Nancy Cunard, yet the image that she presents—inanimate, disengaged, wearing "real emeralds, big as prunes"[6]—seems to deny the giant shifts that changed the twentieth century. Of course great wealth can hold change at bay. It can preserve a lyrical past, as long as it has the means to propagate itself in the real world. The land wealth that had sustained the British aristocracy was finding it increasingly difficult to do this; the Second World War was really the death blow to that system, although extremely rich individuals remained. But Barbara's millions had been generated by a man—her grandfather, Frank Winfield Woolworth—who understood the twentieth century to perfection. He was born in 1852 and died in 1919, yet his five-and-ten-cent stores were, in their way, a Modernist's dream, and the Woolworth company was serenely unaffected by the Wall Street Crash, the Great Depression, and the Second World War. The only thing that depleted Barbara's inheritance was herself.

So that was something else in common with Nancy Cunard; except that Nancy had spent money not on couture and Old Masters but in hectic pursuit of a utopia wherein the class to which she belonged did not exist. It was magnificent, but it had destroyed her as well as her wealth. Had that been inevitable? It seems so now, examining the evidence of her behavior, although a person's life is always a contingent business. It is all too easy—as with the "rewriting" of the story of Daisy Fellowes—to assemble a selection of handy tropes and fit that story around them.

Nevertheless, there is the evidence of what Nancy wrote and what she did; and what can be deduced above all is that she—like Frank Woolworth, whom she would have viewed as the capitalist enemy—was ahead of the game. She intuited the way the wind was blowing. In her case it was a veritable hurricane, but the point stands. The society into which she was born was losing its power, and in 1945 a government committed to systemic redistribution was elected in her own country. The fear created by that seismic victory, and the displacement of Winston Churchill by Clement Attlee, was rife among her acquaintances. The dulled, embittered grief of James Lees-Milne, Cecil Beaton, and Duff Cooper—as recorded earlier—was typical. More hysterical was Osbert Sitwell, who rushed into Heywood Hill bookshop in Mayfair, crying "Labour has begun!" and seizing the till as if to protect its contents. Nancy Mitford, who worked at the shop during the war, had in fact voted for Attlee, and according to Evelyn Waugh had rendered her homeland uninhabitable then moved to Paris. "There are many people puzzled about their futures," wrote Waugh in his diary, an oddly passive remark made two days after the election.

Of course much of this change had been going on, sometimes overtly, sometimes insidiously, for the past seventy-five years. The First World War was a fairly comprehensive wrecking ball; the 1920s had arisen from the carnage like a phoenix but that golden bird had long been dying. In 1931, when there was a run on the Bank of England, the chill penetrated even the centrally heated rooms of Mrs. Greville's Polesden Lacey. During a house party held at the height of the crisis, Gerald Berners burst into tears and Mrs. Greville told her friend Beverley Nichols that if her income collapsed to £10,000 a year she would sell up, that was that, and take a flat in Paris. In fact her wealth, derived as it was from beer, was pretty much bombproof. And the image of those fabulously cosseted people, wringing their hands at the thought of having to sell a spare Fragonard in order to avoid the kind of "penury" for which the average person would have given an arm, is richly comic (or enraging, according to taste); this time it was a false alarm, but it was also a harbinger of what was to come. Soon a growing number of people with country mansions like Polesden Lacey and Faringdon—Lord Berners's home near Swindon—would be looking to the National Trust for help. The Country Houses Committee, established in 1936 with James Lees-Milne as secretary, would investigate ways in which estates could be saved, and the National Trust Acts (of 1937 and 1939) arranged for properties to be transferred while their owners remained in situ—basically, public access was given in exchange for the roof being fixed. After the war, however, the Trust acquired numbers of estates outright, when tax rose to a level whereby people simply handed them over to the government in lieu of payment. When the 11th Duke of Devonshire, husband to the former Deborah Mitford, inherited the title unexpectedly in 1950 and was hit with two sets of death duties, he relinquished the family property of Hardwick Hall in order to be able to maintain Chatsworth House. In London, meanwhile, the town house was increasingly replaced by the service flat, the stately dining room scattered with Sèvres by the restaurant, and the great balls of the old days—the last before the war took place at Holland House in west London—were scaled back. In 1958, the last debutantes would be presented to the young Queen Elizabeth II, thus bringing to an end that ritual of the cars in the Mall, the white vestal virgin dresses, and the gloves handed down through the generations: a tradition both absurd and poignant, although the Queen's sister Margaret is said to have welcomed its cessation on the grounds that by then "every tart in the land was getting in on the act."

This was Princess Margaret's take on the new world, in which wealth was becoming democratized, assets had been nationalized, and the high branches upon which power had long perched were being shaken. Money was under siege. Lord Mountbatten badgered government for a law change that would enable married women (specifically, Edwina Mountbatten) to break a family trust or instruction and access the money. Edwina's income in the early 1920s had been £80,000 a year, which by 1948 was reduced to £4,500: "illustrating," as was said during the House of Commons debate, "the great change in the distribution of wealth which had taken place over recent years." Having been an advocate for socialism during the war, Edwina was now a little less keen. Income tax was nineteen shillings and six pence in the pound, although those with more liquidity and room for maneuver worked out how to play this system. Those who either could not, or did not, found that most of what they possessed was lost to them: that one-woman industry and wealth creator, Agatha Christie, was taxed so heavily after the war that she was twice advised to go bankrupt just to get clear of the rapacious Revenue.

But the rich did not disappear. They never do, in a free society. Just six years after the end of war came the so-called party of the century at Charlie Beistegui's Venetian palazzo: the Aga Khan plus Barbara Hutton plus Salvador Dalí plus Daisy Fellowes plus the film star Gene Tierney plus Winston Churchill, soon to be prime minister once more. Nancy Mitford backed out—"the whole thing would have cost £300 I guess, *hardly* worth it"—but others thought differently, and however boring the actual ball may have been (never enough to drink *chez* Beistegui) the point was not to enjoy oneself but to proclaim one's presence. People spent fortunes on their eighteenth-century costumes—many of which were created by the designers Jacques Fath and Nina Ricci—and on hiring large entourages, plus props, which would turn their arrival along the Grand Canal into a piece of living theater, guests in crinolines and full-bottomed wigs clambering, with perilous bravura, onto the refuge of dry(ish) land. Forget postwar austerity: this was the *Vanity Fair* Oscars party in gondolas. Cecil

Beaton had naturally been in attendance, and in his inimitable, unabashed way he continued to fly the flag for pre-war hauteur. In his diary for 1955 he celebrated the indestructible wealth and élan of Margaret, Duchess of Argyll, who had emerged into society in 1930 as the beautiful heiress daughter of a Scottish industrialist named George Whigham. "Margaret must be one of the few left today who still feels impervious to the approach of the common man," wrote Beaton. "Her money has given her a sense of security, and she is one of the rare examples of someone who has used it well." He then quoted the duchess as saying: "I hate it in America where nowadays your hostess puts on an apron and says she is going to fry a steak. I want other people to do the cooking." Splendid stuff; and an attitude that is by no means extinct, although few duchesses today would be so tactless as to express it.

In the same year, however, Beaton wrote this from the South of France: "Echoes of former glories persist along the now comparatively shabby haunts of the Côte d'Azur," and, from London: "The English have not recovered from the war, and it shows itself in the torpor of their vestments."

* * *

The very rich, like the Duchess of Argyll, wore vestments with no torpor at all. Nevertheless, protect themselves as they might, the forces of egalitarianism were more visible around them. The walls of their castles were more penetrable. This was what Nancy Cunard had perceived and acted upon: a future in which unearned privilege would be up for grabs, or at the very least up for question. Olga Deterding, daughter of a Shell Oil magnate, inherited a portion of her father's £65 million fortune in 1939 at the age of ten. "Do you mean you don't have any *free money*?"

she asked a friend, wide-eyed in wonderment. But in 1956 Olga announced that she had abandoned high society, and was going to work for Dr. Albert Schweitzer at his leper colony in French Equatorial Africa. "Having so much money makes it necessary for me to cleanse myself," she said, in the authentic voice of the anti-heiress.

Twelve years later, during the Paris *évènements*—a bloodless French Revolution in which students hollered for the overthrow of the old order—a young woman was photographed, model-gorgeous, held aloft and waving the flag of Vietnam, staring toward the future with the implacable eyes of a Charlotte Corday. She was Caroline de Bendern, an English-born aristocrat, descended on her mother's side from Oscar Wilde's lover Lord Alfred Douglas. Her grandfather, the Count de Bendern, had inherited the immense fortune of Edward VII's close friend Baron de Hirsch, become a British citizen, moved to Liechtenstein (tax avoidance) where he acquired his new title, and thence to a vast villa in Biarritz, where he lived with more than a hundred cats. Having disinherited his son, on the grounds that he had remarried to a commoner, the count grandly anointed Caroline as his heiress. Nurturing dreams that she would marry into European royalty, like Grace Kelly, he paid for boarding schools and introduced her to the high society of his native Vienna. Then he saw the picture of her in rebel stance. Bang: she too was disinherited. On account of that photograph she lost 450 acres of prime real estate in Paris—"Maybe he thought I'd give it all away to the Communists"—while the young Frenchman who had given her the Vietnam flag became a comfortably rich member of the *haute bourgeoisie*.

Then there were the girls who in 1958 had lined up in their white for that final presentation to the Queen. Among those giggling innocents were two young women who would join creeds that demanded the end, not just of the debutante ritual, but of Buckingham Palace, the monarchical system that it symbolized, and for good measure the government. Teresa Hayter, whose father had been British ambassador in Moscow, became a communist and in 1971 published a book with the punning title *Hayter of the Bourgeoisie*, which called for "World Revolution." Bridget Rose Dugdale, who described her own debutante ball as "one of those pornographic affairs which cost about what sixty old age pensioners receive in six months"—a reasonable observation—became a volunteer with the Provisional Irish Republican Army: the IRA.

She had grown up in Chelsea and in Devon, on a farm with 600 acres, and attended finishing school. Her father was a Lloyd's underwriter and millionaire, which at the time represented a significant amount of wealth. This was not the Cunard shipping line, nor was the family known in the way that Emerald had been—which made Nancy's rebellion akin to that of a minor royal—but there are strong points of resemblance between Rose Dugdale and Nancy Cunard, both of whom believed that extreme activism got one further than the diplomatic variety.

That said, Rose's actions were immeasurably more extreme and less self-destructive. Others, her father included, might consider that she had ruined her lovely heiress life, but she most definitely did not see it that way; she considered that life to be a poisonous anachronism. She kept no foot in the door. If she had turned up to a party, as Nancy did at Grosvenor Square in 1930, she would have dressed as Caroline de Bendern did ("wearing my scruffiest jeans") when she visited her grandfather to be disinherited: in the uniform of the iconoclast, forged in the 1960s as a sign that the times were indeed a-changing. Unlike Nancy, who was intelligent but wayward, Rose had a high-level formal education—studied at Oxford, did a master's at Mount Holyoke

College, had a PhD from London University—and this gave her actions a foundation of cogency as well as emotion. Reason told her that the IRA would, in the end, force its enemies to negotiate. Her character was steelier, less vulnerable than Nancy Cunard's. Nevertheless, her vehement loathing of the class into which she was born, her passionate identification with those whom she believed to be societal victims, her readiness to act in the furtherance of a cause—all that was very much Nancy.

In 1973, aged thirty-two, Rose was convicted of an £82,000 art and silver raid upon her family home in Devon, the proceeds of which probably went to the IRA. The robbery was carried out with three men, one of whom later had his sentence reduced on the grounds that he had been "dominated" by Rose and her lover: Walter Heaton, a militant shop steward and minor criminal with whom she was living in Tottenham, north London, then an immensely deprived area. This is reminiscent of Jessica Mitford's journey from Knightsbridge to Rotherhithe in the late 1930s. Jessica, too, had violently despised her debutante status, and like Rose turned her back on her father, whom she never saw again after her elopement with her communist husband. Rose cross-examined her father at her trial, saying: "I love you, but I hate everything you stand for." To the jury that delivered its verdict, she spoke with her customary rhetorical eloquence. "In finding me guilty you have turned me from a recalcitrant intellectual into a freedom fighter. I know no finer title." The judge did not take her words seriously; he suspended her two-year sentence (Heaton got six years) on the grounds that she was unlikely to offend again.

In the autumn of 1974 the IRA terror reached its peak on mainland Britain. The Guildford and Birmingham pub bombings killed twenty-six people; the Woolwich barracks explosion killed two. At the start of that year Rose—now in Ireland, having joined an active service unit of the IRA—was involved in the hijacking of a helicopter, which dropped bombs inside four milk churns on a Royal Ulster Constabulary station in Strabane. These failed to explode. In April she was a member of an armed gang that invaded and ransacked a Georgian mansion in Co. Wicklow, and stole nineteen paintings—including a Vermeer, a Goya, and a Gainsborough—worth some £7 million. The gang bound, gagged, and pistol-whipped the owners of the house, Sir Alfred and Lady Clementine Beit. Sir Alfred, aged seventy-one, was an industrialist and former politician. Clementine, twelve years his junior, was a first cousin of the Mitford sisters and a patron of the arts in Ireland.

Demands were made for the release of republican prisoners. However, an informant led the police to a farmhouse in Co. Cork where they found the paintings, plus Rose, who was charged under the Offenses Against the State Act. During her sentence—nine years, of which she served six—she married Eddie Gallagher, by whom she was pregnant at the time of her imprisonment. Gallagher was convicted of leading a gang involved in the violent kidnap of a Dutch businessman, held for eighteen days, during which time the release of Rose and other prisoners was demanded. He received a twenty-year term. His wedding to Rose took place in 1978, in the heavily guarded oratory of Limerick jail.

At her trial in Dublin, Rose Dugdale had spent much of the proceedings reading a newspaper with her feet up on the dock. She pleaded guilty to receiving the stolen paintings but, although she had been charged with possession of an automatic pistol, the prosecution could not prove that she had taken part in the armed robbery. After sentencing, she made a speech in which she described Britain as a "filthy enemy." "Yes, I am guilty," she said, "and proudly so, if 'guilty' has come to describe one who takes up arms to defend the people of Ireland against the English tyrant, who would deprive the people of this land of their wealth."

This speech to the Special Criminal Court, delivered in June 1974, was a rebel's cry straight from the heart of the Irish struggle. But it also held unconscious echoes of the words of another rich girl, Patricia Hearst, who four months earlier had been kidnapped by a radical left-wing organization and who, from her place of captivity, announced in a recorded message sent to a radio station in San Francisco: "I have chosen to stay and fight."

* * *

When she moved to Tottenham in the early 1970s, Rose Dugdale cashed in her share of the family syndicate at Lloyd's, a sum of around £150,000, and in true anti-heiress style used it to advance the cause. She even handed out cash directly to impoverished people in north London. The Hearst case contained a parallel with that particular redistributive action. Within a few days of her kidnap, Patty Hearst's captors demanded that her parents should give food—about $70 worth per head—to tens of thousands of people in the poor districts of San Francisco and Los Angeles, a scheme that would have cost somewhere in the infeasible realms of $400 million. Patty herself relayed this demand in her first taped message, recorded in February 1974. "Mom and Dad, I'm OK," she said. "I want to get out of here but the only way is if you do what they say, and do it quickly . . . I'm not being tried for crimes I'm not responsible for. I'm here because I'm a member of the ruling class." The Hearst name did indeed carry huge weight in America. Patty's grandfather William Randolph, upon whose life the film *Citizen Kane* is loosely based, established the media giant Hearst Communications and owned a castle, San Simeon, which stood like an epic film backdrop in the Californian sunlight. His son Randolph, Patty's father, longtime manager of the *San Francisco Examiner* newspaper, at the time of the kidnapping had just become chairman of the company board. He was one of five brothers, however—the family wealth was disseminated, not concentrated—and, with the story of the Lindbergh baby now part of sad and distant folk memory, he had not seen fit to give his daughter personal protection. Aged nineteen, a sophomore student at Berkeley, she had been living unwittingly close to the headquarters of a group of urban guerrillas that called itself the "Symbionese Liberation Army," whose leader, the radical black activist Donald DeFreeze, took on the name "Cinqué" in honor of the leader of a slave rebellion. The group's stated aim was that of reaching "unity between black, white, rich and poor," with which it is hard to disagree, although the means whereby this might be achieved were less Haight-Ashbury, more Altamont. For instance, it transpired that the SLA's original motive for the kidnapping had been to exact the release of two of its imprisoned members, with the Hearst Corporation minded to exert political pressure in the right places. These two prisoners were later convicted of murder. The food plan, with its Dugdale-like public-spiritedness, was bought on the back of extortion.

It was on February 4, 1974, that Patty Hearst was seized from her apartment, where she lived with her fiancé. He was badly assaulted during the operation, which was carried out by two black men and a white woman, and which he described as "commando-like." The SLA claimed responsibility in a letter to the Hearsts sent immediately after the kidnap, which described their daughter as a "prisoner of war."

Yet the prisoner, famously, was about to make common cause with her kidnappers; or so it seemed.

In response to the demand for food distribution, Randolph Hearst had instantly arranged a $2 million loan to put the scheme into place. The SLA was soon in touch again, however, dismissing these efforts as "throwing a few crumbs to the people" and demanding that $6 million be spent. A couple of weeks later the group left a tape recording in a restaurant, and this time the tone from Patty herself had changed. "I do not believe you are doing everything you can, everything in your power," she said to her parents, in a voice that sounded like a bored, possibly drugged, teenager: a Valley Girl who had fallen in with the worst crowd in town and was starting to enjoy it. "I do not believe you are doing anything at all." The food that had already been sent out was criticized for being "of poor quality . . . I know you could have done whatever the SLA asked. I mean, I know you have enough money."

Then came the message that was played on San Francisco radio in April 1974, in which Patty Hearst proclaimed her desire to "stay and fight" with her abductors. She was now—she said—a revolutionary, who had taken the nom de guerre of Che Guevara's comrade and companion: Tania. Still in the relentless "you're so lame" tone of the self-righteous SJW, "Tania" addressed herself directly to the father who had been driven half mad by the refined torture of silence, followed by a crazy demand from the kidnappers, which he frenetically attempted to meet, followed by silence. "You said you are concerned with my life and the lives and interests of all oppressed people . . . But you are a liar in both areas and as a member of the ruling class I know that your interests and Mom's are never the interests of the people . . . One thing which I learned is that the ruling classes will do anything in their power in order to maintain their position of control over the masses, even if that means the sacrifice of their own."

"We've had her twenty years," Randolph Hearst told the press, "and they've had her sixty days. I don't believe she is going to change her philosophy that quickly, and that permanently, and I'll never believe it until . . . she is free to talk without interference."

Less than two weeks later, Patty was photographed by hidden surveillance in a San Francisco branch of the Hibernia Bank, wearing a Che beret and holding a semiautomatic rifle. As the FBI succinctly put it, the only question at issue was whether she was acting of her own free will. She herself sent another tape, stating unequivocally that she was "a soldier in the people's army." Her parents, she added, were "pig Hearsts," and her father was "Adolf." Any suggestion that she had been brainwashed into committing an armed bank robbery was "ridiculous to the point of being beyond belief."

The following month, May 1974, events moved fast toward a bloody conclusion. After an incident in which two members of the SLA, William and Emily Harris, were caught shoplifting in a sports store, Patty fired repeatedly into the overhead of the shop front. Then she and the Harrises hijacked two cars and drove off with the owners. It was later reported that Patty had chatted pleasantly during the drive about what life was like in a radical gang. While she was thus engaged, police were moving in on the main headquarters of the organization; it is impossible to know whether they did so in the certainty that the scion of the Hearst dynasty was absent, and thus safe from gunfire in the ensuing shoot-out. The six gang members inside the stucco bungalow were killed, with the police launching a sustained attack that eventually caused the house to catch fire. The confusion and carnage were very great. For some time the identities of the dead were unknown; Donald DeFreeze, it later transpired, had shot himself when the flames took hold. The surviving gang members—William and Emily Harris, together with Patty Hearst—went on the run, and remained so for sixteen months, until they were found almost by accident when following up a routine tip-off. Patty was arrested at the apartment of an SLA associate in the Mission district of San Francisco. "Don't shoot," she said, when the law finally turned up. "I'll go with you." Around ten automatic weapons were found at the premises.

Although the SLA itself no longer existed, its creed of anarchic warfare had lived on undaunted during those fugitive months, and indeed it was then that the most serious crime with which Patty was involved took place. During a bank robbery in Carmichael, California, a customer was shot dead. Patty, who was driving the getaway car, was thus at risk for felony murder charges, on top of the many others that she had already accumulated: the federal charges of bank robbery in San Francisco and illegal use of firearms in Los Angeles, plus nineteen state charges including kidnapping (the hijacked cars) and armed robbery.

Small wonder that, a few weeks after she had given her occupation cheerily as "urban guerrilla," her loyalty to the Symbionese Liberation Army underwent a violent volte-face. And, in the same way that Patricia Hearst began to re-emerge from beneath the freedom fighter persona of Tania, so a defense appeared. When it had been suggested eighteen months earlier by her sorrowing, terrified parents, she had laughed the notion to scorn, but now she herself was saying it: that she had committed all those fearsome acts under extreme duress from her kidnappers, that effectively she had been brainwashed by them to act as they did, because she believed that they would kill her if she did not become one of them.

* * *

Was this the truth, or not? It was the question that the FBI had asked when it all started, and even officialdom struggled to answer it—it disbelieved her, then it hedged its bets, and finally it accepted her story. At her trial in 1976, Patty was found guilty of bank robbery and given a term of seven years' imprisonment.

Natalie Barney, fearless creator of a new design for living.

The heiress as artist: Romaine Brooks, whose lovers were the subjects of her finest paintings.

The ineffable Mrs. Greville (*right*), the "social Napoleon" who commanded the battlefield of her drawing rooms.

Polesden Lacey (*below*), Mrs. Greville's centrally heated paradise near Dorking—now a National Trust property—where the future George VI and Queen Elizabeth spent their honeymoon.

Emerald, Lady Cunard, the mistress of reinvention and queen of Grosvenor Square, in a 1924 illustration for *The Sketch*.

Lord Mountbatten with his glittering prize, the superrich Edwina.

Daisy Fellowes:
never a dull moment.

Wild things: Alice de Janzé and her beloved Samson.

Ice-cool Nancy Cunard in her bangles, at the Harlem hotel where she took up residence in 1932.

Rose Dugdale, on her release from prison in 1980. The following year she campaigned in support of the hunger-striking Irish Republican prisoners led by Bobby Sands.

The image of the rebel-heiress: Patty Hearst and her gun.

Christina Onassis—plus
Jackie, whose former
brother-in-law Ted
Kennedy walks behind—
at the funeral of her father
Aristotle in 1975: the third
bereavement in the space
of two and a half years.

Barbara Hutton with
her first husband, the
unabashed heiress-hunter
Alexis Mdivani.

Barbara in *Vogue,* 1937, during her marriage to Count Haugwitz-Reventlow.

Barbara Hutton at her villa in Tangier, photographed by Cecil Beaton in 1970, by which time her marrying days were done.

Winfield House, Barbara's house in Regent's Park, on which she spent almost $7 million but owned for less than ten years.

Angela Burdett-Coutts, the bejeweled philanthropist, eyes weary with the weight of the heiress's burden.

In 1979 this sentence was commuted by President Carter. In 2001, one of the last acts of Bill Clinton's presidency was to give a pardon to Patricia Hearst Shaw, as she then was, a married woman with two daughters, active in charitable organizations and a successful dog breeder: so complete a reversion to type, it was as if the events of the 1970s had simply never happened.

She had been, before the kidnapping, an unremarkable young woman. Attractive, average, apolitical. She had refused to become a debutante, but post-Vietnam and the Summer of Love that system was as vieux jeu as powdering one's nose. To have been engaged to be married at so young an age showed an excess of conventionality, if anything. If she had found in the SLA a means to escape that particular trap—well, there were easier ways of doing it. Heiresses were no longer commodities to be bartered without their consent in the marriage market.

At the time of her arrest she was revealed to be seriously underweight, smoking compulsively, and with an IQ that had dropped alarmingly. In her mugshot she looks oddly beautiful— with the stony glamor of the renegade—but at her trial for the Hibernia Bank robbery, by which time the euphoria in her had died down, she appeared weary and almost apathetic. There was a great deal against her; not just the case itself, but the way in which it was being framed. Interviews with psychiatrists had revealed no diagnosed mental illness, therefore she was deemed responsible for her actions. "Brainwashing" was dismissed by her first counsel as being no defense in law. The replacement attorney asserted a defense of coercion or duress, which would—or should—have been relevant to the question of intent. The judge, however, was not sympathetic. As only a judge can do he pushed detrimental testimony to the fore, and affected indifference to evidence that was helpful to the accused.

With regard to the armed robbery at the Hibernia Bank, Patty Hearst testified that she had shown enthusiasm for the crime because she dared not do otherwise; in support of this, photographs were shown of other gang members pointing their guns at her in the bank. The counter-argument was equally plain to see, however, and it was the image of Patty holding the semi-automatic. It said that her dead-eyed zeal had been genuine, that she had been possessed with the true spirit of rebellion, and that—in the words of Emily Harris, a dangerous adversary—the brainwashing was being done now, by the Hearst family, who were turning her away from her beliefs. That, said Harris, is what the rich and powerful do.

Patty was not tried on this occasion for the incident at the sports shop. Nevertheless a question was asked about it. Why, when William Harris was caught shoplifting and in the hands of the shop manager, had she not seized the chance to escape, but instead had fired an entire magazine from her gun to force Harris's release? It was a good question. It was *the* question. "When it happened I didn't even think," she told the court, "I just did it, and if I had not done it and they had been able to get away they would have killed me." The reply was credible in relation to that one instance, which would have taken her by surprise and quite possibly removed the capacity for thought. Yet it was alleged that she had had at least ten opportunities to flee the SLA, particularly throughout the sixteen-month period when she was on the run. This is perhaps the most extraordinary part of the story; although the kidnap victim who no longer knows how to live beyond even an invisible perimeter is now a more familiar phenomenon than it was almost fifty years ago. In fact "Stockholm syndrome"—in which a victim forms a powerful and primitive bond with a kidnapper—took its name from a case that had happened not long before the Hearst trial, in 1973, when four Swedish bank workers were taken hostage, and one woman begged to be allowed to leave the premises with her captors. But this was still too recent for the judge and jury in the Hearst trial, the mysteries of which were ill-suited to being pondered in a court of law. In a television interview in December 1976, when Patty was on bail pending appeal, she was asked why she had not seized the chance to escape. She replied: "It's crazy. It doesn't make any sense at all, and it's something that I'm still working on myself." She also described Donald DeFreeze as a "complete maniac, alcoholic, egotistical, raping, murdering, horrible person."

At her trial, she stated that she had been threatened with death "hundreds of times" by her captors. She was given the choice of fighting with them or dying. For the first two weeks of her captivity—during which, she said, she had little hope of getting out alive—she was kept in a cupboard wearing a blindfold, only removed when she went to the bathroom, to which she was escorted by an SLA member in a ski mask. She testified that she had been given four black eyes, and that when the gang changed hideouts she was carted to and fro in a dustbin. In a bizarre episode during the trial, she escorted the jury on a tour of these hideouts and pointed out a cupboard—around five feet by eight—into which holes had been drilled. She also said that she had been sexually assaulted in the cupboard by several members of the SLA, including a man named William Wolfe. Yet in one of the taped messages sent during her time with the gang, she had described Wolfe as her lover: "the gentlest, most beautiful man I ever knew."

The conundrum posed by her relationship with Wolfe—had she been forced? Had she been willing?—contained, in microcosm, the entire question of Patty's relationship with the SLA. And it acquired still greater significance when Emily Harris gave a magazine interview from her prison cell, in which she alleged that Patty had kept a trinket that Wolfe had given her.

This was damaging. So too was Patty's explanation in court, that she had kept it because she believed it to be of archaeological significance. Pushing further, the prosecution in its final speech averred that the women in the SLA—staunch feminists—would not have stood for Patty being raped; if it seemed that she might actually have enjoyed sleeping with members of this gang, then all bets were off when it came to her other activities. Meanwhile the closing speech for the defense—"there was not anything close to proof beyond a shadow of a doubt that Patty Hearst wanted to be a bank robber . . . There was talk about her dying, and she wanted to survive"—sounds more like the oratory of Donald Trump than Clarence Darrow.

What was lacking throughout is *any sense at all* that this whole thing—the trial, the questions, the agonies of the Hearst parents, the image of the heiress with the semiautomatic—had happened because a young woman had been abducted; from that all else proceeded, just as it had for Ellen Turner, Clementina Clerke, Sibble Morris . . . Ellen Turner in 1826, taken from her school, carted from pillar to post by a plausible rogue against whom she was forced to defend her reputation in a sensational trial; Clementina Clerke in 1791, abducted and twice impregnated by a man whom she dared not betray, because if he were hanged her marriage would be annulled and her children illegitimate; Sibble Morris in 1728, kidnapped and forced to marry by a gang of women who pulled off her "Cloaths," saved only by the fact that her rapist-husband ran away, and therefore nobody could say she had wanted him to do those things . . . Were those ancient stories so different from that of Patricia Hearst? If she had formed a relationship with her captors, if she had even been stirred for a time by the glinting certainties of their radical nihilism, did not that still proceed from the first cause: the sudden outrageous displacement from the life that she knew?

Not until May 1977—when she pleaded no contest to the charge relating to the sports shop incident—did anybody in a court of law acknowledge this. Patty Hearst was placed on probation for five years by a judge who stated that she had, in his opinion, been subject to extreme coercion. She may have had no legal defense of "brainwashing," said California Attorney-General Evelle J. Younger, but why had this all started? Because she had been kidnapped. The following year her bail was revoked and she was returned to jail, where a dead rat appeared on her bed on the day that the Harrises, the last remaining members of the SLA, were arraigned for her kidnapping. Calmly reiterating the counter-argument, the one that had by then taken hold, the Harrises testified that Patricia Hearst had been treated with "compassion, sensitivity and respect" before she too became a member of the Symbionese Liberation Army. The prosecution dropped the more serious charges relating to the kidnap, and the couple were sentenced to ten years—just three more than Patty—of which they served eight.

The California Attorney-General, who had cut to the heart of the matter regarding this case, had made another remark. There was, he said, a double standard for the rich, and it worked in the opposite way from the one that people believed: had Patty been poor, her own sentence would have been lighter. Contentious, yes. In that particular instance, not without foundation.

Patricia Hearst, heiress and bearer of a renowned American name, was a member of the class that dominated the courtroom in which she was tried. How to deal with her, given that the evidence was too complex for complete exoneration? How to cope with what she represented, the young woman who had, in some way, made common cause with those who threatened destruction and terror? Perhaps it was easier to dismiss her outright for having "betrayed" her background. For what she represented was truly fearful, in an age when militancy, both to left and right, was threatening to tear its way through society and was now—it seemed—seducing the daughters of the rich with its brave-new-world absolutism. If only there had not been that photograph! If only Patty Hearst had not looked so damn good, so dangerously alluring, in what the fashionistas would have called her Radical Chic. Perhaps, in the end, it was the optics that did the greatest damage: the image of the girl in the beret, with the family millions and the semiautomatic rifle.

BARBARA

AND SO, IN a way, the story is back to where it started. Abducting an heiress, as in the old days. There was no sure means to seal up that particular chink in the rich girl's armor. Ultimately it depended upon how determined a kidnapper was to exploit her vulnerability.

There had been a prominent case six years before the Hearst affair, involving Barbara Mackle, twenty-year-old daughter of a Florida businessman. In December 1968 Barbara had been staying with her mother at a motel in Atlanta. Mrs. Mackle opened the door to a man claiming to be a detective; he chloroformed and gagged her, then absconded with Barbara. A ransom demand for $500,000 was paid instantly by Mr. Mackle. However, the drop was inadvertently intercepted by the police, who scared the kidnapper away from a car containing the money—the officers claimed to have been left uninformed about arrangements made by the FBI. A second attempt was made to deliver the $500,000, this time via the intermediary of a priest from Miami, who left the cash—it was reported—at the West Palm Beach home of Joe Kennedy. Four days after her abduction, Barbara was released. The kidnapper had given instructions as to where she would be found, by a hillside in Georgia, where searchers heard a repeated knocking from underground. She had been held for eighty hours in a ventilated box.

Her abductor—an escaped prisoner named Gary Krist—had stowed the ransom money in the hull of a rotting boat on Hog Island in Florida, where he was captured after a chase through swamplands and jungles on the Gulf of Mexico; a drama that can be appreciated because this story, unlike that of most kidnappings, had a happy ending. Less so in the case that it was thought to have "inspired," through these highly publicized tales of underground hiding places—that of the 1975 kidnap and murder of the British heiress Lesley Whittle.

There was nothing to be done about this kind of victimhood. It was a risk that went with being an heiress, just as other risks went with being poor. What *could* be avoided, because it depended upon the heiress herself, was that other old area of weakness: the bad relationship. Mary Davies, Mary Stoney Bowes, Catherine Tylney—they had all been vastly foolish when it came to men and money; astoundingly so, given that they knew that marriage would leave them with next to no rights. Later heiresses did have legal protection, together with a freedom of choice unknown to almost every woman who had lived before them. Yet they were capable of behaving with that same staggering folly. The law did not compel them to give their money to a husband, but they did it anyway; and not just to a husband, of course, but to anybody clever enough to work upon them (in the case of tobacco heiress Doris Duke, her butler*). The strong among them were strong

---

* This extraordinary man, Bernard Lafferty, managed to penetrate the defenses of a woman who had been told by her father on his deathbed: "Trust no one." Doris had listened, and had kept two acquisitive husbands at bay. In the few years before her own death in 1993, aged eighty, she revised

indeed—Winnaretta, Daisy, Natalie Barney, Mrs. Greville, Emerald Cunard, Rose Dugdale—yet they were outnumbered by the vulnerable; as perhaps is true of any group of people, because strength is more difficult, although these women had every advantage to *make* them strong. But there was always boredom, the ineffable melancholy, the shadowless sameness of another beautiful fucking day. There was guilt. And there was the weakness at the heart of so many heiresses, the fatal flaw, the desire to be loved *for herself*; which led, oh so often and with oh such excruciating irony, to the shortcut of buying love instead.

In 2002 a woman named Tania Campbell, described in *The Times* as an "heiress"—that word, that signifier—married a man

---

her will five times, thus keeping hopeful legatees at bay also. Would she have changed her mind yet again before she died? Or was it her definitive decision to name her butler as her executor, and moreover to place him in control of the Doris Duke Charitable Foundation, which was to receive most of her $1.2 billion fortune? In 1995 Lafferty relinquished this control and agreed a settlement with Doris's disinherited adopted daughter. Nevertheless, the mystery of the will remains.

Lafferty, who was born in Co. Donegal in 1945, had been Doris's butler for the last seven years of her life. He was flamboyantly gay, a big heavy man who carried out his duties in uniform, barefoot, with an earring and a ponytail. He had mixed easily in show business circles—within the inevitable avalanche of legal challenges to the will, the singer Peggy Lee was among those staunch in Lafferty's defense—and must have had a great deal of careless charm. Whether Doris Duke knew of incidents such as the one when he was found naked among several empty bottles of Grand Marnier (of such distinguished vintage that the labels were handwritten)—whether if she *had* known, this would have changed her view of Lafferty—is impossible to say. There is no reason to think that she had lost her mind, but her reasoning otherwise is impenetrable.

Inevitably, it was suggested that Lafferty had murdered his employer (the butler did it), but the accusations came to nothing. Just three years later, he died at his Bel Air mansion at the age of fifty-one. Again, the death was officially deemed to be unsuspicious.

named Chad Johnson, thirty-eight years her junior. They had met at an art gallery in her home town of Cheltenham. Johnson managed never to consummate the marriage—he spent most nights with the mother of his four children—but instead to steal £250,000 from his wife, whom he also persuaded to cash in her shares and put her flat into his name. When she was declared bankrupt he sold the property to an associate, as a means to keep it away from her creditors.

Johnson was sentenced to three and a half years in 2007, but was out in time to be imprisoned again in 2008, along with four family members, for a succession of burglaries in which antiques with an estimated worth of £80 million were stolen from a number of country mansions. "I feel I have got the fucking right to rob the lords, the sirs and the ladies" was the philosophy of Johnson's father.* The Symbionese Liberation Army would have certainly approved; so too a couple of the anti-heiresses.

Tania Campbell, by comparison with these highly planned operations, had been mere useful small change. Her delusions about Chad Johnson were monumental and pitiable. Such blindness is not unique to heiresses but, when money is involved, a particular quality of self-deception is required. At Johnson's trial in 2007 she had begged the judge not to jail him. She had, she said, a compulsion to spend her money—another heiress trope—and on one occasion had bought twenty-one refrigerators, but thanks to her husband she had stopped such wastefulness. Yes, he had sold her flat, but the fact was that she had given it to him as a wedding present.

"All I know," she said, "is that we are in love."

---

* Ricky Johnson was invited to express this view on BBC television, which in 2005—before the full extent of the traveler family's criminal activities was known—made a series entitled *Summer with the Johnsons.*

* * *

A woman in Cheltenham, shopping addictively for fridges rather than Ferragamo, deprived of a birthright worth a small percentage of the $50 million–plus inherited when Barbara Hutton came of age; yet this story reminds one irresistibly of the last of Barbara's seven marriages, in 1964, to a man named Raymond Doan. She was fifty-one by then, prematurely aged by the same *régime* favored by Nancy Cunard—no food and enough drink to sink a private gondola. Doan was half-French, half-Vietnamese, working for a French oil company but by inclination a painter, living in Marrakech with his wife and children. Barbara was at her palace in Tangier, which Doan painted from outside its high walls for a solo exhibition that opened in 1963, with Barbara in attendance. She bought the work, plus everything else on offer, and moved Raymond Doan into the palace.

She had been lured by the fact that this man—whom she had met once before, just briefly, again when he was trying to sell paintings—had sent her some effusive poetry, written in French (the language of love). She adored poetry and wrote it herself. What she did not know was that Doan had been encouraged to compose these verses by his brother Maurice, also living in Marrakech, who had identified Barbara as the easiest target in Morocco and come up with a plan to reel her in. As with Chad Johnson's approach to Tania Campbell, this was not complicated. It did not have to be. Doan's wife and children were sent off to the Canary Islands, preparatory to a divorce being set in motion, and all was set fair. It might not have been, because prior to the exhibition Barbara was told by a friend exactly what had been going on with the Doans (the gossip was rife); she must have recognized the truth of it but, being what she was, that made her all the more determined to ignore it. A couple of months later she swept into the Laotian Embassy in Rabat and offered £50,000 for a title for her new boyfriend, who thenceforth was known as Prince Raymond Doan.

This went on for two years, at the end of which the prince received $2 million. Maurice, the architect of the whole affair, received a flat in Paris. Quite a normal transaction by the standards of Barbara Hutton, but a hell of a payday for a couple of people who she knew had marked her down as a human cashpoint machine.

Oddly enough there are similarities with her first marriage, in 1933, to the Georgian-born Alexis Mdivani. It too lasted two years, and Mdivani also bore the title of "Prince"; not because Barbara had bought it for him, although his use of the title was dodgy nonetheless. To be frank, very few people in the smart, silly, transatlantic society to which Mdivani belonged had the first clue where Georgia actually was, let alone whether it had princes, kings, or possibly tsars. But he was a man of aristocratic bearing and vaguely noble ancestry, and with his polo playing plus nodding acquaintance with the Prince of Wales he carried the thing off. He was at one with the heiress-hunters of old, the sexual swashbucklers and dandies who had rampaged through earlier centuries looking for rich girls to bedazzle. Before marrying Barbara he had been the husband of Louise Van Alen, who was related to a complexity of Astors and Vanderbilts; according to Elsa Maxwell, a close acquaintance of all parties, he swapped wives but always remained "the same queer, ambitious, reckless character." This was the Mdivani way. He and his brothers, Serge and David, were called the "marrying Mdivanis," male equivalents of the "magnificent Morgans." For sure they must have had something. Serge's third wife was his former sister-in-law Louise (they married in 1936, a month before his death in a fall from his polo pony). Before that, he had been married to the silent-film star Pola Negri, whom he dumped when she lost her money in the 1929 crash; then to the opera singer Mary McCormic, who described him as "the world's worst gigolo." David, meanwhile, also married a film star, Mae Murray, who claimed in a divorce court that he had assaulted her and spent her $3 million fortune. So one could hardly say that Barbara hadn't been warned.

Alexis was probably a smoother operator, scanning the Lido and the Riviera for the daughters of multi-millionaires—an activity in which he was silkily encouraged by his sister, Roussadana, wife of the Spanish painter José Maria Sert, who, with the skill of a Madame de Merteuil, befriended twenty-year-old Barbara Hutton and pushed her into Alexis's path. Despite her greater refinement, Roussie played the same role as the female accomplice to the eighteenth-century heiress-hunter, preparing the ground before the man moved in to reap his reward. "HAVE WON THE PRIZE" was the key phrase in a telegram sent from Alexis to Roussie in April 1933, when Barbara accepted his proposal.

She was still underage by seven months. And therein lay a danger of which her father, financier Franklin Hutton, became quickly aware. The blissful couple intended to marry in Paris but, according to French law, if a woman married before she was twenty-one, her property would come under the control of her husband. The old days really were back with a vengeance; whether or not Roussie and Alexis were aware of this law, and one rather suspects that they were, it was a very nice piece of leverage. Franklin Hutton, whose stewardship of his daughter's Woolworth trust fund had been exemplary, moved into action, and strong-armed Alexis into waiving this particular legal right. Instead, the groom-to-be received a dowry of $1 million and a substantial annual allowance, on top of the millions that he had received from Louise Van Alen. Then Barbara began to spend on him in earnest: a wedding present of two strings of polo ponies; Alexis's wedding present to her—a $40,000 necklace—for which she of course had paid; and a Venetian palazzo, the twelfth-century Abbazia di San Gregorio, whose deeds were registered in her husband's name.

From that point, early as it was in her life, the course appears to have been set. Marry, spend, marry, spend, until both emotionally and financially—with Barbara the two walked in uneasy tandem—there was pretty much nothing left.

In the mid-1930s, however, there was a spectacular amount. Only Doris Duke had more. The Woolworth Corporation, built by Barbara's colossus of a grandfather, had begun as a string of small stores—the first of which opened in 1879—and by 1905 the company was grossing $10 million per annum. Frank Winfield Woolworth, who like Isaac Singer was looked upon askance by New York society, had no intention of retreating in defeat to Europe, as Singer had done. Anyway he had a business to run. He built a Fifth Avenue mansion (plus more houses around the corner, on East 80th Street, for his three daughters and his servants) and the sixty-two-room Winfield Hall, on Long Island. He also raised the great Woolworth Building in lower Manhattan, whose fifty-nine stories made it for some years the tallest skyscraper in the world. It was completed in 1913, the year after Barbara's birth.

Her mother, Edna, had married money, as the rich so often do. Franklin Hutton was shrewd, successful, a heavy drinker and a womanizer. In 1917 Edna was found dead at the Plaza Hotel, where the family was then staying; no autopsy was ordered, and officially the cause of death was "suffocation" caused by mastoiditis, although it was later revealed that the police had reported the presence of an empty vial of strychnine. It also recorded that Edna's dead body had been found by Barbara. She went to live with her grandfather—Franklin Hutton had no objection to this arrangement—and, after Frank Woolworth's death in 1919, moved between the homes of various relations. When her grandmother died in 1924, the $76 million Woolworth fortune was divided between two surviving daughters and one grandchild.

The $28 million that Barbara inherited, aged eleven, had by 1933 increased to $42 million, and was further supplemented by money direct from her mother's estate. Her first action was to give $5 million to her father, who had since remarried, as a thank-you for handling the trust fund. This, too, set a tone: of compulsive generosity, and of spending as though the money sprang from a well (an oil well) that it was impossible to stamp down. There was a flagrancy to her extravagance—an invitation, as it seemed, to criticize what was merely a luck of birth—as if it were easier to welcome opprobrium in, than to wait for it to storm the battlements. Barbara knew that her life would be scrutinized, and that a woman in particular could rarely win with the press, nor indeed with the public. This, too, she confronted head-on (unlike Doris Duke, who—until *l'affaire Lafferty*—maintained an elegant distance from her own heiress status). It was as though she were trapped, from the first, in a kind of masochistic relish. In the midst of the Great Depression, when people who had kept their money were best advised to keep quiet about it, she did the very opposite. Every aspect of her wedding—the eighty couture outfits brought to the Paris Ritz, the honeymoon in the royal suite of the Excelsior on the Venice Lido, the un-American suavity of her dubiously titled husband—was detailed in the newspapers, which knew perfectly well that they had found a perfect hate figure to alleviate the dire times. Barbara was the "Million Dollar Baby" in the era of "Brother, Can You Spare a

Dime": popular songs, both perceptive little masterpieces, both covered by Bing Crosby, with the first seeming to constitute a satire upon the second.

A woman like Daisy Fellowes, who felt no guilt at all about her wealth, would have been untouched by such criticism. For that reason alone, it is unlikely that it would have been leveled at her—hitting a target is no fun if the arrows bounce straight off again. With Barbara, however, the newspapers were deliciously aware that she knew she was being pierced. Like the other "symbolic" heiress, Christina Onassis—who married four times with what seemed like a knowing, sorrowing delight in her own recklessness—Barbara carried the scent of vulnerability, and there was not enough Mitsouko in the world to cover it.

* * *

The day after her divorce from Alexis, granted in Reno, she married Count Kurt von Haugwitz-Reventlow; like Henry VIII with Jane Seymour she saw no point in waiting. Reventlow was a genuine count, a Danish aristocrat with a bona fide castle plus 16,000 acres, and, although more than happy to have so rich a wife, he was not a blatant fortune hunter. Indeed, as Franklin Hutton's spies reported back, he was a considerable step up from her first choice, and it thus seemed possible to dismiss the Mdivani affair as a sex-crazed youthful folly, a hugely expensive starter marriage (Alexis's death in 1935, from a high-speed crash in his Rolls-Royce, marked the final chapter in that lurid novella). The fact that the Reventlow marriage produced a child—Lance, born in London in 1936—gives it a more stable and adult appearance, although the birth itself was a disorientating event. During the caesarean delivery, then much more of a rarity, Barbara ruptured a blood vessel and nearly died.

BARBARA

As with Nancy Cunard, who endured her own gynecological trauma, Barbara was not a healthy specimen. Only youth was on her side in the battle to regain her strength. She was a vicious dieter, who had diminished from the plump, pretty creature at her 1930 coming-out ball to a wraith of a woman, as skinny as her cigarette holder and as insubstantial as the smoke that came out of it. It has been suggested that anorexia set in after a casual, cruel reference to her weight from Alexis Mdivani—this would be quite in tune with what one knows of his character, and eating disorders can indeed proceed from a one-off remark. Barbara began to endure days on end with no food at all (interspersed with inevitable periods of gorging), which alarmed Reventlow and caused him to dread meals. She became immensely smart, in that bodiless way favored by certain society women, but there was an unhappy look to her spindly silhouette and dissipated eyes. In newsreel footage she is as faint as a smudge, kept together only by her clothes and her courteous manner; one has the impression that even to collapse from hunger would be too much effort.

Unlike Nancy, who really did not want to eat, Barbara strove continually not to want to. Dieting in that way can take over a person's life. The debilitating, exhausting, soul-warping effect of constant starvation cannot be underestimated in the story of Barbara Hutton; nor in that of Christina Onassis, who believed herself to be unattractive and whose heavy body looked all the clumsier against that of her stepmother, Jacqueline Kennedy, whom her shipping tycoon father Aristotle married in 1968, when Christina was aged eighteen. She fought constantly to be thin—to be beautiful, in fact, which she saw as synonymous with thinness: an attritional war that, together with her dependency upon barbiturates and amphetamines, surely contributed to her death from a heart attack at the age of thirty-seven.

331

With Barbara, that came later. For the time being, when she still had a young woman's natural energy reserves, there was couture and art and a joy in beauty. She mixed with the hostesses of London, in those splendid drawing rooms where privilege was sufficiently fertilized with intelligence to create a last fabulous flowering of high society, and met the same people—the Coopers, the Prince of Wales and Mrs. Simpson, Daisy Fellowes—in Paris and Venice. She wrote poetry, some of which she published in two separate collections, *The Enchanted* in 1934, and *The Wayfarer* in 1957. She acquired a property in the middle of Regent's Park—the dilapidated Hertford Villa, set in twelve and a half acres of prime London land—which she demolished, rebuilt, and renamed Winfield House, after her grandfather's mansion on Long Island. She spent some $4.5 million on the house and grounds, around $2 million on interiors (such as a Gold Room, brimful of carats), and $250,000 on the real purpose of the exercise: a security system. Bulletproof windows, strong rooms, the lot.

Security was one thing; Gold Rooms another. Just four years after coming into her inheritance, Barbara was displaying clear signs of being unable to handle it. She received around $2 million per annum from investments, a sum that in 1936–7 she spent on jewelry alone. In that year she also bought Winfield House, four cars, and a $250,000 yacht with two elevators, kept on the Lido. It was a kind of madness: it is scarcely bearable to compare this excess, this superfluity of cloying luxury, with the situation of the Woolworth workers who went on strike in 1938 demanding a minimum weekly wage of $20. When Count Reventlow proposed that, in order to put her financial affairs to rights, Barbara should renounce her US citizenship and take that of his native Denmark, the uproar in America was loud indeed. The desertion of New York for Britain by William

Waldorf Astor in 1899—which had gone down very badly—was as nothing compared with this. Tax avoidance, even when entirely legal, touches a powerful nerve. And this was avoidance on a Woolworth Building scale: an estimated $45 million's worth. Comparing Barbara with the striking workers, a Scripps-Howard newspaper columnist wrote: "In a way it was none of the shopgirls' business whom Miss Babbie married, but in a sort of way it may be that. Because even shopgirls have dreams of love on $10 a week . . . And furthermore, these shopgirls . . . had been contributing their mites toward the income of $2,000,000 a year without which their own 'princes' might never have aroused the love of her ideal. Now she has betrayed them for all time."

Later, it transpired that the Danish citizenship ploy had been urged by Barbara's husband in order to protect their son's inheritance, and that Reventlow—who was revealing himself to be a highly controlling individual—had made refusal difficult. That is all too believable, although it has little bearing upon the deranged spending that had put Barbara so far on the back foot.

The marriage ended in 1938. There would be an unpleasant custody battle for their son, a fight between two parents who were both fairly hopeless in their different ways. Lance intensely disliked his father and never forgave Barbara for failing to attend his graduation from school in Arizona (the following day she gave him a Cadillac: a gesture entirely typical in its cluelessness, guilt, and desperate fingers-crossed hope that money might make her forgivable). The person who did take a proper interest in Lance was his mother's third husband, Cary Grant, whom she married in 1942. The war had allowed Barbara to redeem her reputation somewhat, through financial donations to the Red Cross and the Free French movement and the gift of her yacht to the US government; this tentative new start, underlined by her marriage to a handsome, gloriously talented, complex but down-to-earth man, gives a sense that here was the moment at which her life could have steadied itself and moved happily forward, if she had only been able to let it. Grant was openly bored by Barbara's weakness for the sneery-weary drawlers of Eurotrash café society ("if one more phoney Earl had entered that house, I'd have suffocated") and preferred smaller evenings with fun, relaxed people like Jimmy Stewart, David Niven, and Marlene Dietrich. Possibly Barbara felt intimidated by the ease with which these particular stars negotiated their celebrity. Possibly she felt inadequate with Grant, whom by definition she could neither impress nor buy. Possibly she did not know how to get through the days in what was, despite her husband's fame, her first "normal" marriage: he went to work, earned a living, and came home wanting peace and quiet—certainly not in the mood to eat caviar with somebody like Barbara's cousin Jimmy Donahue, a wild homosexual addicted to cruel practical jokes, and—for all his barbed-wire wit and close friendship with the Duchess of Windsor—as pathetically unable to handle great wealth as Barbara herself (Donahue died aged fifty-one, in a rumored act of suicide).

In any event, with her peerless gift for screwing up and shooting herself in the Blahniks, Barbara divorced Cary Grant in 1945. The following year she donated Winfield House to the US government, a gesture acknowledged by President Truman as "most generous and patriotic." It was a further rapprochement with her homeland. But it was also a sign that she had changed, that she had abandoned any dream of leading a settled life, a family life, in a home like the one that her grandfather had owned on Long Island. Instead Barbara kept moving—from country to country, husband to husband. In 1947, for reasons unknown, she married Prince Igor Troubetzkoy, an amateur cyclist of Lithuanian descent. In 1953 came the craziest marriage yet: a fifty-three-day ride on the helter-skelter with Porfirio Rubirosa, a former diplomat from the Dominican Republic, late of Doris Duke's wedding bed, then of Zsa Zsa Gabor's bed, bath, and anywhere. He was School of Mdivani—a polo-playing gigolo, famed for his sexual prowess—although more charming; one senses the presence of a sense of humor, something that Barbara herself could have done with. It is sad to think of him crashing fatally into a tree in the Bois de Boulogne in 1965. He was out for what he could get, such as the $500,000 that Doris Duke gave him as a wedding present, but there was something disarming about the openness with which he did it. And these women did not have to succumb to him (the list of those who did includes Joan Crawford, Dolores del Rio, Veronica Lake, and Christina Onassis's mother, Tina Niarchos). They knew his reputation. He was a "playboy," as such men were then called. The term was banded about readily in the mid-twentieth century—it was a very 1950s word, indeed Hugh Hefner founded *Playboy* magazine in the year that Barbara married Rubirosa—and was not necessarily synonymous with gigolo: Prince Aly Khan was the archetype, with his marriage to Rita Hayworth, his racehorses, his affairs with everybody from the Duchess of Argyll to Gene Tierney, and he had plenty of money of his own. The type descended directly from the Regency buck, but differed in that twentieth-century women had acquired the power to deal with him. One could even perceive a feminist dimension in the phenomenon of the playboy. Was not Rubirosa, who offered his services to all these alpha women, the male equivalent of the 1960s groupie who moved from Jagger to Richards to Clapton to Page? When Barbara had had her turn—which could not possibly have been worth the $66,000 a day that the marriage cost her, but she had known that was the deal—she moved on and left him to Zsa Zsa, while she herself married her old friend Gottfried von Cramm, a German tennis player whose preference for sleeping with men ensured that this marriage, too, would be of short duration. Then came Doan. He was not her final lover, but he marked an ending to a turbulent quest for something that Barbara had craved and did not know how to accept. Her last three marriages imply that she was aware of this inability, and was almost having a defiant laugh at her own expense. But these moribund, cynical transactions were a long way from her 1930s poem "The Enchanted," with its sad, sweet dignity:

> Will you remember when day / Has died upon my leaving
> Will you stay in loneliness / And silent grieving . . .

Noël Coward, who had read Barbara's poems to her in 1957, and had concluded that money was always between her and happiness, finished his diary entry for that evening in understated fashion: "It does seem a shame." How right he was. Given such an intractable situation, her solution was to keep spending in the hope that her money might *buy* happiness. Increasingly it was used to buy an illusion of love. Those husbands, all bar Grant, extracted their huge pay packet. Then there were the husbands' friends and her own friends and the friends of friends, the people she met in cafés and the people who worked for her and the people who wrote begging letters . . . to the point where the existential question, of whether she could ever be loved for herself, had acquired a part b): could she even be sure of being *liked* for herself? This was Nancy Mitford to her sister Diana Mosley in 1956, describing the behavior of the Parisian writer and socialite Louise de Vilmorin.

"The latest coup de Louise de V is rather funny. She began to smother Barbara Hutton with *presents*, canchia trees, truffles, valuable-looking bibelots, & so on, invited her to Verrières &

made her read out her (B. H.'s) poems. Nobody has ever thought of this approach before & the net result is said to be 5 millions [francs] *so far*. La Silvia very nervous and Jean, we hear, NOT PLEASED."

Silvia de Castellane and Count Jean de Baglion were just two more of the people who had come to expect handouts; this scattergun approach was typical of Barbara's manner of giving, including to charity. It was impulsive, unpredictable, easy to exploit, and hard for her to keep track of. It made her a target, and it gave her an uncomfortable power.

Five years later, this toxic mixture of insecurity and might was captured in the diary of Cecil Beaton, who attended the annual ball held at her palace in Tangier, which she had bought—outbidding General Franco—after the Second World War. It was a much anticipated event, with orchestras, belly-dancers and the like, and hundreds of gate-crashers would turn up at the gate. Yet Beaton described a desultory, wayward occasion, strongly redolent of Barbara herself, who picked up life and dropped it again as if it were a book by which she were gripped and bored in turn. "By 11:30 a hundred ill-assorted people of all ages wandered aimlessly from room to room wondering when the hostess would appear to greet them . . . Suddenly [she] was on view, dazzlingly illuminated in a greenish light . . . The egg-size pearls at her neck had an unholy brilliance; her dress was heavily embroidered in diamonds. It was a little Byzantine empress-doll. Her gestures of greeting and affection, her smiles, the look of surprise or delight, were all played in the grand manner. An arm was extended for the hand to be kissed, a graceful turn of the head to greet a Moroccan 'big-wig,' a wide, open-armed welcome to an old friend, head thrown back with lowered lids and a move of the mouth— every sort of smile and coquetry.

"I watched, as did quite a number of others, as if she was in reality playing a scene on the stage . . . As the evening progressed, she overplayed her role. She was in need of a director to tell her that she was forcing her effects too much. Nevertheless, I was fascinated.

"This perfect oval face was seen at its best with the Helen of Troy hair do and the fillets above. I could not discover why I did not think she looked utterly beautiful. Any minute the curtain might come down forever. But, meanwhile, the delicate little child's hands applauded, and the exquisite little feet, shod in the tiniest Cinderella sandals, were beating time ineffectually, with the toes turned in."

A strangely moving description of one of the richest women in the world, steeped in sophistication to the tips of her fillets and twirling for her guests at her party.

* * *

In 1972 Lance Reventlow was killed, along with three others, when his single-engine plane flew into a mountain north of Aspen, Colorado. Barbara, who was in Tangier, did not attend his memorial service; quite simply she felt unable to do so.

Like Christina Onassis, with whom she shared the fatal flaw of vulnerability, she had also been assailed by outward events. Christina lost three members of her family in the space of two and a half years—her brother Alexander died in a plane crash in 1973, her mother, Tina, from a suspected drug overdose in 1974, and her father, Aristotle, in 1975. From this succession of terrible griefs her life was forged. When her brother died, she was given a large role in running the Onassis shipping empire. From Tina she inherited $77 million, from Aristotle $500 million, part of which she donated to the American Hospital of Paris. Therefore, Christina was a great heiress whose inheritance was entirely bound up with appalling loss: the wealth and the horror were inseparable. At the age of just twenty-five she had experienced a cataclysm, comparable with the final relentless act of a Sophoclean drama from her own Greek culture. It is tempting, as with the multiple griefs that have assailed the Kennedy family, to see in these events a significance that goes beyond the indifferent workings of coincidence, to discern hubris. This is not really accurate—sometimes a list of events is just that: a list—yet it has, in the case of Christina Onassis, brought depth and dimensionality to the myth of the tragic heiress.

With Barbara, the story is more complicated. Yes, one can play the game of Heiress Bingo and tick off the familiar tropes. She was motherless, and she was not a good mother. She had a father who caused her mother extreme unhappiness, and who was emotionally distant with Barbara herself. She was susceptible to the lure of a European title, however specious, and alert to the snobbery that would dismiss her wealth as "trade." She was careless of her health—over the years she became addicted to drink, then drugs, and by the end weighed little more than her jewelry. She was still more careless in her choice of men. She was unable to resist buying anything that took her eye—she bought entire couture collections, Rolls-Royces, a tiara once owned by Empress Eugénie, all in the same discriminating way, yet with a desirousness that evaporated as soon as the object was hers. She was plagued by people who wanted a piece of her money, and she often gave it to them. She had a love of high society, although some of its manifestations were wholly without charm, and when she "escaped" to her palace in Tangier, society was soon invited to join her there. She married men who she knew would make poor husbands, and left the one with whom she had a chance of stability. She was creative and imaginative and had a powerful sense of beauty. She felt guilt and boredom and made a couple of suicide attempts. Partly through mismanagement on the part of the advisors who replaced her father, but mainly through her own extravagance, when she died from a heart attack in 1979—en route from the Beverly Wilshire to the Cedars-Sinai Medical Center, at the age of just sixty-six—almost all her money was gone.

Yet she had had so many advantages. So many! Before the death of her son, that knockout blow, might not her life have been splendid—despite the dreadful men, the dreary hangers-on, the wretched father (who did at least look after the millions)? Might she not have been a Daisy Fellowes, whose life could be interpreted as a secret tragedy but was, in fact, a triumph over all those damn tropes?

Not Barbara. She is the ultimate heiress—The Heiress—because her story is indeed that of the poor little rich girl, the million dollar baby, the female rake making her fateful progress through the Hogarthian tableaux, the fiction that is so richly satisfying for the rest of us to read. And why is this her story? Because she saw it that way too: that was her own interpretation.

EPILOGUE

ANGELA

THERE WAS, HOWEVER, another way of doing this.

Angela, 1st Baroness Burdett-Coutts, one of the great nineteenth-century philanthropists, neither fought nor squandered nor suffered over her immense inheritance. Instead, she made it her life's work. Queen Victoria, her near contemporary, regarded her role as monarch as a destiny and a duty (even if she sometimes shirked it); Angela took the same view about her role as heiress. And *that*, if you like, was revolutionary.

She was born in 1814, to a politician named Sir Francis Burdett and to Sophia Coutts, whose Scottish-born father, Thomas, had established Coutts & Co. as a prestigious London bank; the Royal bank, in fact, from the days of George III to the present Queen. Thomas had three daughters—his sons had died—and, as he grew older, so the question of inheritance became more complicated. His solution was an intriguing one, evidence of the shrewd and sometimes unconventional attitudes that had driven his career to such heights.

Thomas's first wife had been one of his brother's servants, a kindly woman who in later life became mentally incapacitated. His second, Harriot Mellon, was a Drury Lane actress, forty years his junior, not notably gifted but extremely appealing, with whom Thomas had fallen in love toward the end of his first marriage. Although the relationship was said to be friendship only, Thomas bought Harriot a "country" house in Highgate—the very lovely Holly Lodge—and, aged eighty, married her four days after his wife's funeral. Naturally none of this went down well with his daughters, but he held firm and was blissfully happy for his remaining seven years of life. When he died in 1822 he left everything to Harriot, "for her sole use and benefit." She also became a partner in the bank. Most significant of all, however, she was bequeathed the decision as to whom she should pass on the weight of that inheritance.

With a different kind of man from Thomas, one might have suspected that the old fool had gone doolally over a young woman's embonpoint and that his apparently left-field judgment would lead to familial warfare and carnage at Coutts Bank. What actually happened was that Harriot, although later silly enough to marry the much younger Duke of St. Albans, was in other ways extremely sensible. She spent fifteen years observing every contender for the prize of the Coutts inheritance, and she eventually decided that the most worthy recipient would be her step-granddaughter, Angela. How much Harriot imagined, or guessed, of what Angela would do with the money is impossible to say; all one can think is that she knew the girl would not waste it. In any event, she had chosen better than she could ever have realized.

What had led her to this decision? Angela was apparently unremarkable; but within that quiet, steady watchfulness lay what made her remarkable. She had a modest demeanor, fitting to the Victorian-female ideal, shielding a will as unyielding as the whalebone in her corsets. She was very tall and thin, rather plain but with a certain physical grace, the sixth and last child of her parents' sometimes turbulent marriage (during which her father had a long relationship with another woman, Lady Oxford). Her mother, Sophia, who took to invalidism—perhaps in revenge for the affair—was a somewhat commonplace woman, poorly suited to Sir Francis. He too had money, as well as the Burdett baronetcy; he was, however, attracted to progressive politics, which luckily for Angela included the proper education of his five daughters. In 1807 he took the seat of Westminster for the Radicals. He made speeches about Ireland, about the terrible conditions in prisons; Lord Byron admired his oratory and cartoonists lavished their adoration upon him. He was a hero in the way that the British most love—good-looking, gallant, raising a fist to Them on behalf of Us. The defining year of his life was 1810—four years before Angela was born—when, with typical righteous flourishes, he challenged the legality of the imprisonment of a fellow Radical in the House of Commons, was accused of breach of privilege, and condemned by the Speaker to the Tower. Ever the showman, he remained for four days in the family house on Piccadilly, allowing the anger against his sentence to bloom, as the crowds grew ever larger and the wide thoroughfare was filled with people shouting "Burdett for Ever!" It was the high point of his radicalism. During his weeks in the Tower, to which he was escorted by the troops summoned to control the crowds, he realized that he disliked the scene that he had part-engineered; his subsequent shift rightward meant that he ended his parliamentary career as a Tory, and was despised for it by many who had worshipped at his shrine, including Angela's future friend Charles Dickens. She, as yet unborn, would grow up with the mystical legend of the four-day Piccadilly siege, and the sound of the crowds outside the windows chanting her father's name.

She was aged twenty-three when, in August 1837, she learned that she was chief beneficiary in the will of her step-grandmother Harriot, and thus heiress to the fortune of her grandfather,

Thomas. It was worth around £1.8 million, but was not a fixed sum, as it included half the shares of the Coutts banking house in the Strand. She also received Thomas's house in Stratton Street off Piccadilly, plus its glorious contents, together with Holly Lodge in Highgate and all Harriot's "watches, trinkets, jewels, and ornaments of the person." She was required to take her grandfather's name, which by royal license was added to that of her father, although she was generally known as "Miss Coutts." She had become one of the richest women in Europe, and was said to be the richest heiress in England.

There is no suggestion that she had any intimation of how Harriot had chosen to leave her money, although they had been close toward the end. Almost certainly the will was a shock, yet somehow unsurprising. What the rest of the family thought—Angela's parents, aunts, four sisters, and brother—may well be imagined; her father had turned irascible (as disillusioned radicals sometimes do) and at first handled the situation badly, unable to hide his jealousy, while her sisters had to be paid off. Yet Angela was up to it, right from the off. She was prepared to take her time, which in itself was a sign of wisdom, and to understand what her new position signified. When she had done this, it became clear that she regarded the inheritance in a way that sounds very simple, yet is almost unique among heiresses. The money was hers, but it was as though she were holding it in trust, because it had been left to her as an *act* of trust: she had been given it because she was trusted to do the right thing with it. As yet she did not know what that was, but she trusted herself to find it.

* * *

She was besieged, of course, by those who sought to divert her. Begging letters, suitors: "the world set to work, match-making, determined to unite the splendid heiress to somebody," was how *Punch* described the reaction to her sudden financial elevation. One young man in her circle, Lord Houghton, who remained a friend, later explained that "Miss Coutts likes me because I never proposed to her. Almost all the young men of good family did: those who did their duty by their family always did." He described the little code invented by Angela and Hannah Meredith (later Browne), her former governess and lifelong companion, in order to deal with the plague of would-be husbands that came swarming into Stratton Street. "Mrs. Browne used to see it coming, and took herself out of the way for ten minutes, but she only went into the next room and left the door open, and then the proposal took place, and immediately it was done Miss Coutts coughed, and Mrs. Browne came in again."

These languid aristos looking for some unearned thousands were easy enough to deal with. More problematically, the publicity that Angela and her inheritance received also brought her a demented stalker: a bankrupt Irish barrister named Richard Dunn, whose campaign of persecution, as described in *The Spectator*, has a horribly contemporary ring.

"Dunn had blockaded Miss Coutts for two mortal years. If she went to Harrogate he followed her; if she returned to Stratton Street he entrenched himself in the Gloucester Hotel; if she walked in the Parks, he was at her heels; if she took a walk in a private garden, he was waving handkerchiefs over the wall, or creeping through below the hedge. With his own hands he deposited his card in her sitting-room; he drove her from church, and intruded himself into the private chapel in which she took refuge . . . he bombarded her with letters, smuggling them into her hands under all sorts of disguises."

Angela's father, still being tetchy, accused her of styling her hair in too severe a way; she wore it sleeked down and plaited away, an apparent suppression of her sexuality that may have been connected to the Dunn episode. Even before the arrival of this maniac, however, she had been wary of attracting male attention. She knew it to be the heiress's lot, and was rigidly determined to keep it at bay. If she chose the man, that was different; but she was fully aware that the power of choice, which in theory belonged to the heiress, was all too easily removed from her. Catherine Tylney Long—whose inheritance was squandered and children were stolen by a man whom she had married of her own free will—would have constituted a famous, alarmingly recent cautionary tale. Its moral was that an heiress was prey, exposed like a deer on bare moorland when the hunters were gathering, and that she must take steps to find cover. Richard Dunn was merely the most lurid symbol of that ongoing truth.

Yet Angela was not averse to men, and thus it was that she conceived a tenacious, slightly bizarre passion for one who, above all others, represented safety and doughtiness: the Duke of Wellington. He lived near the Burdett-Coutts house, his immense mansion Apsley House on Hyde Park Corner—"No. 1 London"—being just a few minutes from No. 1 Stratton Street. A closeness developed between the two throughout the 1840s. When the duke was aged seventy-eight and Angela thirty-three, she proposed to him.

"My dearest Angela," he wrote in reply, "I have passed every Moment of the Evening and Night since I quitted you in reflecting upon our conversation of yesterday, Every Word of which I have considered repeatedly. My first Duty toward you is that of Friend, Guardian, Protector. You are Young, My Dearest! I entreat you again in this way, not to throw yourself away upon a Man old enough to be your Grandfather . . . My last days would be embittered by the reflection that your Life was uncomfortable and hopeless. God Bless you My Dearest!"

An admirable letter, which did not put an end to their romantic friendship, nor indeed to Angela's hopes, which were based upon a fantasy that Wellington—for all his plain speaking and deployment of emphatic capitals—did not absolutely want to dispel. He was fond of her; he was flattered. Not long after his rejection of her proposal, he wrote from his home in Hampshire, Stratfield Saye, informing her that he had been "looking out and measuring walls with a view to break out doors and make passages, with a view to make fresh communication with my Apartment. In recollection of what you said to me some time ago as to your wishes." In other words, she made the running and he was quite happy to be caught—in this instance, by assigning Angela an apartment above his private study, with the two rooms connected by a small winding staircase. Rumors that the duke was, in fact, going to marry this young heiress inevitably abounded. The renown of both parties meant that their companionship—including at public events—was a riveting diversion to high society. There were even whispers of an affair, which seems supremely unlikely, and a persistent story of a secret marriage, although Wellington's later letters—"I wish that it could occasionally occur to your reflections that I am eighty-two not twenty-eight years of age"—show an irritability that suggests he had grown a little tired of playing Antony to his relentless Juliet. When he died in 1852, Angela's grief was accorded great general respect. Yet one has the sense that she had deliberately lost herself in this widow's role: believing in it, as unworldly people can.

Obviously she had seen the duke in the image of her grandfather, who had married a much younger woman and whose marriage had succeeded despite the age difference (enormous, but smaller than in the alliance that she contemplated). Her attachment can also be traced to the death in 1844 of her father, that glamorous, difficult, semi-absentee man. And the aging hero of Waterloo was an ideal figure for an inexperienced woman to fixate upon; still dynamic, but completely unthreatening. Then there was the fact that *she* was able to pursue *him*. It was a perfect psychological riposte to the sensation of being under siege, particularly from Richard Dunn; with Wellington, who did not want her money and was confident enough to handle anything, she could be the predator, and this seems to have reassured her.

For despite its wonderment, the inheritance was deeply destabilizing. It had isolated Angela in one way, and surrounded her with a clamor of attention in another—a fundamental problem for heiresses, and marrying the Duke of Wellington was not a bad way of dealing with it. Nevertheless, to have had the idea of doing so was remarkable, and to have followed it through to the point of proposing still more so, particularly in an age that valued the demure and the passive in women. It was, however, wholly typical of Angela. She was defined by a stubborn innocence, which enabled her to be bold and direct as a child; for all her intelligence she was indifferent to repercussions, consequences, or how a thing might look. There was perhaps no better temperament for a person who sought the betterment of the world.

* * *

And even as she was pursuing her girlish obsession with the Duke of Wellington, her deeper engagement was, in truth, with the relationship that enabled her philanthropic quest: a partnership of singular beauty between a man and a woman, but with a third party in the mix, which was their common cause. It was through her meeting with Charles Dickens that Angela Burdett-Coutts first understood what her life's work could be, and in the fire of his imaginative compassion the future of her inheritance was forged.

Dickens, flawed and married and all too human as he was, was her natural companion; not necessarily in a lover-like sense, although the young Dickens was a very attractive man; but with a closeness that led him to write in 1860: "I think you know how I love you." In January 1845 she sent a wonderful cake to celebrate both his son's eighth birthday and Twelfth Night: "which you made a proud night for Charley," wrote Dickens, "and a happy night to me in the more secret quarter of my own breast."

They had met soon after she came into her money. She could meet anybody, really, after that happened: Queen Victoria, who frequently visited her at Stratton Street and Holly Lodge; the scientist Michael Faraday and the mathematician Charles Babbage, whose work fascinated her, and who were among the first people to whom she gave financial assistance; Gladstone and Disraeli, the two men whom her father tipped for the highest office (Disraeli had an eye briefly on Angela, upon whom he modeled the heiress Adriana in his novel *Endymion*); and, from around 1838, the novelist whose *Oliver Twist* had been greatly admired by Sir Francis Burdett, who read it as coruscating social comment as much as a brilliant work of fiction.

In 1843 Angela, who was making charitable gifts but not yet involved in any formal schemes of her own, began working seriously with Dickens. She started with the "Ragged Schools" in which the very poorest children, the kind who worked for men like Fagin, were educated: she immediately offered to supply public baths and bigger schoolrooms. It was an unglamorous cause, but that was the point, and it was also what Dickens liked so much about Angela. She was, he wrote, "very, very far removed from all the Givers in all the Court Guides." That year he dedicated *Martin Chuzzlewit* to her. Later he would use her as the model for Agnes Wickfield in *David Copperfield*. He was susceptible in every way—his marriage would later break down on account of his passion for the young actress Nelly Ternan— and brimming with the empathy that was at the heart of his genius; his headlong, high-energy temperament meant he was incapable of holding back in any way. Working with this woman of his own age, upon causes that he had brought to a pitch of novelist's intensity—how could his feelings about her not be infected by all the emotion that was flying around? What, indeed, could have brought two people together more effectively? As for her: she too was susceptible, beneath her reticence and control, and it seems impossible that she should have been indifferent to this man. Yet the relationship remained what it was—a friendship of fervent intimacy, in which the cause kept them detached as well as unified—and Angela's vast capacity for ardor was instead directed toward a man almost three times her age.

She and Dickens embarked upon their first major plan in 1846: a home for what were then called fallen women, whom Angela had seen from her windows as they paced Piccadilly and sidled into Green Park. "There is a lady in this town," Dickens would later write to residents of the home, "who from the window of her house has seen such as you going past at night, and has felt her heart bleed at the sight. She is what is called a great lady, but she has looked after you with compassion as being of her own sex and nature, and the thought of such fallen women has troubled her in her bed."

Again, how remarkable she was. It was a singularly rare Victorian woman who actually looked upon prostitutes, who did not turn her head away, or close the curtains, or tell herself that if their existence was not acknowledged then they did not exist. If one is honest, this would be the prevalent attitude today. To look out of one's protected cage and actually notice what is there—

that is unusual. And this was a woman without experience, a closeted child in some ways, yet whose naivety pushed through convention in a way that her father's rebellions had not. She had, said Dickens, the gift of "seeing clearly with kind eyes."

The home, Urania Cottage in Shepherd's Bush, opened at the end of 1847. One of the first residents cried when she was shown her pretty bedroom. Dickens, ever humane, had insisted upon details such as a piano in the house, which he had obtained secondhand for £9, and whose presence caused amazement even among the more liberal-minded reformers; had he really bought such an instrument for ex-prisoners? "I shall always regret," Dickens wrote, apropos this exchange, "that I didn't answer, 'Yes—each girl a grand [piano], downstairs . . . besides a small guitar in the wash-house!'" Wellington was also skeptical about the scheme, and perhaps saw it clearly in a different way: that by association it might be damaging to Angela. This was the year in which she proposed marriage to the duke, yet the joint venture with Dickens continued. It *was* a daring thing to do; the cause commanded little sympathy and huge stigma (as would have been the case as recently as the 1970s, when the prostitutes murdered by the Yorkshire Ripper were treated with scant respect compared with his other, so-called innocent victims). Angela's financial backing for Urania Cottage was anonymous, which might be seen to imply caution, but in fact this was quite usual: most of her giving was attributed to "a Lady Unknown."

By 1853 fifty-six girls had passed through the home, of whom thirty had remained thereafter on the straight and narrow: "Two to one are consolatory odds," as Dickens put it. Given that some of the young women were serious recidivists and/or alcoholic—one was described by Dickens as a girl who "could corrupt a nunnery in a fortnight"—the success rate was in fact very high, and a testament to the hands-on nature of the enterprise. This was the hallmark of both Dickens and Angela, another of whose minor schemes was to source a huge rudimentary spin-dryer and transport it to Florence Nightingale in the Crimea, where the hospital had been struggling with sodden linen—sensible practical help, of the kind that grander schemes so often sail over on their elevated cloud. At Urania Cottage, meanwhile, Dickens listened to the stories of the inmates, and was shocked. So too was Angela. This was an education that she did not get in a Mayfair drawing room. She had had a hard, quick knock against reality when a young woman, claiming to be her father's daughter by Lady Oxford, wrote to ask for the continuation of her regular allowance; which Angela had refused. For all her goodness she was not a saint, and could not bear to extend charity to the girl who had destroyed her fine illusions about Sir Francis. And the daughter of an aristocrat would have seemed like an undeserving case compared with what she was seeing at Urania Cottage, these people for whom a safety net—of the kind that she supplied— was all too often too late to rescue a tumbling body. She began to want to do more, to reach further: to get closer to the first cause that separated poor from rich.

With Dickens's full support and praise for her "moral bravery," Angela Burdett-Coutts moved eastward, to Bethnal Green, where streets are now named in her honor and which, in the mid-nineteenth century, was a place of fathomless squalor, where people slept on straw and the streets were strewn with dead animals. She planned and financed a new development called Columbia Square, comprising four blocks of flats (Dickens had advised flats), with proper sanitation and another of her favored spin-dryers; although not the first of its kind, it was a pioneering influence upon later philanthropic housing bodies like the Peabody Trust. She tried to do the same in Bermondsey, but got nowhere. Nevertheless, her life's work was becoming an ever larger thing; it was near infinite, in fact, the world being as it was, but she kept on with it.

She was deeply engaged with Ireland, which had been one of her father's causes, and where the potato famines of the 1840s had killed around one million people. She financed emigration schemes—this was also done with the Urania girls—but, in the end, she simply bit the bullet and sent a check for £250,000 for the purchase of seed potatoes. She gave large sums to cities such as Edinburgh, Newcastle, and Liverpool, and strove to revive the cotton trade in Lancashire—thinking perhaps of her long-dead grandmother, Thomas Coutts's first wife, who had come from just that background. But it was the East End, always, that obsessed her. She could not forget that a short journey would take her from the lustrous, embellished house at Stratton Street to the hellish alleys and squares where, in her lifetime, Jack the Ripper would kill the kind of women whom she had tried to help. Knowing the importance of a skill, she set up sewing schools and gave support to the silk weavers of Spitalfields. She employed a bursar, whose annual budget might be as high as £20,000 and who, during a cholera epidemic in 1867, organized a detailed aid program that "in one week distributed on Miss Coutts's behalf one thousand eight hundred and fifty meat tickets of the value of a shilling each, five hundred pounds of rice, two hundred and fifty pounds of arrowroot, fifty pounds of sago, fifty pounds of tapioca and oatmeal, twenty gallons of beef tea, thirty pounds of blackcurrant jelly, eighty quarts a day of pure milk supplied from her own farms, four hundred yards of flannel, two hundred garments and a hundred blankets, twenty five gallons of brandy and fifty gallons of port wine." Her gift was still for direct action, which before the age of state aid was frighteningly necessary, and which worked. This was the thing about Angela; what she did worked. Usually.

* * *

Sometimes her innocence let her down. She was a religious woman, despite her fascination with science (she read Darwin with great interest), although that was hardly noteworthy in the Victorian era. She would have felt the presence of God in a way that is hard to understand in a secular age, but she was not self-righteous; she did good, but she was not a do-gooder. Yet for all her sympathy with—say—the plight of the prostitute, she could be unworldly in her quest for solutions. Sometimes she took the philanthropist's wrong turn of planning for people as she would like them to be, rather than as they were. In 1869, for instance, the Prince of Wales opened the splendidly ornate Columbia Market, which she had conceived as an adjunct to the development in Bethnal Green; a wonderful idea marred by the fact that swearing and Sunday trading were forbidden. No swearing in the East End? She was thinking in a way that Dickens would have modified and humanized. Since the early 1860s, however, he and Angela had become more distant. She was not judgmental about the breakdown of his marriage to Catherine Dickens, which was happening—calamitously—around this time; with the blessing of distance she had accepted her father's transgression, and now she saw why her friend might have fallen out of love with his intellectually insubstantial wife. Nevertheless, when Catherine turned up at Stratton Street and begged her to intercede with Dickens, she felt compelled to send a messenger asking him to call. The reply came immediately: "How far I love and honour you, you know in part, though you can never fully know. But nothing on earth—no, not even you, can move me."

They continued to write to each other. He missed her, that was very clear. Her own feelings, as so often, are opaque. If she understood the lack of love for Catherine, how did she feel about the excess of passion for Nelly Ternan? It is impossible to know; the relationship between Angela and Dickens had been so intense yet so subtle. It would be too strong an inference to say that she was jealous (although Dickens was certainly jealous of the Duke of Wellington), but what is certain is that the ending of the Dickens marriage fractured their own connection. It also killed off Urania Cottage, the little house in Shepherd's Bush, which had contained an indomitable belief in the transformative power of kindness. In 1862 Dickens, by then something of a lost soul, assailed by scandal and guilt, was visiting Paris and walked past the Hotel Bristol, where he knew Angela to be staying. Like Newland Archer at the end of *The Age of Innocence*, he decided not to enter. Instead he left a message to "Miss Coutts" with her companion Hannah Browne, in which he wrote that he continually "lived over again the years that lie behind us." He died eight years later, aged just fifty-eight.

Angela, meanwhile, kept the flame alive. An early connection with Dickens had been their shared love of animals; now she became President of the Ladies' Committee of the RSPCA and, throughout the 1870s, was deeply engaged with animal welfare. She had always owned dogs, and the sight of her gray parrot in the window at Stratton Street was, like the flag at Buckingham Palace, a sign that she was in residence. "Life whether in man or beast is sacred," she wrote: "inhuman treatment of animals should be held to be a wrong and a sin." Again, with that characteristic emphasis upon practicality, she installed water troughs and dog drinking fountains throughout many cities, built donkey stables at Columbia Square, provided cattle trucks to improve animal transportation conditions—which distressed her greatly—and campaigned successfully for a closed season on the shooting of birds. In Edinburgh she erected a fountain in honor of Greyfriars Bobby, a Skye terrier who had guarded the grave of his owner until his own death. In her middle years Angela's ambition had been immense, at one point extending even to Africa; she had given financial support to the 1858 Zambezi expedition led by the explorer David Livingstone, who became a good friend. She attended his lectures in London and was galvanized by his motto of "Christianity, Commerce and Civilization." He had sought to establish the Zambezi as a commercial route, in the belief that trade routes would "strike an effective blow at the slave trade, the scourge of Central Africa." A different world, in every sense, from water troughs and sewing schools. Yet it was in the accumulation of such small, compassionate details that her legacy truly lay; and despite the façade of the "Lady Unknown" it was bringing her fame among the general public, thousands of whom would later file past her coffin before she was interred in Westminster Abbey.

To her old friend Gladstone's surprise, she took two days to consider whether to accept the title of Baroness in 1871, the first such to be created in her own right. The following year she became the first female Freeman—a contradiction in terms, but that was the nineteenth century for you—of the City of London. In her old age the accolades flowed like good wine until, on the evening of Queen Victoria's Diamond Jubilee in 1897, a scene re-created itself like the legend from her childhood, in which her father's name was chanted by the people on Piccadilly; a commentator described the massed crowds on that same street, and the gradual perception among them of the presence of the woman known as "the Queen of the Poor":

> Suddenly a hush spread over the vast sea of people. A slim form, supported by several ladies and men, was seen silhouetted against the light; it stepped on the balcony and stood there leaning tremulously against the window. A great

hoarse roar spread over the night, cheers, snatches of songs and wild cries of welcome and delight . . . in the tiniest of tiny barrows a fat woman struggled to her feet . . . and yelled above all the clamor—"The best woman in London—God bless her!"

Angela had not been a rebel, nor a political animal. She had not deprived herself of clothes from Worth, nor splendid jewelry: on one occasion, in 1845, she had appeared at Court in a tiara that had belonged to Marie Antoinette and, when asked by a friend the total value of her outfit, "she answered, in her quiet way, I think about a hundred thousand pounds."[1] She had not spent inappropriately on impossible utopias. Yet she had made a difference to the lives of others: to a girl who glimpsed an alternative to walking the street, to an East End family with a bed to sleep on rather than sawdust, to a nurse in the Crimea with clean dry sheets on which to tend her patients, to a cotton mill worker or silk weaver whose job had been saved, to a thirsty donkey or an exhausted horse. She had given more than £3 million, almost twice the sum of her original inheritance. She had had good friends, an educated mind that she had striven to improve, relationships with two national heroes, and the consciousness, whose value cannot be calculated, that she had wasted neither her money nor her life. She had fulfilled the trust placed in her with that great inheritance, which she had taken so seriously—as a destiny and a duty.

Yet she, too, remains incalculable, with her air of a bony governess and her mysterious seething passions; which her life's work did not sublimate, so much as intensify. What had made this work possible was that her inheritance had remained her own. For all the advice and support upon which she relied, she had handled it alone and dealt with it alone. She had been a burning spear of independence, spreading the warmth of philanthropy because there was nobody stopping her. It is unsurprising, therefore, that during the years of their collaboration at Urania Cottage, she had disagreed with Charles Dickens when he suggested that the girls should be given hope that they might marry: it would encourage them, he said. No, replied Angela, it is possible to be single and saved. Indeed single and saved might well be the clarion call of all those heiresses, both before and after, who had found themselves married and damned.

* * *

However: in 1880, at the age of sixty-six, Baroness Burdett-Coutts announced her engagement. Her fiancé was one of her secretaries, a former actor named William Ashmead Bartlett, aged twenty-nine. Her grandfather had done something very similar, but a worldlier woman would have known that it is different for girls. The rumored marriage confounded those who knew and admired her, including Queen Victoria, who proclaimed that "Lady Burdett really must be crazy" and—possibly relishing the putative fall from grace of her rival "Queen"—wrote excitedly for confirmation from Angela's cousin.

"The Queen is anxious to learn from Lord Harrowby privately whether a report that has reached her as to Lady Burdett-Coutts's marriage is true . . . She trusts that Lady Burdett-Coutts has given the fullest consideration to this step before making her final decision."

At Coutts bank, meanwhile, a decorous panic had set in. A partner wrote to a colleague: "I wish our Lady had come back to her senses and would wait until after her death to bestow £10,000 a year on Mr. A. B.—I should not object to that—far more respectable than bestowing it with her hand." It was, came the reply, "a pretty kettle of fish." Those around Angela grabbed tight hold of a loophole in Harriot's will, which stated that she would forfeit the inheritance in the event of her "marrying an alien." Ashmead Bartlett was half-American. Was that alien enough? He himself thought that it might be, or at any rate that too many people would insist that it was, and offered to release his fiancée from her engagement. "That may be so," said Angela, "but I don't release him and I mean to carry it out."

In early 1881 she ventured out into London society with Ashmead, where they caused a predictable giggly sensation. Hogarth or Rowlandson would have relished the chance to render the scene: the aging bride with her Jane Eyre hairstyle, the Most Loved Woman in the Country with her noble schemes and her pet parrot, turning her love upon a dashing blade, a strutting player, who declaimed his affections while his eye roved toward a nubile creature upon whom he might spend his wife's fortune . . . Benjamin Disraeli was one of those who observed the couple. "I thought Angela would have become classical and historical history," he wrote to the queen, in a letter designed to delight and tantalize, "and would have been an inspiring feature in your Majesty's illustrious reign. The element of the ridiculous has now so deeply entered into her career that even her best friends can hardly avoid a smile by a sigh!"

Finally an arrangement was reached whereby, to honor yet semi-circumvent the "alien" clause, Angela retained her position at Coutts but took just two-fifths of her income, with the rest going to one of her sisters. Ashmead, whom she married in February 1881, had predictably expensive tastes—breeding horses, for one, which is about as ruinous as it gets—and this meant that her charitable enterprises were greatly reduced. She had done more than her share, however, over the past forty years: truly a life's work. And she had not been forced to marry a half-American man who would trigger the "alien" clause in her step-grandmother's will, thus depriving her of her own money. To do so had been her own choice, freely made. Her husband became Conservative MP for Westminster—Sir Francis Burdett's old seat—and worked hard at representing causes that Angela cared about, even the doomed project of Columbia Market. As the husbands of heiresses had traditionally done, he took her surname. They remained married until her death in 1906.

A couple of months after their wedding the couple had, in accordance with procedure, been presented to Queen Victoria, who remained obsessed with their relationship. "That poor foolish old woman Lady Burdett-Coutts," she wrote in her journal, "was presented on her marriage with Mr. Bartlett forty years younger than herself. She looked like his grandmother and was all decked out with jewels—not edifying!"

Angela had never felt the numbing weight of public opinion; in her way she had always done what she wanted. This was no different. The "truth" about the marriage can never be known, and it strains credulity to think that Ashmead would have been a faithful husband. Nevertheless it was reported that, much to the disappointment of the watching world, she had lost her air of withdrawn perplexity and looked ten years younger.

Having released herself of the heiress's burden, in fact, she was happy.

NOTES

INTRODUCTION

1. From *Victorian Women* by Joan Perkin (John Murray, 1993).
2. In an interview given to the Hearst magazine columnist Adela Rogers St. John.

PART I

1. By Charles Gatty, published by Cassell & Company, 1921.
2. *Original Weekly Journal*, September 26, 1719. Cited in *Road to Divorce: England 1530–1987* by Lawrence Stone (OUP, 1990).
3. *The Times*, August 1, 1825.
4. From *Mary Davies and the Manor of Ebury* by Charles Gatty.
5. From *Road to Divorce: England 1530–1987* by Lawrence Stone.

PART II

1. As reported in *The Times*, July 11, 2020.
2. From Lady Diana Cooper's *Autobiography* (Michael Russell Publishing, 1979). She first stayed with Laura Corrigan in 1931 at the Palazzo Mocenigo, which had been Byron's home in Venice.
3. From Consuelo's memoir *The Glitter and the Gold* (Harper and Brothers, 1952).
4. From a letter to Lady Mary Lygon, June 28, 1954.
5. As said by a goddaughter, quoted in *Queen Bees: Six Brilliant and Extraordinary Society Hostesses Between the Wars* by Siân Evans (Two Roads, 2016).
6. From *Loved Ones* by Diana Mosley (Sidgwick & Jackson, 1985).

7. By her friend, the writer Beverley Nichols.
8. *The Times*, November 27, 1908.
9. The judgment of "The Saunterer," anonymous and often withering gossip columnist in the society magazine *Town Topics*, quoted in *The Husband Hunters* by Anne de Courcy (Weidenfeld & Nicolson, 2017).
10. By Hugo Vickers in the *Daily Mail*, May 25, 2019.
11. Cited in *The Churchill Who Saved Blenheim: The Life of Sunny, 9th Duke of Marlborough* by Michael Waterhouse and Karen Wiseman (Unicorn, 2019).
12. In a 1979 article for *Books and Bookmen*, which also recalled Gladys asking Diana's father, Lord Redesdale, if he had read a book that she was then enjoying. "I haven't read a book for three years," was the reply.
13. Ibid.

PART III

1. From a letter to Evelyn Waugh, March 13, 1948.
2. In *The Times*, October 18, 2000.
3. Her unpublished memoir, "No Pleasant Memories," which she began in 1930 when confined at home with an injured leg.
4. *The Times*, August 28, 2004.
5. In a letter to her sister Jessica Treuhaft, January 11, 1962.
6. To Gerald Berners, November 3, 1947.
7. From *Cecil Beaton's Diaries: The Happy Years 1944–8*, ed. Hugo Vickers (Weidenfeld & Nicolson, 1972).
8. Ibid.
9. In a letter to Harold Acton, April 27, 1948.
10. To Lady Dorothy Lygon, April 16, 1932.
11. In a letter to Diana Mosley, March 4, 1945.
12. From *Margot Asquith's Great War Diary 1914–1916* (OUP, 2014).
13. Philip Ziegler, in his biography *Diana Cooper* (Hamish Hamilton, 1981).
14. In a letter to Harold Acton, July 1957. That month, during her annual holiday in Venice, Nancy received a letter from Palewski informing her that he was leaving Paris to become French ambassador in Rome.
15. As cited in *Second Son: An Autobiography* by David Herbert

(Peter Owen, 1972). The Hon. David, whose older brother was Daisy's mark the Earl of Pembroke, was also a close friend of Barbara Hutton.

16. John Richardson in his *Sacred Monsters, Sacred Masters* (Jonathan Cape, 2001).

17. Diana in conversation with the author, 2002.

PART IV

1. In *The Temptress: The Scandalous Life of Alice, Countess de Janzé* (Simon & Schuster, 2010).

2. By the writer and former QC John Mortimer.

3. As described by Selina Hastings, in her *Evelyn Waugh: A Biography* (Sinclair-Stevenson, 1994).

4. In a letter to Lady Dorothy Lygon, April 1932.

EPILOGUE

1. Quoted in *Lady Unknown: Life of Angela Burdett-Coutts* by Edna Healey (Sidgwick & Jackson, 1978).

BIBLIOGRAPHY

Acton, Harold. *Nancy Mitford* (Hamish Hamilton, 1975).

Amory, Mark (ed.). *The Letters of Evelyn Waugh* (Weidenfeld & Nicolson, 1980).

Brock, Michael, and Eleanor Brock (eds). *Margot Asquith's Great War Diary 1914–1916* (OUP, 2014).

Barrow, Andrew. *Gossip* (Hamish Hamilton, 1978).

Clifford, Naomi. *The Disappearance of Maria Glenn: A True Life Regency Mystery* (Pen and Sword History, 2016).

Cooper, Lady Diana. *Autobiography: The Rainbow Comes and Goes / Light of Common Day / Trumpets from the Steep* (Michael Russell Publishing, 1979).

de Courcy, Anne. *The Husband Hunters: Social Climbing in London and New York* (Weidenfeld & Nicolson, 2017).

Evans, Siân. *Queen Bees: Six Brilliant and Extraordinary Society Hostesses Between the Wars* (Two Roads, 2016).

Gatty, Charles. *Mary Davies and the Manor of Ebury* (Cassell and Company, 1921).

Hastings, Selina. *Evelyn Waugh: A Biography* (Sinclair-Stevenson, 1994).

Healey, Edna. *Lady Unknown: Life of Angela Burdett-Coutts* (Sidgwick & Jackson, 1978).

Heffer, Simon (ed.). *Henry "Chips" Channon: The Diaries 1918–38* (Hutchinson, 2021).

Herbert, David. *Second Son: An Autobiography* (Owen, 1972).

Heymann, C. David. *Poor Little Rich Girl* (Hutchinson, 1985).

Lees-Milne, James, and Michael Bloch (ed.). *Diaries, 1942–1954* (John Murray, 2006).

Mackrell, Judith. *The Unfinished Palazzo: Life, Love and Art in Venice* (Thames & Hudson, 2017).

Mitford, Nancy. *The Pursuit of Love* (Hamish Hamilton, 1945).

Mitford, Nancy. *Don't Tell Alfred* (Hamish Hamilton, 1960).

Mosley, Charlotte (ed.). *The Letters of Nancy Mitford and Evelyn Waugh* (Hodder & Stoughton, 1996).

Mosley, Charlotte (ed.). *Love from Nancy: The Letters of Nancy Mitford* (Hodder & Stoughton, 1993).

Mosley, Diana. *Loved Ones* (Sidgwick & Jackson, 1985).

Mosley, Diana. *The Pursuit of Laughter* (Gibson Square, 2009).

Payn, Graham, and Sheridan Morley (eds). *The Noël Coward Diaries* (Weidenfeld & Nicolson, 1982).

Perkin, Joan. *Victorian Women* (John Murray, 1993).

Richardson, John. *Sacred Monsters, Sacred Masters* (Jonathan Cape, 2001).

Roberts, Geraldine. *The Angel and the Cad: Love, Loss and Scandal in Regency England* (Macmillan, 2015).

Spicer, Paul. *The Temptress: The Scandalous Life of Alice, Countess de Janzé* (Simon & Schuster, 2010).

Stone, Lawrence. *Road to Divorce: England 1530–1987* (OUP, 1990).

Thompson, Laura. *Newmarket* (Virgin, 2000).

Vanderbilt, Consuelo. *The Glitter and the Gold* (Harper and Brothers, 1952).

Vickers, Hugo (ed.). *Cecil Beaton's Diaries: The Happy Years 1944–48* (Weidenfeld & Nicolson, 1972).

Vickers, Hugo (ed.). *Cecil Beaton's Diaries: The Restless Years 1955–63* (Weidenfeld & Nicolson, 1976).

Waterhouse, Michael, and Karen Wiseman. *The Churchill Who Saved Blenheim: The Life of Sunny, 9th Duke of Marlborough* (Unicorn, 2019).

Waugh, Evelyn, and Michael David (ed.). *The Diaries of Evelyn Waugh* (Weidenfeld & Nicolson, 1976).

Ziegler, Philip. *Diana Cooper* (Hamish Hamilton, 1981).

ACKNOWLEDGMENTS

For their kindness and exemplary patience, I thank my two editors, Georgina Blackwell at Head of Zeus and Charlie Spicer at St. Martin's Press. Thanks also to my splendid agent, Georgina Capel; Sarah Grill; Kate Appleton; and to the handful of precious people whom I saw in the dismal year of 2020, during which this book was mostly written: my mother, my brother John, Nick, and Milo.

PICTURE CREDITS

Section 1

p. 1 Bridgeman Images; p. 2 Mary Evans Picture Library, © The Trustees of the British Museum; p. 3 Alamy Stock Photo; p. 4 © Illustrated London News Ltd/Mary Evans, Keystone/Getty Images; p. 5 ullstein bild/Topfoto, © National Portrait Gallery; p. 6 © National Portrait Gallery, ullstein bild/Getty Images; p. 7 Library of Congress, Wikimedia Commons; p. 8 Album/Alamy Stock Photo, Wikimedia Commons.

Section 2

p. 1 Library of Congress, The History Collection/Alamy Stock Photo; p. 2 The History Collection/Alamy Stock Photo, Wikimedia Commons, © Illustrated London News Ltd/Mary Evans; p. 3 Hulton/Getty Images, © Illustrated London News Ltd/Mary Evans; p. 4 Wikimedia Commons, Bettmann/Getty Images; p. 5 PA Images/Alamy Stock Photo, Bettman/Getty Images; p. 6 UPI/Alamy Stock Photo, Hultonn/Getty Images; p. 7 Horst P. Horst/Condé Nast/Shutterstock, Photograph by Cecil Beaton/CAMERA PRESS London; p. 8 Bettmann/Getty Images, Corbis/Getty Images.

INDEX

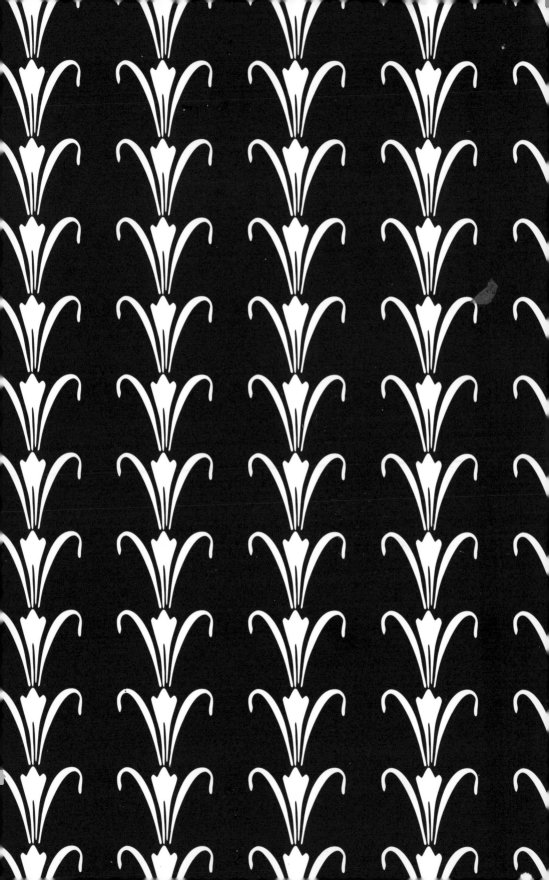